Patriots and Redeemers in Japan

George M. Wilson

PATRIOTS AND REDEEMERS IN JAPAN

Motives in the Meiji Restoration

THE UNIVERSITY OF CHICAGO PRESS
Chicago & London

The University of Chicago Press, Chicago 60637
The University of Chicago Press, Ltd., London

© 1992 by The University of Chicago
All rights reserved. Published 1992
Printed in the United States of America
00 99 98 97 96 95 94 93   5 4 3 2

Library of Congress Cataloging-in-Publication Data

Wilson, George M. (George Macklin). 1937–
    Patriots and Redeemers in Japan : motives in the Meiji Restoration
 / George M. Wilson.
        p.   cm.
    Includes bibliographical references and index.
    ISBN 0–226–90091–6. — ISBN 0–226–90092–4 (pbk.)
    1. Japan—History—Restoration, 1853–1870. I. Title.
DS881.3.W55   1992
952.03′1—dc20   91–20448
                                                            CIP

The frontispiece comes from the *Illustrated London News* for December 15, 1860 (p. 570; reproduced in Kanai Madoka, ed. and trans., *Egakareta bakumatsu Meiji* [Tokyo: Yūshōdō Shoten, 1973], p. 61). The scene depicts the war god of ancient Japanese mythology riding on a sacred wild boar as he descends onto the shogun and assorted mortals.

For David and Elizabeth

Contents

Chapter Five

Chapter Six

Chapter Seven

Preface

> The final trait of effective history is its affirmation of knowledge as perspective.
> —Michel Foucault

> The working class did not rise like the sun. . . . It was present at its own making.
> —E. P. Thompson

This book asks the question, Who took part in making the Meiji Restoration? By arguing that there are many answers, that many groups of agents participated, it offers a novel perspective on the decade of the 1860s in Japan, one that identifies and develops multiple lines of thought and action. Both ideas and deeds figure prominently, and no attempt will be made here to assert an order of priority (or sequence) between them.

The perspective offered here arises from a conviction that the different players in Japan acted from different motives. In the total discursive field of late Tokugawa Japan, these agents acted as bearers of rival discourses vying for supremacy. On the one hand, the samurai heroes who survived to join (or to reject) the new Meiji government in the years following the imperial restoration of 1868 pursued a patriotic muse that had beckoned ever since Commodore Perry broke the scrim of Japanese seclusion in 1853–54. On the other hand, the common people of Japan responded to conditions of internal unrest—fueled by the arrival of foreigners and the start of external trade—with a burst of activities vaguely but energetically aimed at redeeming society from the troubles it had engendered. But others also played roles in this contest: the foreigners who came to Japan sought stability to exploit the Japanese in trade; and those who ran the Tokugawa political system, the feudal authorities in Edo and the more than 250 han, also strove to preserve stability as befitted their venerable mandate to keep order.

The gathering crisis heightened the prospect of conflict. It has also had the effect of highlighting the patriotism of the imperial loyalist samurai who were responsible for "restoring" the young Meiji emperor to power and ending the era of Tokugawa bakufu hegemony that lasted from 1603 to 1868. But the crisis also calls attention to the common people's search for redemption in Japan's time of troubles. In the perspective developed here, the twin themes of patriotism and redemption play upon one another dialectically. So too the victorious samurai and the common people worked on each other, and both in turn were worked upon by the behavior of the foreigners and of the bakufu and the leading han, headed by daimyo in baronial positions. All of these different agents may be viewed as participants in a total set of activities, a concert of mutual interaction: it is this interaction that shaped the nature of the restoration that followed.

This study contends that the samurai elite cared as much about the effort to redeem the realm from disarray as it did about responding to foreign pressures, and that redemption does more to explain the extent and timing of the later restoration reforms than does the classic emphasis on patriotism. The reforms that followed 1868 carried revolutionary overtones even though they were reactions to stress executed by one sector of the traditional social elite. The samurai who thus reacted were launching Japan upon an era of unprecedented change. National goals took shape from deep-seated concerns about society's capacity to control itself. It was not just a desire to emulate the West with its superior technology that occasioned the drive for change; it arose also from the hope of redeeming Japan from the danger of internal chaos.

Everybody who writes history has a bone to pick with the past. Sometimes veiled by the process of accumulating knowledge through the exposition of newly recovered historical facts, that contentious bone remains at the heart of a historical writer's enterprise. My quarrel with past treatments of the Meiji Restoration lies not with what they put in but rather with what they leave out. I want to make a concern for the common people a normal part of the task borne by historians of this episode. Not a monograph, but an extended topical essay on the agenda for Meiji Restoration historiography, this study uses secondary and tertiary (historiographical) sources—and some primary ones as well—to look at ways of appreciating the behavior of some of Japan's more than thirty million commoners on the eve of a true sea change in their history. Every group in society had some relation to the Meiji Restoration. All such groups were participants in the sense that their motives and actions fed into the reservoir of circumstances that came together to produce a transformational process.

The point of this historiographical exercise is to connect Japanese popular behavior in its various forms to the rest of what was happening in mid-nineteenth-century Japan. The book centers on the time that historians invariably call *bakumatsu:* the last *(matsu)* years of the Tokugawa bakufu *(baku)* from about 1850 into the 1860s and the difficult months on the eve of the restoration's public pronouncement on January 3, 1868. For our purposes *bakumatsu* will figure as the temporal site where the rival discourses then at work in Japan intersected and were contested.

The argument sounded here recognizes but downplays the role of the Japanese warrior status group, the *bushi* or samurai, who normally get the lion's share of credit for making the restoration and transforming Japan afterward, during the Meiji period from 1868 to 1912. Both Western and Japanese scholars point to the samurai as agents of change, and indeed they were. They guided the new nation after 1868, creatively if willfully manipulating their monopoly of the lawful uses of force—police, army, navy. So it was they who determined the direction that the whole reform project would take.

But great events like the Meiji Restoration are too vast to be attributed solely to political elites. They alter the history of whole populations. In the course of such events, ordinary people express their feelings about the situation in which their lives are caught up and played out. Some kind of intentionality shapes their attitudes and attends their activities, even though it may end up being formally unrepresented in subsequent acts and policies of government. Intent, I am saying, is too important to be left unplumbed.

It is on this matter of intent that intellectual history enters into the inquiry: looking for intent, motive, purpose helps to identify the work of an intellectual historian. Both thought and action will occupy us, but the fact that there is no necessary correlation between them, nor any between expressed goals and achieved objectives, tells us only that history is something other than an exact science.

This is a lesson that comes as no surprise: R. G. Collingwood, for instance, wrote that history is neither *noesis* nor *aesthesis,* not science and not art, but a "third thing" connecting these two (artificial) categories. Perhaps the surprising thing is the way thought becomes embedded in actions. Historical actors reveal their thinking in their actions, by what they eschew as well as by the acts they finally perform. The historian's task is to think through these actions to get to the thoughts behind them; Collingwood said it was "to discern the thought of [the] agent."[1] Indeed, he emphasized ideas almost to the exclusion of acts, but the point is that we can "read" thought in the "text" of action. Or, as the hermeneuticist Paul Ricoeur expresses it, human action can be seen as an "open work" on the model of the text.[2]

Now, ideas do not in any precise way manifest themselves in events. It may be that we expect to see them "reflected" there, but skepticism about cause and effect—and about reflection—precludes making ambitious assumptions of this sort. History as sequence, whether in the direction of "progress" or anything else, must remain forever in doubt. Teleology is a matter of faith, not fact. Dubious too is the proposition that historical events can in sheer reality be reduced to "narrative" accounts. Yet the organization of data and the imposition of order are obligatory tasks in the craft of any historian who means to write so as to enable readers to follow what is written. The imputation of cause is so firmly embedded in the spoken and written languages of our discourse that we find ourselves obliged to engage in some degree of causal attribution if we want to communicate a coherent message.

Edward Gibbon wrote in 1782 that "diligence and accuracy are the only merits which an historical writer may ascribe to himself."[3] For me it would suffice to have it known that I cultivated diligence and prayed that accuracy really was a virtue. The practice of intellectual history obliges us to be accurate about what was said or done, and when as well as by whom. Saying this, however, does not convey the necessary corollary: to demand utter accuracy would generate a breakdown of our ability to narrate and explain; indeed, it would vitiate the achievement of so accomplished a writer as Gibbon himself. For in the end he may only have imagined that "the triumph of barbarism and religion" ruined the world's greatest empire (as Carl Becker implies in *The Heavenly City of the Eighteenth-*

Century Philosophers).[4] If accuracy be served, but not worshiped, and diligence praised as the more forgiving of the two, then we may find the freedom to interpret the data, and to discern the multiple avenues of thought and action that necessarily inhere in the great events of history.

Acknowledgments

Thanks are due to the *American Historical Review* and Princeton University Press for permitting me to include two of my articles that they previously published: "Time and History in Japan," *American Historical Review* 85 (1980): 557–71; and "Pursuing the Millennium in the Meiji Restoration," in *Conflict in Modern Japanese History,* edited by Tetsuo Najita and J. Victor Koschmann, pp. 177–94 (Princeton: Princeton University Press, 1982). These appear here as chapters 2 and 5. Some changes and additions have been made for the sake of style and consistency.

Chapter 6 originated as a paper called "Dancing toward Millennium," which formed part of a panel at the 1983 annual meeting of the Association for Asian Studies. Chapter 7 was presented as a paper for a panel, "Imagining the Meiji Restoration as a Revolution," held at the 1989 annual meeting of the American Historical Association.

When I began this book, I benefited by a period of sabbatical leave and a research grant from Indiana University. Early in the project I drafted several chapters on the Florida gulf coast thanks to the hospitality of my mother, Dorothy M. Wilson. Since then I have been fortunate to receive support for research expenses from the Office of Research and the University Graduate School at Indiana University.

Horiuchi Hisao owns the Fujisawa scroll that inspired chapter 7. I am grateful to him and to Ishii Osamu of the Fujisawa City Archives for allowing me to see it.

I wish to thank the Japan Foundation for awarding me a research fellowship in 1985. I appreciate the help given by my editor, Alan Thomas; thanks go as well to the two readers whose reports to the University of Chicago Press resulted in publication. Harold Bloom offered timely encouragement for this project. These and others with whom I have discussed the book are not implicated in the views expressed here: for what the book says I am responsible.

My children, David and Elizabeth, have given me countless motives to do creative work. Now they are grown and engaged in doing their own work; with all my love I dedicate the book to them. The arbiter of this project is my wife, Joyce Wilson, who has been both sustenance and inspiration. No better critic can be imagined, and I am ever thankful for her love and support in all that we have done.

Chapter One

Prologue: Agency and Structure in the Meiji Restoration

Question and evidence, in history, are correlative. Anything is evidence which enables you to answer [the] question you are asking now.
—R. G. Collingwood

The meaning of an event is the sense of its forthcoming interpretations.
—Paul Ricoeur

Who makes history? Is it the actor on stage, or the conditioning structure that surrounds and shapes the act? Do "men make their own history," as Karl Marx put it, only not "just as they please"? When we assign causes to historical events, shall we credit the agency or the structure, the persons who act, or the ambience that envelops them?[1]

These classic questions inform all parts of the present inquiry with a caution to be wary of explanatory patterns that leave out human beings, their motives, their passions and foibles. It will no more do to ignore the agents who perform historical acts than to omit the structures that enable or impede their occurrence.[2] First things first: the actors have to act before the history can be made, no matter how great the degree to which external circumstances or unconscious drives condition or impel people to do what they do. We shall therefore focus here on *agency,* the actors and their acts, rather than structure, the arena in whose conditioning web the agents acted. This is finally a matter of text and context: both exist in any historical situation, but we will concentrate on the "text" of ideas (and of actions), leaving the "context" of shaping institutions in a secondary if necessary role.

1

This study argues that love of country was complemented by redemption as a motive for making the Meiji Restoration of 1868. My thesis is that a pervasive urge to remedy distress at home was just as compelling to most participants as the patriotic intent to elevate Japan in the international arena.

Others have not always seen the matter this way. Most writers in Western languages stress nationalism as the intellectual driving force behind the Meiji Restoration.[3] To pursue the issue we need to consider a series of questions about the process that led to the restoration.

To begin with, why did the Meiji Restoration eventually result in the vast changes that made Japan a modern nation? Are there genetic connectors between the events that led to the coup d'état in 1868, which was intended to "restore" direct imperial rule, and those events that followed the coup and became the reform program? If there are, could these connectors help us understand the duration and intensity of Japan's sustained leap to world prominence by the turn of the twentieth century?

Such questions lie behind any inquiry concerning the Meiji Restoration. They undergird all efforts to understand it. Only the Japanese, among nations that do not derive from west European civilization, accomplished an industrial revolution and the makings of advanced capitalist society during the heyday of world imperialism, which ended with World War I and has persisted since then in altered and attenuated form. Only the Japanese crossed from a closed and introverted fixation on their own great and little traditions into the *terra nova* of mass society based on the mechanized industrial sector of the economy, an economy pressed into the service of urban populations governed through the institutions of the nation-state, whose inception and rise to prominence had taken place in early modern Europe: only Japan became "modern."

If the root questions have engendered only partial responses, it is because the available evidence cannot sustain complete ones. Historical evidence is invariably flawed, from the historian's point of view, because it could not have been assembled for the purpose of answering questions that later generations alone would put to it. Evidence did not arrive already catalogued into libraries. The Japanese who lived through the Meiji Restoration knew nothing of the process of events that subsequently would be assigned to them as originators—the industrial revolution, creation of an empire, tenure of a rapidly modifying society. Such consequences of the restoration do not necessarily evince causal links to the events that led to 1868; perhaps the connections are purely genetic rather than causal. One event follows another according to the hallowed rules that writers observe in assembling annals and chronicles.

But chronology, useful as it is to all historians, has never yielded reasons to explain the development of any sequence of events. Reasons are causal statements imposed by historians in the course of arranging and narrating events. Narrative strategy may be the key to historical explanation. Without narrative there would be fewer "reasons" used in the vocabulary of historians; we would see fewer references to factors, forces, trends, or the climate of opinion. Without interpretation—the effort to characterize or evaluate a narrative series of events and explanations—it would not be possible for reasons to assume importance. For it remains problematic whether any set of events, any "event-process" of the magnitude of the French Revolution or the Meiji Restoration, could ever be apprehended as more than a series of accidents unless historians in search of causes dare to name and articulate the elements of a story and to interpret them as the basis for a set of results. When we do this, of course, we not only interpret but also judge, as Hayden White reminds us with the dry query, "Could we ever narrativize without moralizing?"[4]

Here we shall be wary of cause-and-effect explanation. Yet no one writing readable history can actually avoid it. Our languages oblige us to account for things that happen, and our human curiosity spurs us to do so. The very act of "fashioning" a narrative is a willful intrusion on the part of the historian into the domain occupied by the inert data that inform the treatment of a topic. Yet antinarrative, though in vogue among some literary critics and writers of fiction, leaves any event-process essentially incomprehensible. The problem of treating historical topics without using a narrative format is therefore one I will not raise. What is germane is the dual thrust I mean to pursue: on the one hand, to present an essay on the significance of the Meiji Restoration in Japanese history, while resisting the impulse to attribute linear causality to the process of historical events; on the other, to narrate events, attitudes, and behavior from the perspective of the groups of historical actors then active on the scene in Japan.[5]

The effort to proceed in such a way rests on a conviction that historians tend to be too finely attuned to the demands of a closed narrative: the pieces have to fit and the story must go smoothly. Against this attitude I propose to set a historical style concerned with motives and moments that were important to their protagonists and are useful for interpreting the period we are studying.

The Myth of the Meiji Restoration

Scholarship in recent years has sought to recuperate "myth" as a good thing, a vital force acting as a powerful archetypal story that drives and motivates human behavior.[6] But equally common usage recognizes myth as fabrication, mere fiction, a waste product to be sloughed off by seekers after truth. So we have two common conceptions of myth, and both apply to the restoration as an object of historical inquiry.

In the first place, the restoration has always suffered in translation, because it should not be regarded chiefly as an event that "restored" the emperor to actual rule. The actors who surrounded the throne "seized the jewel" and ritually put the successor of the sun goddess Amaterasu, a sixteen-year-old boy named Mutsuhito (1852–1912), into a technically sovereign position at the power center that dominated all Japan.[7] Yet in practice it was not the emperor, whose Japanese titles *mikado* or *tennō* signify more of a religious than a political role, but those who spoke for him who actually ruled the country; subsequent events and arrangements such as the Meiji Constitution of 1889 only solidified their position. They are therefore collectively known as oligarchs, a small group of high officials, self-selected on the basis of political and military influence, who wielded power in the emperor's name. Those among the oligarchs who survived into old age came to be called *genrō*—original elders, or elder statesmen, who were present at the creation of the Meiji system. So in a sense there was no "restoration" at all. Instead we find an age-old stratagem at work, whereby those who held power first appropriated the symbols of authority and then used them for the purpose of legitimating their own rule.

In the second place, however, a novel arrangement of this sort does not happen without some credible basis, and the oligarchs correctly judged that the trappings of the emperor and the old imperial court at Kyoto would serve their needs better than other possible instruments could. The general appeal of the imperial myth gave these rulers just the basis they needed to grasp and exercise power. Skill and experience and dexterity aside, the oligarchs could dominate politics because the emperor, whom they dominated, represented or, more properly, *constituted* political legitimacy in Japan. A long heritage vindicated those who used the emperor thus, and their faith in that heritage was not misplaced. The myth of imperial grandeur that associated the court with the distant past, and even with the temporal creation of Japan as a physical and political space, was a force that no other challenger for power could hope to match. Not even the Tokugawa bakufu, a venerable institution that had endured as the chief political arbiter in Japan, could challenge what was after all the nominal basis of its own legitimacy—the imperial court that pronounced the bakufu's original authorization in 1603.

We thus encounter two uses of myth, both of them valid. We have to adjust to these uses if we want to understand the restoration. First, it is not adequate to say that the emperor was restored to power, for his officials ruled in his name, and he personally remained powerless. Yet the myth of the Meiji Restoration is not false, for the institution of the emperorship was in fact restored to temporal rule over the whole of Japan, something it had not had for a millennium. Second, the widespread acceptance of the myth of imperial legitimacy resulted from the established currency of that myth: it was well known and not regarded as false. The myth carried enough force to justify the central government's efforts in the daring policies it undertook. The mandate of the emperor, sanctioned in myth, allowed the oligarchs to suppress opposition from every quarter as well as to build a new nation-state after the Western manner.

The very terms for "restoration" that were first used among the samurai—*isshin* (innovation) or the more formal *ōsei fukko* (restoration of imperial rule)—were soon supplanted by more supple phrases that allowed a wide range of interpretations. Two terms—*goisshin* (imperial innovation) and *ishin* (from the Confucian classics, connoting "to promote the new")—may have originated among the mixed commoner-samurai military units that fought in the Chōshū Civil War in 1865. The commoners in these units also fought off bakufu armies in 1866 and kept on playing a part right through 1867–68. The government did not refer to *Meiji* as the reign title of the new era until late in 1868, when court scholars chose it in time-honored fashion from classical Chinese sources. The use of *Meiji ishin,* the commonest phrase by which Japanese have referred to the restoration for more than a century, awaited the issuance of an imperial proclamation in 1870. In that document the term was merged with Shinto connotations to produce a maximal sense of venerable politico-religious authority.[8]

The myth of the Meiji Restoration will accordingly receive high regard here. For our purposes it indicates the social force produced by imperial government. The fact that the emperor and his court had languished reclusively for many centuries did not inhibit the Meiji oligarchs from building a nation on the basis of the imperial mystique. They did so with admirable inventiveness.[9] But their skill should not inhibit us from seeing that the emperor, though not restored to true power, carried in his role and person such symbolic significance for Japanese culture that power relationships were literally defined by means of their proximity to him. For the Japanese such a web of symbols and signs of authority was no stranger than the American appeal to the overriding importance of liberty and all of its attendant symbols. However abstract, the emperor's emotional appeal was both valid and real. We must therefore respect the myth of the Meiji Restoration: it encompassed the symbols that authorized political prestige and the exercise of power in Japan.

The Meaning of the Meiji Restoration

What then shall we make of the restoration, and especially of the event-process that led to it? Addressing this question takes us into areas where arguments rage and historians disagree. Issues arise of (1) epistemology, (2) historiography, or theory of history, and (3) methodology; they all pose vexing problems. First among these issues is the epistemological, the matter of what we can know about relatively underdocumented popular phenomena such as rebels, revels, and new religions.

Looking for ways to probe the motives of the actors who took part in the restoration, I have sought to identify story lines that express the intentions of the different groups that were active at the time. (This method and its underpinning in contemporary intellectual history will form the basis of chapter 4.) I chose this tack, as readers will see, from dissatisfaction with synoptic approaches to restoration history as these have developed in Japan and the West.

The historiographical tradition in Japan rests on a conflict model of social change. It has been basically Marxist, and it views the outcome of the Meiji Restoration as a flawed bourgeois revolution carried out by elements of the dying feudal aristocracy in league with nouveau riche lower-middle-class types in rural and to a lesser extent urban Japan. The result of this kind of inherently unstable class alliance was Japanese "absolutism," a trough between stages of history, leading to imperialism abroad, to authoritarianism and suppression at home, and predictably enough to catastrophe from 1931 to 1945.[10]

Western historians, on the other hand, have typically proceeded on a consensus model of social change. This model views conflict as an aberration and not a prime mover of great events like the restoration. Following this approach, historians have stressed the key role of Western imperialist pressures on Japan during the *bakumatsu* years as well as the overarching need of the Japanese to develop a consensus to enable the leadership to carry the country safely into a hostile world environment without sacrificing national unity.

My chief difficulty arose when I could not reconcile the motives of historical actors before the restoration with its amazingly vast consequences. Conflict and consensus both came into doubt as inappropriately narrow strategies for plumbing the sudden abrupt set of sweeping political, economic, and social transformations that the new government introduced and promoted after 1868. It was easy enough to see why the Tokugawa bakufu and the feudal system *(bakuhan taisei)* that supported it had to come tumbling down. I could also see why something had to replace those long-lived institutions that kept order and gave structure to society. Why, however, should the replacement for feudalism have been a government that made a revolution from above and by 1900 had converted Japan into a fully centralized, rapidly industrializing regional military power? The foreigners never required such a performance of Japan during the years when the Tokugawa bakufu was trying to hang onto the reins of authority. Why not a more modest response from the basically elitist samurai rebels who became the Meiji oligarchs, but who after all hailed from the same samurai status group as the bakufu officials?

Searching for answers led to immersion in reexamining the subdiscipline of intellectual history. Recently, intellectual history has come under attack as a method of explaining historical change. To many, ideas appear to operate as by-products of the actions of groups, or as outcomes of the turning points in event-processes that represent broad institutional change. But newer trends in philosophy of history and social anthropology, as well as hermeneutic approaches to the analysis of the production of meanings, offer promise of reviving intellectual history as a primary basis for reasoning through the unsmooth and discontinuous process by which Japan actually experienced the Meiji Restoration and then set out on a truly "national" course.

In this realm of new approaches to the use of ideas in historical constructs, one encounters certain thinkers who are not always thought of as compatible, or even thought of together: R. G. Collingwood, an Oxford metaphysician and historian, joined Claude Lévi-Strauss, Michel Foucault, Northrop Frye, and Hayden White as touchstones of these new attitudes and approaches. Carl Gustav Jung and his notion of "synchronicity" became involved. Myth and religion, always taught as central to behavior patterns by Max Weber, Talcott Parsons, and Robert Bellah, took on new importance in the hands of Mircea Eliade, Victor Turner, and Clifford Geertz. Operating under a name its foremost practitioners were always disavowing—*structuralism*—I had worked from a deductive mode of reasoning, à la the Cartesians, towards a model of motivation and behavior among participants in the events of the several restoration dramas.

Structuralism causes enormous if unnecessary difficulties for people who insist that it must be an ideology or philosophy. At root it seems rather to be a method.[11] The method is to use various kinds of alternation, whether of polar opposites or merely binary combinations, to explain phenomena in relation or juxtaposition to other phenomena. It is thus perforce a comparative method, and it attempts to explain interphenomenal relationships synchronically, following the lead of the parent discipline, linguistics, which reflected the distinction between philological diachrony and linguistic synchrony as exemplified in the thinking of the Swiss linguist Ferdinand de Saussure. It locates meaning in sentences and documents (texts) and groups of documents (discourses) or other commensurable systems of thought (epistemes, discursive formations, paradigms) by analyzing the simultaneously prevailing (synchronous) relations of the binary components to one another and to other occupants of the field in question, not by tracing and explicating the origins and "evolution" of those parts diachronically, as time "passes." Peculiarly ahistorical in appearance, this mode of signification is not so blind to history's needs when it comes to assessing the motives or intentions of groups of actors who are party to making history happen. Such people scarcely think of themselves as living a story or a narrative line. Yet everyone has motives, difficult as these often are to identify, and everyone fashions plot structures just to make sense of the passing scene.

So it came about that I sought to marry Collingwood's precept that the historian "reads" action in order to perceive the thought of historical actors to the structuralist project of isolating and analyzing discrete synchronous sets of (coincidental) acts. Every event has an exterior—what happened—and an interior—the hope or idea that animated it—said Collingwood in a famous formulation; the convergence of exterior and interior constitutes an action whose agent's thought the historian must discern.[12]

Meanwhile, the postwar French conspiracy of thinkers who consummated structuralism got an assault going on everything from causation to narrativity, but in places this line of thought still allows for the harmonious fusion of the forms of an event. Paul Ricoeur, for instance, writes of the philosophic harmony of the theory of the text, the theory of history, and the theory of action.[13] I began to think of ideas as communication events, whose action component consists in conveying the thinker's thought or intent to an audience. Similarly, thought itself is a kind of text, just as actions may be "read" as texts, to be studied as contributors to the context of historical situations.[14] Foucault, in an unwonted display of clarity, is quoted as saying, "Thought [once expressed] is no longer theoretical. As soon as it functions it offends or reconciles, attracts or repels, breaks, dissociates, unites or reunites. . . . Thought, at the level of its existence, in its very dawning, is in itself an action—a perilous act."[15]

More perilous an act than thought itself may be the attempt

made here to connect diverse strands of popular thinking and forms of Japanese popular behavior into a set that we may credit with the making of the Meiji Restoration. I do not insist on causality, only on contemporaneity. But the presence of these "texts" within the ensemble of texts that go into the makeup of the Meiji Restoration says something about the nature of the whole process. It was, for example, not a revolution of elites vis-à-vis other elites. Yet it was no simple intraelite realignment of power, with authority shifting from the tired old bakufu to the new and energetic heroes from the southwestern territories, the han of Satsuma and Chōshū. Nor was the Meiji Restoration's class base as narrow as many have supposed.

Popular consciousness in its dream of *yonaoshi*—a millenarian remaking of the world to redeem the disarrayed clutter of late Tokugawa Japan—comes ironically into concurrence with the thrust of the romantic quest by imperial loyalist samurai to redeem Japan not only from defilement by the foreign powers but also from further depredations by those who had proved unworthy to conduct the affairs of state. Both impulses were ultimately redemptive, and both responded to internal differences associated with keeping the peace of the realm—Japan writ large—rather than principally constituting responses to outside stimuli and pressures.

This quality of redemption is what matters most. If there is a paramount impulse among the universal social motives, perhaps it is redemption. Future and present are obviously affected by the drive to redeem, but the meaning we give to the past also has a bearing on that drive. As Walter Benjamin notes, "Our image of happiness is indissolubly bound up with the image of redemption [*Erlösung*]. The same applies to our view of the past, which is the concern of history. The past carries with it a temporal index by which it is referred to redemption." [16] Less a move to restore the past than to rescue the present, less an economic than a social conflict, the Meiji Restoration witnessed coincident struggles to attain goals that were not at all the same. Yet they were driven by the same redemptive motive, and their human agents necessarily interacted. What finally eventuated in the restoration after 1868 was a "revolution" that turned upon itself to erect a modern nation-state based on containment of the vast energies that had been released in the *bakumatsu* period. Popular energy did not vanish, nor indeed had it ever been lacking in the dramas of *bakumatsu;* it was absorbed, canceled and elevated into the reform program of the victorious samurai, "sublated" in a manner suggested by the philosophical concept of *Aufhebung.*

To say that the common people caused the imperial loyalist samurai to act as they did in the Meiji Restoration is unsustainable. To say that their shared motive of redeeming the realm coincided is undeniable.

Chapter Two

Time and History in Japan

It is not space that rules
this form of existence,
but time, duration,
spontaneous change.
—Kurt Singer

In Japan time and history are abstractions: their palpable representation is the imperial line. A cultural rather than a formal or a sacred view, the Japanese attitude to the line unbroken for ages eternal links all generations past and future. As such it conforms to linear notions of historical time. This attitude resembles European ones after the Middle Ages waned in historiographical stereotype.

"Modern" linear conceptions of history harbor a vulnerability not shared by cyclic historical thinking. Cycles recur, and repetitions preclude an end to history. But for a linear model, time passing is conceived as history "unfolding." What will be the result if the core of belief in a linear scheme breaks down or, worse, appears to complete its prescribed mission during the course of events in an actual historical process? When the scheme cracks and the mission stops, the shock to historical consciousness resembles a geological cataclysm. Because time *is* history for a linear model, the realization of the model's central goal will "stop" history, temporarily divorcing it from the sense of time passing. A sensitive observer of such a cataclysm, possessed of an idea of history, will be vulnerable to profound feelings of discontinuity and a loss of historical bearings.

In Japan, as in other cultures of long duration, occasions arise when crisis has blurred the identity between time and history. Never did such a crisis erupt so forcibly as in the Meiji Restoration of 1868. Improvising to cope with coincident domestic and foreign difficulties, Japan's new leaders legitimated their program by "restoring" the imperial throne to secular rule and invoking the authority of the crown. The restoration thus appeared to fulfill Japan's historic destiny, graven on Japanese minds through oral and written transmission from the protohistoric past, that a sacred line of emperors descended from the mythical creators of the cosmos should rule the country. In meeting this ancient test, however, the new Meiji government ironically engaged a dilemma that has bedeviled the Japanese ever since: how to reconstruct a sense of purpose in a people whose central historical myth has come to fruition.

In this chapter I will argue that Japanese historical consciousness is indeed linear in form and has been linear since the dawn of Japan's recorded history. But the residue of an earlier and simpler sense of time always conditioned the linearity of Japanese perceptions about history. A comparison of Japanese notions of time with those of China and Europe will help illuminate the relationship between time and history in Japan. The essential questions are three. What is the nature of Japanese historical consciousness? How have the Japanese construed the passage of time? And under what indigenous and external influences did the idea of time-as-history become established in Japan?

Time so bewilders physicists and philosophers that humanists rarely venture into its intricate conceptual domain. A prominent historian of Western antiquity says that "perhaps it is as well for the average historical student's peace of mind that he is even less aware of the degree of personal bias implicit in his temporal framework than he is conscious of the problems of causality in his reconstruction of the past." But the same author avoids so cavalier a dismissal by observing that "the historian deceives himself who feels that in fixing his dates he has completely dealt with time." [1]

Normally time is treated as a "scientific" problem, outside the scope of the historian, who must accept temporal parameters as given. Yet time, like space, is a fundamental boundary condition of life. Perception of time depends on available technology, the climate, what people do to make a living, and the rituals they celebrate. But everyone perceives it, and in every culture time has a poignant quality that suffuses human affairs. Time marks off the parts of our lives, our youth and age, our fullness and death. Time affects the way people choose to organize their communities, as it does the values they want to live by, die for, and bequeath to posterity. When a society articulates a sense of time, "history" is apt to follow. Put another way, a community aware of time passing is likely to display a historical consciousness. This is what happened to the Japanese during the protohistoric era (third through seventh centuries A.D.).

Such a transition had occurred earlier in China, where it became the practice to chronicle the passage of time by political reign periods, an approach that the Japanese later adopted.

In English we are accustomed to saying that "time flows" or "time flies," or we may refer to the "passage of time"—without considering the implications of such harmless metaphors. Zeno's paradoxes go to extreme lengths to illustrate how complicated the subject of time can be, but there is no easy way to dispose of time's riddles. In the Western tradition the most famous observation ever made about time belongs to Saint Augustine: "What, then, is time? If no one asks me, I know what it is. If I wish to explain it to him who asks me, I do not know."[2] But Immanuel Kant's opinion that time is an "inner intuition [that] yields no shape" may be the shrewder insight. Like space, time is an a priori form by which the mind intuitively sorts out the sensory impressions derived from phenomena, and we can have no absolute knowledge of it. Far from being a thing-in-itself, time has no phenomenal aspect; it has no image and cannot be represented because it relates to neither shape nor place.[3] But time is a condition without which objects and their appearances cannot be perceived. Experience therefore occurs only within a transcendental and unknowable temporal framework.[4]

Recent scientific pronouncements do little to improve on Kant. Although the startling implications of relativity theory have expanded our knowledge of the way time functions in the physical world, neither classical nor modern physics has produced a synthesis of knowledge about time (or the space-time continuum) as a dimension of human existence; for time remains indefinable except intuitively, even in physical theory. Many philosophers of science find that they must approach time, apart from formal theory, in basically commonsense terms. G. J. Whitrow, a thoughtful mathematician and cosmologist, has said that "the essence of time is its transitional nature."[5] Whitrow's position requires that time continue its Kantian role of enabling biological and physical events to occur. We can measure time metaphorically but not literally. Nor can we situate it. A. S. Eddington speaks of "time's arrow" and its one-way movement, but there is no ultimate test of a unidirectional time. Furthermore, the argument that time moves implies a need to establish some sort of index against which to plot this "movement," setting up the mathematical dilemma of infinite regress.[6]

Custom and written evidence indicate that Japanese conceptions of time and historical change are more linear than cyclical. No overt teleological theme marks Japanese views of history, but nothing in those views suggests that time is reversible. The Greek concept of *eschaton,* denoting finality and the ultimate end, has no indigenous equivalent in Japanese, and the translation of *eschatology* is *shūmatsuron,* "doctrine of the conclusion." The character for *matsu* does, however, carry deep philosophical associations. It comes from the Buddhist canon and appears most prominently as the first half of the two-character compound *mappō,* which is the Mahayana Buddhist idea of the "law" in its late and deteriorating phase.

Japanese tradition in mythology as well as in the early versions of Shinto offer no philosophical concept for end or purpose in the passage of time. By contrast the Hebraic tradition from the Covenant onwards required a shift from cyclical to linear thinking. Christian theology, by asserting the uniqueness of the Crucifixion and Resurrection, inexorably compelled historical thinking to take linear form, though it took the scientific revolution and the doctrine of biological evolution to inculcate the idea of linear time in Western thought.[7] Nothing so dramatic punctuates the Japanese religious heritage. Ceremonies end, as do lives, but the ultimate nature of this ending is not the subject of speculation in Japanese mythology.

It may be a Western conceit to juxtapose linear and cyclical views of history. Some anthropologists label certain peoples "primitive" and characterize their sense of time as underdeveloped. They usually depict such peoples against a background of ceremonial rites based on myths—true stories exaggerated over long duration for their effect and their utility as models for human behavior. Mircea Eliade's phrase "the myth of the eternal return" refers chiefly to the propensity of these primitive peoples to mark time according to mythical events that they reenact in periodic rituals and utilize as the basis for their societal values.[8] In this context the argument that the Japanese have tended to favor a linear view of history implies an "advanced" character for their historical consciousness. The contrast that suggests itself is with China, where linear considerations appear less emblematic and cyclical thinking may be viewed as predominant. It is not necessary, however, to insist that linear history is advanced and cyclical history primitive, or to argue that

Chinese historical thought runs exclusively in circles rather than in lines. The sophistication of Chinese written history belies any notion of simple cyclical didacticism.

Here we must affirm that all conceptions of history contain both linear and cyclical elements. Every society at whatever scientific or technological level fantasizes repetitions in history, not literal perhaps, but repetitions in form. Giambattista Vico, for example, based his "new science" of 1744 on repetitions and "filiations," as Edward Said calls them; yet Vico enjoys nearly universal acclaim as the forerunner of rational historical consciousness in Europe on the eve of the Enlightenment.[9] Neither Japanese nor Chinese speculations about history show an exclusive bent towards linear as opposed to cyclical projections, but Chinese philosophy (which is coterminous with historical writing under the aegis of humane letters) stresses the recurrent aspects of human interaction with nature. And China differs from Japan in the emphasis of its discourse on this issue.

Joseph Needham has explicitly argued that the basic Chinese worldview conceives of time in linear, not cyclical, fashion. Linear will out, so to speak, though the issue is close: "it has elements of both conceptions, but broadly speaking . . . linearity . . . dominated."[10] Nathan Sivin chooses to stress the cyclical nature of Chinese thinking about time.[11] Frederick W. Mote states no opinion on this question, but he implies that the Chinese sense of line and circle may be immaterial. What counts is Chinese cosmology as a preponderant humanism. Chinese thought does not contain a full-blown cosmogonic myth. Western analogistic thinking and ethnocentrism are responsible for the effort to imbue China with such a myth, but in fact there is none. Centered on humanity in nature, Chinese cosmology, in Mote's view, calls for a world order dependent on interpersonal relations and harmony between human institutions and natural phenomena.[12]

From this standpoint it is reasonable to contend that cycles become just as important as linear ideas. Not just rituals of spring, the harvest, and the coming and going of life but also cycles of good government and bad, or rebellion and tranquillity, fill the Chinese historical record. The emphasis on a golden age in the past resembles a myth of eternal return, but Chinese thought should in no way be construed as primitive, for it did not include any expectation of actual physical recurrence. Nevertheless, the golden age always served as a standard for later Chinese, and on this point the Japanese notion of their own distant past differs precisely because they saw it as an age of superhuman beings, of mythical heroes, rather than of politicians and philosophers, as in China.

The Japanese sense of history differs from the Chinese but owes its origin to the process of adapting Chinese thought to Japan before and during the Nara period (710–94). Japanese cosmogonic myths were set down in writing at that time, mainly in the *Kojiki* (Record of ancient matters) and the *Nihon shoki* or *Nihongi* (Chronicles of Japan) of 712 and 720.[13] Chronological records of imperial rule delivered through the medium of the Chinese written language allowed the Japanese government centered in the Yamato plain to construct and propound its own version of the way the world began.

At about the same time the rise in literacy at the Yamato court enabled Shinto to assume formal identity as an indigenous set of beliefs that may be referred to as religious. It also retained its role as a form of folk behavior associated with recurring ceremonies and rituals. Over the centuries a complex interplay of ideas led to changes in Japanese thinking about history. These changes arose from Buddhist theology mediated by the Chinese and Korean texts in which it came to Japan; such changes also issued from Confucian philosophy, which entered Japan in the same way. Of course, Chinese and Korean thought—especially Confucianism—underwent modification over time, but the Japanese also made incursions into the intellectual substance of the doctrines they imported. Through all of this activity a linear mentality persisted, connecting the Japanese state to its mythical origins. So did an East Asian sense of time that appears to differ sharply from Western conceptions.

In Western thought, being or existence happens "in time," and time therefore defines the limits of finitude within which life goes on. In Buddhist thought, however, transcendence of life as well as living existence may be characterized *as* time: time "spent" *is* existence. Finality comes only through escape from the cycle of rebirth (by means of nirvana) or through "the awakening of insight" beyond mundane expectations (what the Japanese mean by *satori*). The Buddhist view of time therefore has no need of sequence; events are all existential and transcendental at once.[14] Such a characterization neatly accords with Mote's comparative assessment of the Chinese approach to time and history: events in the West are viewed as moving one after another in causal sequence, whereas in China they have their own contemporaneity. Not causality, Mote suggests, but Carl Gustav Jung's idea of "synchronicity" signifies the relationship of events to time in China.[15] When Jung coined the word *synchronicity,* he meant "meaningful coincidence," and like the "collective unconscious" with its inherited "archetypes," this Jungian term poses difficulties for logicians and epistemologists.[16] But taken simply as the willful abandonment of insistence on direct causal connections between discrete events, synchronicity represents an effective way to denote the Chinese view of time and history. It also applies to Japan.

As their sense of history became multilayered, the Japanese seem to have grafted Confucian precepts onto indigenous thought, then made great strides by adapting from Buddhism, and returned again to Confucianism only in the Tokugawa period (1600–1868) when various schools of Confucian ethics constituted the ideology of both state and society. To narrate history they combined the timeless Shinto creation myth with the idea of an imperial line of rulers. This concept of imperial rule was borrowed from Chinese political thought, but unlike Chinese rulers the Japanese imperial line was never to change; unchanging succession within the imperial family assured a nobility of origin and a legitimacy of authority. The chronicles—the *Kojiki* and *Nihon shoki*—lay out the imperial reigns in good Confucian fashion, and the usual exemplars of proper and wicked monarchical behavior dot their pages. The initial reign periods were superhumanly long, and the reigns grow shorter, more human in scale, as the chronicles approach the era when they were actually composed.

Soon the early histories were supplanted as models of Japanese historical thinking by other chronicles, prepared by monks or warriors under the influence of Buddhist teachings. Perhaps the most interesting example is the *Gukanshō* (Random writings), written about 1220.[17] The *Gukanshō* amounts to a conflation of Buddhist doctrine and Japanese ideas drawn from the Shinto tradition of the state. It sets Japanese history on a straight line and points it towards the future. The reflections are everywhere hedged about by gloom and a sense of impending doom (not surprising in Buddhist literature), but the reasons given to account for the current state of affairs do not proceed in sequential expository form. The situation is outlined, and timeless laws are invoked to explain it.

Written during a crisis in relations between the imperial court and the military government—the bakufu—at Kamakura, the *Gukanshō* might have had a politically didactic purpose. We may surmise that its author, Jien (1155–1225), a gifted monk and four-time abbot of the Tendai sect, wanted to cite lessons from the past and so warn both the imperial family and the court aristocracy against just the sort of confrontation with the military that did occur in the Jōkyū uprising of 1221.[18] Despite the close connection between Jien's political interests and his view of history, the conflation of Buddhist macrocycles and Shinto linearism presented in the *Gukanshō* defies simple cause-and-effect explanation. Jien created his system of historical interpretation out of multiple motives, some personal and some doctrinal. The work combines his intellectual faith in Buddhism with his emotional allegiance to Shinto and the Japanese imperial tradition.

Jien recognized the political authority of the imperial line descending from the creation myth, which he accepted at face value and made an article of faith. But he discerned three phases in the evolution of Japanese government: direct and personal imperial rule, imperial rule with aristocratic assistance, and imperial rule with the aid of both civil and military aristocrats such as the Fujiwara family of Kyoto and the heirs of the Minamoto family of Kamakura. The unfolding of this pattern was ordained by both Buddhist principle *(dōri)* and the spirit of the imperial ancestors *(sōbyō no kami)*.[19] Jien was well schooled in the manifold cycles of Buddhist doctrine, which are very long indeed, lasting several tens of thousands of years or longer; as such they could have no more immediate bearing on human affairs than the extended cycles that Western geologists and astronomers have devised to deal with the formation and development of the earth, the Solar System, and the galaxies. Jien could construct a sophisticated narrative, and in parts of the *Gukanshō* he did so. But the "causes" of events seem to emerge more from the author's deep faith in Japan and the Japanese Shinto tradition than from the order of those events as he describes them.

This feature also marks the military tales, the *gunki monogatari* or *gunkimono,* which began to appear in the Kamakura period (1185–1333). Perhaps the most celebrated and certainly the most repeated (and filiated) of these stories, the *Heike monogatari,* opens with dramatic energy: "The sound of the bell of Gionshoja echoes the impermanence of all things. The hue of the flowers of the teak tree declares that they who flourish must be brought low. Yea, the proud ones are but for a moment, like an evening dream in spring-time. The mighty are destroyed at the last, they are but as the dust before the wind." [20] Up and down go the fortunes of individuals and families, a cycle in tune with both human and Buddha nature. But nothing need deter the Japanese imperial line in its mythic-heroic flight across the tawdry terrain of earthly history.

The creation myth is so compelling and original that it stands as a chief feature of Japanese thought. It appears in the *Kojiki* and *Nihon shoki,* and the political provenance of these chronicles does nothing to diminish the appeal of the mythological base. Certainly the creation myth transcends the state. It contains vivid and beauti-ful tales, pulsing with so much life that a Victorian translator chose to clothe a few sentences demurely in Latin rather than offend En-glish delicacy.[21] And, as Joseph Campbell says, "The freshly fledged literati of Japan still had the dew of youth upon them." The myth's power, its Japaneseness, cast a spell. Campbell calls the result "the most remarkable history of the world-as-fairytale that the literature of [mythology] knows—which . . . befits Japan, where . . . the ex-traordinary earnestness and profound gravity of the ideal of life [are] masked by the fashionable fiction that everything is only play." [22] These are archetypal stories.[23] They consist of "idealized episodes in the lives of the heroes whom the nobility appreciated and emulated as models of the sublime and desirable in human life." [24]

The creator gods, including their lustrous offspring, the sun goddess Amaterasu, paid attention to the green islands of Japan. Amaterasu's brother Susanoo, a complicated character who seems to embody violent forces of nature such as wind and storms, did his mischief but was banished before he could loose devastation on the islands. Amaterasu's grandson, Ninigi, purposely descended to Ja-pan, and Ninigi's grandson (or great-grandson) became Japan's first emperor and founded the Japanese state. He is known from his reign title as Jinmu Tennō, the "divine warrior." His dynasty's power consolidated in a great "eastward expedition" to the Yamato plain area, his claim to sacred authority clearly established, Jinmu initiated the history of the Japanese state.[25] Nothing intervened between politics and other aspects of official life. Religion in the strict sense of the word had no independent existence as it did in the West. What was political was also religious; the religious was equally political. The first Japanese term for government, *matsurigoto* or "ceremonial affairs," covered both politics and religion and worked to preclude a schism between the civil and the sacral. So it means something like "the business of worship" (as George Sansom puts it).[26] The official creation myth fairly assured this result by infiguring the tales about the "heavenly ancestor" into the transition to their human successors on the imperial throne.[27]

How did these gods and early emperors live? Like mortal men and women, generally: their lives were not specially sacralized. In those times the gods were metaphoric concentrations of human traits: joy, love, ambition, and also greed, lust, and envy make appearances in the stories. The very nature of Shinto was vivacious, even playful, and its deities, the *kami*, were so mundane that early Western commentators treated them with derision.[28]

Whatever Shinto possessed in the way of theology was implicit. Some years ago a Shinto priest in a party that included Mircea Eliade replied to a question about Shinto's lack of doctrine by stating, "We have no theology. We dance." Further reflection moved Eliade himself to decide that the Japanese seem driven by a need to confront the divine incarnate. "Everything in the cosmos can be transfigured, no one is unworthy to receive the visit of a god: a flower, a stone, a pillar of wood." Time is neither a limiting nor an enabling factor, because temporal duration never catches the *kami*. Shinto showers the universe with "an infinity of instant epiphanies."[29] The stories capture this conspicuous vivacity and celebrate the rites of life. Death is notably played down. Of a definitive ending of life there is no trace. This fits in well with the Japanese proclivity not to dwell on death or the afterlife. John C. Pelzel notes that the mythmakers treated death with equanimity: they "quite simply denied death as a final or different state [and] saw life [as being] universal in time as it is in space."[30] Synchronicity again: life does not "lead" to death in the causal-sequential sense, nor is it necessarily conclusive. Even after Buddhism was fully integrated into the Japanese scheme of things, the bloom remained on life despite its transient and ephemeral nature. The high and mighty become lowly after a while, but they may rise to power and glory again. The finitude of John Donne's formulation is missing.

Not merely human nature and individual destiny but history and historicity in Japan also partake of this temporal sense of separate segments rather than sequential series. The emperors reigned, it is said, one after another, but it makes no apparent difference in what order the reigns occurred. The line itself is clear and sharp, a thread running through all the chronicles as well as the more cosmopolitan *Gukanshō*. But its ultimate fate, what will finally become of the imperial line, does not arise as a subject for consideration. Time in the form of existence cannot run out.

In the *Gukanshō* Jien pondered the future of the emperors, reflecting a general fear that only one hundred reigns would be allowed. Originally the phrase "one hundred reigns" indicated an indefinite number extending ad infinitum, but political commotion had changed confidence into anxiety. Eighty-four reigns were already on record, and Jien sometimes worried about the forthcoming lapse of continuity. Given his stated conviction that Japan was in the deteriorating phase of a long Buddhist cycle, it was natural for him to speculate in this way, but the telling point is that Jien found the resources to obviate the unwanted possibility. Secular improvement within long-term deterioration, he proclaimed, could replenish a depleted supply, just as paper is restocked when the number of sheets runs low.[31] As he actually plotted the story of the imperial line, Jien never questioned its heroic character—yet he was writing around the time of the troubled year 1220![32] A century and more of bitter disputes among the emperors and retired emperors as well as the civil and military nobility had not shaken this pillar of the Tendai sect. He hardly expected the emperors to rule without the aid of courtiers, monks, and warriors. It was enough that the imperial line existed and would continue to exist through improvement and replenishment even as the barely perceptible deterioration of the long Buddhist cycle continued.

A later history, more famous but not as sophisticated as the *Gukanshō*, evinces a similar approach but ignores Buddhist fears of decline. *Jinnō shōtōki* (Record of the orthodox succession of divine rulers), written in 1339 by Kitabatake Chikafusa (1293–1354), introduces the imperial line as the hallmark of Japan and the touchstone of its genius as a culture. The book's initial phrases capture

the point: "Japan is the divine land, the land of the *kami*. The original heavenly ancestor [Ninigi] laid the foundation, and the Sun
Goddess will forever transmit the succession. Only in our country
does this situation exist. In other dynasties its like is not to be
found. This is why we call it the divine land."[33] George Sansom
brands *Jinnō shōtōki* "a polemic treatise rather than a history [even
though its] general attitude reveals influence of the *Gukanshō*."[34]
But this chronicle again reaffirms the orthodox succession as the
characteristic trait of Japanese political history. From the clouds of
myth to the fourteenth century this principle was reiterated, and it
permeates Japanese thought in the subsequent Tokugawa period
right to the Meiji Restoration.

In an elegant and almost forgotten manuscript, Kurt Singer
fixes Japan with the epithet "the realm of time." Singer compares
Japan with China, which to him is more a "realm of space."[35] The
dichotomy is stark but revealing. Neither Japanese nor Chinese
thought attaches much importance to the specific duration of any
particular historical process, whether the life of a dynasty in China
or a political style in Japan. For China, however, time's relative sim-
plicity contrasts with the pervasive vastness of space. The space of
the Middle Kingdom was crucial. Culturally, the space not comprehended by China was of no great significance unless the outsiders in
such peripheral areas were to invade the Middle Kingdom. But the
central space itself held real life, universal life, where Chinese culture held sway. "Chinese civilisation seems one with China's wide
plains.... It is not man who dominates in this world, but Space
itself, ... a timeless presence."[36] Yesterday, today, and tomorrow
commingled, but China built its culture in spatial terms. China's
human generations were important, to be sure, yet five of them
formed a unit. Forever was a vacant notion.

Japan, however, lacked space, and nature had peevishly left the
mountain-clad islands wanting in resources. Not niggardly space
but infinite time was the cosmic gift to Japan. Ordained by divine
myth and symbolized by the mirror, sword, and jewel belonging to
the imperial family, Japan's spirit moved through time even while it
"existed" in time—without conceivable end. No one devised an intellectual framework for an ending; no contingency provided for
the unthinkable prospect of closure. If some dreamlike act of wish
fulfillment were to occur, the conversion of myth to hard political

reality would leave the human actors unsure where to turn or what to do next. A return to the golden age of the original superhuman heroes was out of the question. Their light shone on and on as time passed unbidden. Then along came the Meiji Restoration.

Nothing in the annals of Japan before 1868 prepared those who thought in historical terms for the divorce of time from history that accompanied the Meiji Restoration. One prior attempt to reestablish the monarch as the actual ruler of Japan, the Kenmu Restoration of 1334–35, had collapsed in military defeat. It is instructive to consider the difference in intent between these two restorations. Emperor Godaigo (1288–1339) had sought to reimpose the Kyoto court's supremacy over the eastern provinces at a time when Japan was becoming too fragmented politically and militarily to allow effective control from the center. Aristocracy at the center was giving way to feudal rule by landed warriors on the periphery. Godaigo overreached himself and lost his bid to rule as well as reign. But his aim was traditional, if reactionary. He had intended to consolidate the eroded prerogatives of the imperial court and its military allies.[37]

No such underlying continuity of intent was at work in the Meiji Restoration. By 1868 the restoration of "direct" imperial rule required the dismantling of a massive and historically effective configuration of Japanese people, places, and institutions—the Tokugawa bakufu, whose authority as first among equals in politics had been paramount since the early seventeenth century. Such a restoration also made it necessary to take apart the entire system for distributing power and perquisites that had permitted the Tokugawa bakufu to share its authority without losing it.

No matter how ardently the new Meiji leaders tried to demonstrate the compatibility of their government with Japanese historical tradition, in practice their restoration broke with precedent and embarked upon a novel journey. The transcendent element in Japanese mythology could now be fully politicized, but at the cost of its hold over the collective historical consciousness. So, for example, "We have no history," a Japanese friend told the startled German physician Erwin Baelz in 1876 when Baelz arrived in Japan. "Our history begins today."[38] The premise for the restoration undeniably came from Japan's own philosophical heritage. The *Gukanshō* and *Jinnō shōtōki* as well as the ancient chronicles attest to it; so do the philosophical writings of the Tokugawa era. But the indigenous provenance of the premise did not soften the blow to continuity struck when the central myth of Japan's history had to end, if it were to be used. The premise was, after all, grounded in myth. Converted to reality, the myth of the premise dissolved. Actual politicians had to recapture it to use as an organizing principle with which to build an entirely new political structure—a national state on the European-American model.

At this point time and history diverged, the Japanese sense of historical purpose became veiled, and succeeding generations down to the present have labored to revive it. They have failed: oligarchs, militarists, and plutocrats—inter alios—all had their opportunities along the way in the past century but could not recover a durable Japanese past to ignite public emotion and establish an ultimate goal in Japan's future. These elites of the generations that followed the restoration have bequeathed the quest for meaning and value to the current generation of Japanese. Today many visions compete, and the competition is fierce. Perhaps a complex industrial society cannot be brought together by any single sense of historical destiny or mission and, therefore, cannot settle on a dominant "myth of concern" to guide it.[39] The ambiguity of the situation only intensifies this dilemma of identity and purpose, assuring Japan of further decades of tension and uncertainty.

It may be ironic that a linear model of history in Japan should be vulnerable to such a crisis before the "modern" West lost faith in the secular religion of nationalism. The Japanese after all came late to nationalism. Europeans and Americans inaugurated the age of national states under the secularizing impact of science as it exploded into prominence from the Renaissance to the Enlightenment, culminating in the nationalistic surge of the nineteenth century in the wake of the French Revolution. This transition was relatively calm because nation could be substituted for church and secular values projected as religious ones. But in Japan the Meiji Restoration demanded a very rapid transition and a deliberate expropriation of myth for concrete political purposes. Everything happened so fast that Japan became a laboratory for experimentation with new values (or old ones revisited) to support competing existential strategies.

The state and its ideology of mass nationalism constituted one among several such strategies for survival in a hostile world, and not all Japanese embraced the nationalist crusade that followed the restoration. But the fulfillment of old verities in an epochal event like the Meiji Restoration robs those verities of their power to inspire. Traditionalists must embellish them in order to achieve a specific definition of their rule in a postmythic age. Societies tremble when such changes occur, and "world history" finds its paradigms. Because the remaining advanced industrial societies all face similar dilemmas as the force of nationalism inevitably wanes, Japan's problem with its sense of historical mission may be at once ironic and prophetic. Defeat in the Second World War vitiated the particular nationalist-imperialist style that Japan had borrowed from Europe and America.

Late to reach and early to leave this style of nationalism, the Japanese continue to pursue their elusive mission, while other "modern" nations extend their own national histories. Today time and history have resumed their joint procession in Japan. But the direction in which they proceed remains shrouded.

Chapter Three

Pax Tokugawa

In every epoch of humanity certain great tendencies are expressed [and] every epoch is immediate to God.
—Leopold von Ranke

Historians have made it clear how even at that moment of *sakoku,* Japan created a wonderful world of *closed culture.* . . . But we must also know *how much we lost* in order to pay for those [beautiful] things.
—Watsuji Tetsurō

It can be said of Japan from 1600 to 1850, as it could of Fernand Braudel's Mediterranean world, that here was a cosmos, self-contained and regulated, functioning through durable systems that absorbed change and persisted.[1] The volume of change varies as the historian sifts among the topics to be considered, yet the structures of historical certainty that were expressed through the political system, the social system, the economic system, and the several stratified cultural systems were to last a quarter of a millennium and even then succumbed only to a powerful affiliation of challenges both internal and external to Japan itself. Unlike the Mediterranean in Braudel's history, Tokugawa Japan was not marked by widespread or frequent eruption of warfare or military action of any sustained kind. That does not make it an unmixed blessing in the long record of humanity's efforts to create a stable and peaceful world, but it was an age typified by both peace and stability.

Characterizing Tokugawa Japan

John W. Hall remarks that "the Tokugawa period . . . has suffered a bad press from modern historians."[2] The Tokugawa era seems to suffer also from a variety of misleading labels. "Unchanging," "frozen," and "rigid" are a few of the more charitable (or less invidious) ways in which writers have chosen to characterize this vibrant and tense but also highly creative epoch in world history. Other stereotypes, such as "centralized feudalism," the "military-bureaucratic state," and "integral bureaucracy," succeed in catching key elements of the makeup of institutions in this era but are not cast widely enough to render the whole period easily understandable.[3] Those who call Edo-period Japan a "police state" or an authoritarian dictatorship miss the point that a balance of tensions between freedoms and restrictions perpetuated the systems of the era in a state of basic social equilibrium. A lot was going on, but the visible surface of events was usually tranquil. Maybe there is no adequate characterization of an age. Perhaps we should say that it will do to acknowledge the long peace, the growth of cities, and the general production of wealth, as well as the stunning cultural accomplishments of Tokugawa Japan. It is a fascinating era for the student of a stable social order.

This is not at all to contend that Tokugawa Japan was some unblemished paradise on earth. It concealed its share of suffering, and it revealed various instruments of terror. Lives were lost to the dangers that afflicted the precarious Tokugawa arrangements for social balance. The leaders of the political system perpetuated far past the need to do so a picture of a feudal society, ever in want, self-sufficient but barely. Economic and other kinds of behavior gave the lie to such a picture, yet it remained an ideological fixation of most Japanese down through the Meiji Restoration.

We will do well to treat Tokugawa Japan as a synchronic episode for purposes of making comprehensible the wave of shocks that its survivors underwent in the mid–nineteenth century. Their world abruptly cracked. Why it was that change suddenly appeared so dangerous can best be grasped if we realize how much of one piece the Tokugawa experience had come to seem. Analytically separable, the parts (systems) of the Tokugawa configuration fitted the unspoken structures of order that governed social behavior. This network of structures was elaborate and precise, forming a balanced basis for long duration.

The assumption behind this mode of analysis is a simple one. Structures are the rules and regulations that control behavioral patterns, whereas the patterns themselves are the systems through which that behavior occurs. Thus a system of alternating red and green lights, for example, governs traffic flow on our roads, but this pattern of conducting vehicular and pedestrian traffic is itself subservient to the principle that alternating red and green lights constitute a visual linguistic protocol instructing us when to stop or go and in which direction. Other metaphors are available, such as the use of pain and pleasure as a basis for halting or going on with a particular kind of behavior, but the principle of structural underpinning for the systems through which society functions is present in any similar coding method that might be adduced. It is the notion of such a code that holds us here. How were the codes of Tokugawa Japan established? How can we decode behavior so as to grasp the structures that give it significance and meaning?

Claude Lévi-Strauss and others have set forth myths as keys to the code of human behavior.[4] In pursuing such a line for the analysis of Tokugawa Japan, we must posit certain guiding ideas whose prevalence ensured the continuance of the Tokugawa order. What follows is an attempt to distinguish some of the permanent structures from more transient phenomena in the Tokugawa period.

The Tokugawa Feudal System

Two opposed features of the Tokugawa settlement strike every observer. On the one hand, the political system erected during the seventeenth century provided a framework for containing centrifugal tendencies and allowing the orderly pursuit of economic and cultural interests throughout the several hierarchical layers of Japanese society. On the other hand, so much real change can be detected from early in the period that one wonders how the system managed to contain all the pressures that built up within it.

A device deliberately installed (but not always strictly observed) to promote stability, the *sakoku* or closed-country system, kept external influence under specified controls. But the very stability that the "closed" system encouraged and the political order reinforced had the unintended effect of affording ample opportunities for innovation and change. As John W. Hall has put it, a kind of "social entropy" occurred during the Tokugawa period, and this entropy resulted in the diffusion of some political power and cultural advantages to peripheral parts of the realm.[5] Social constraints, while never undone, were loosened, and cultural creativity increased throughout Japan along with literacy rates, especially among males, who were encouraged to read and attend local schools. Pursuing the physical metaphor of entropy, this chapter examines the broad institutional framework built in Tokugawa Japan, in order to understand how it held in check the entropic redistribution of political and, especially, economic power.

"Japanese feudalism" is a universal metaphor of the twentieth century. It appeared first in the research conducted by Western-trained Japanese scholars of the late Meiji period who sought both to characterize Japan and to suggest a basic analogy with the Tokugawa period. Many definitions of feudalism have been employed, ranging from the legalistic formulations of Frederic W. Maitland's generation to various Marxist-Leninist formulas, but all of them have one thing in common. They are metaphors for describing Japan and also for postulating its likeness to Europe.

If we remember that feudalism is a metaphor, it can be useful in looking at those Tokugawa Japanese structures that need to be considered here. Recently it has occurred to Western historians that the Tokugawa period retained almost nothing of earlier ("medieval") Japanese feudalism except its shell, because economic and even social change so affected Japan that its very face had changed and so had some of its deeper structures in the two centuries between 1600 and 1800. There is no doubt as to the degree of change and its widespread extent.

Feudalism, however, continued to characterize the formal exterior of the Tokugawa political system from its inception in 1600 through various modifications down to its last decade in the mid–nineteenth century. Those who actually played historical roles in the politics of Tokugawa Japan used language and expected formal behavior conforming to seventeenth-century prescriptions, which may appropriately be labeled feudal. Sham modes of expression may survive for centuries; sham modes of behavior rarely do. And there is no mistaking the serious way in which nineteenth-century political actors regarded the feudal ties that bound them. Even when they were seeking to break those bonds through appeal to old or new justifications for action, their circumspection is a motif that runs through the whole period and even the *bakumatsu* years. (Signifying the "end" [*matsu*] of the "bakufu" [*baku*], *bakumatsu* as we have seen is a generic periodizing code that always refers to the "late" Tokugawa period and differs in usage among historians only as they differ in assigning dates to periods. It covers something like the years from about 1825 to 1868, but some writers who are fond of stressing the Western impact on Japan tend to date it from 1850 or 1853. No matter when they elect to begin it, all writers must end *bakumatsu* with the demise of the bakufu in late 1867 and the start of 1868, when a proclamation issued from Kyoto declaring the "restoration of imperial rule" [*ōsei fukko*].)

Tokugawa feudalism: the phrase rings old and hollow, calling to mind pictures of outmoded land relations as well as "premodern" class relations. Leaving these aside, however, the shell of the old feudal system, its symbols and trappings, must have had meaning for the politicians of the time because generations of them followed the rules and acted according to symbolic prescription. Let us take them as they took themselves—seriously.

A simple model of feudalism will serve our purpose. Joseph Strayer, for example, used one that specifies (1) political decentralization in which a (divine) central authority no longer has the power to rule, so local lords wield effective political control; (2) economic decentralization in the sense of relative local self-sufficiency; and (3) a pattern of social stratification in which the lord-vassal relationship of the military profession determines the hierarchy of social groups.[6]

Viewed against this model, Tokugawa Japan shapes up as a feudal society. Imperial authority in Kyoto was vestigial at best and had little effect on politics in Tokugawa times, certainly not until the *bakumatsu* years. The Tokugawa house and its consanguineous branches were *primus inter pares* (first among equals) but not technically superior to the two-hundred-plus daimyo who controlled their own smaller and larger domains throughout the realm—the domains that came to be known as han. Economically, no political or local unit could ever be even proximately self-sufficient in the real world, but the objective of feudal control devices, to restore the agrarian basis of society and therefore regulate social and economic relations as if a farming economy prevailed, was met, at least on the face of it, and the ideal retained its attraction well into the nineteenth century. The economy had changed so much by 1700, or again by 1800, that the idea of an agrarian natural or physiocratic form was merely that, an idea. Yet even in the cities, among the mercantile houses that erupted into economic prominence during the seventeenth century, lip service was always paid to the original ideal.

Socially, the whole Tokugawa period reverberates with assertions and reaffirmations of the supremacy of samurai as the highest status group in society, higher than farmers, artisans, and merchants in the four-status hierarchy adapted with other Confucian doctrines from China and applied to Tokugawa needs. Never mind that in the course of two centuries the samurai had changed from warrior to administrator, bureaucrat, or teacher. The bureaucratization of the samurai made him a civilian and converted his status group into relatively one of the largest aristocracies in world history: 5 to 10 percent of Japan's population at any given time from the mid–seventeenth to the mid–nineteenth century consisted of samurai families. Thus the sword-carrying samurai were brought close to the classical Chinese ideal of the "warrior as a gentleman-scholar" *(bushi)*.

The performance of Tokugawa institutions also conforms to the Strayer model of feudalism. That is, political, economic, and social functions were carried out in ways that we would predict on the basis of the model. The *sankin kōtai* system of "alternate attendance" by the daimyo in their han and in the shogun's capital at Edo assured political and economic subordination of the daimyo to the bakufu. Alternate attendance had an unforeseen and powerful stimulating effect on economic change. It forced the han into debt and therefore compelled them to find new ways to make money, and as a result the economy expanded into nonphysiocratic activities far more rapidly than it might otherwise have done on its own.[7] But neither the bakufu nor the two-hundred-odd han forswore the feudal basis of economic behavior. All they could do was rationalize new kinds of economic performance and subsume them under the rubric of an agrarian economy. The social status of the samurai never came under direct attack, and the bakufu plus the han retained the military strength necessary to put down all challenges to samurai political and social supremacy. In the *bakumatsu* period such challenges finally began to take overt form, but even those who rebelled masked their intentions (if they had such intentions) and called their rebellions protests. The whole Tokugawa period passed without a single direct challenge to the character and continuity of the feudal system.

Pax Tokugawa: Multistate Balance of Power

"Balance of power" and "the European state system" are virtually synonymous phrases that have enjoyed long currency. Arising out of (European) international law devised from the seventeenth century onward, such phrases have been augmented by others of more recent derivation. At last we hear of "the Chinese world order," or we consider regional political relations among societies as international systems in their own right, such as the "East Asian international subsystem." [8] The circumstances of the first Japanese encounter with Europe in the sixteenth and seventeenth centuries make this sort of nomenclature applicable to the Tokugawa settlement as well. In short, Tokugawa Japan should be regarded as a self-contained and self-regulated system of "states" in much the same way as early modern Europe. This multistate system was subject to an analogous but differently grounded code of conduct that would pass, if need be, for "Japanese international law." All of these states were constituent parts of a greater whole known as the "realm"— the *tenka,* which literally means "all under heaven."

Too much and too little can be made of the Christians and traders who came to Japan after 1543. Efforts to narrate the history of Japan in the sixteenth century, or in the seventeenth century, using the European visitors as the chief construct, miss the frequency and magnitude of indigenous Japanese changes that mark the rise of the hegemons Oda Nobunaga, Toyotomi Hideyoshi, and finally Tokugawa Ieyasu. But to belittle the European encounter as an ephemeral episode involving only a tiny percentage of the population also misses the point. The Europeans brought ideas and guns, and both were important in war-torn feudal Japan of the late "warring states" *(sengoku)* period.

The challenge of Western ideas posed the greater problem, though the Japanese did their best to forget both Western weapons and Western thought after the country was essentially closed in the 1630s. Catholic theology had a leavening effect on a society already in ferment after three centuries of sporadic warfare. The concept of transcendent loyalty beyond all temporal power threatened both the Buddhist establishment and the military hierarchy. The gradually taken decision to close the country and regulate foreign contacts through the port of Nagasaki signified two things: a desire to be rid of weapons that might undo the political settlement, and a need to combat any ideas that might corrode the ideological compromise between Confucianists and the specific requirements of Japanese politics in the feudal mode. The alien quality of Christian theology provoked Japanese authorities to take measures against their own populace, measures that appear to have no parallel in the earlier history of Japan. As both George Elison and Robert Bellah point out, Christianity failed to comport with traditional Japanese political values and therefore became a target for ruthless suppression.[9] Transcendence was reserved for the Japanese myths, which seemed politically supportive to seventeenth-century political leaders, but supervening loyalty to a source outside of Japan—beyond the realm—was unacceptable to leaders who meant to curtail the endemic warfare and stabilize the mobile society of feudal Japan.

Beyond the systems that enabled Tokugawa feudal society to perform, we may perceive a further purpose: to carve out a rank order of internal political units and to keep both that order and the populations of the units in a stable balance. This is good balance-of-power thinking that owes nothing to external influences. Indeed, were European influence—or Chinese, for that matter—significant in this regard, the standard question must surely be, Why did the Tokugawa stop short of centralizing the realm? It was a feat, to all appearances, that was easily accomplished after the Meiji Restoration. Why not in the seventeenth century as well?

The answer is already apparent. A feudal *order* was wanted by Japan's military chieftains, the daimyo. To secure such an order necessitated a *primus inter pares,* but that was no unqualified desideratum, merely a necessary evil to most of the daimyo. If the Tokugawa were to play the role well, they had to avoid stepping on toes, and above all this role meant that they must drop any thought of total centralization. Daimyo acquiescence and constructive cooperation came not despite but because of the Tokugawa willingness to recognize han autonomy in fiscal matters, education, and local military control.[10] Only when facing the outside world did the bakufu speak for all Japan, and then because the daimyo had agreed that it was necessary to have a spokesman. Given the extent to which European traders and missionaries had traversed Japanese waters and coasts, only the *primus inter pares* of all the daimyo could handle such a role. So the tradition of *seii tai shōgun* (the "barbarian-subduing shogun") assumed a new function, that of fending off the European aliens rather than domestic or Mongol intruders.

Again it is useful to consider the *sankin kōtai* arrangements. The system whereby the daimyo were made to alternate between Edo and their home han strengthened the bakufu's hand whenever it came to dealing with foreigners. The related mechanisms of levying supportive military forces from the daimyo and obligating them to build defenses also helped the Tokugawa bakufu to command universal (that is, in Japan) respect as lord protector of the realm. On the other hand, there was no "national" or centralized system of taxation. Each han represented, as it were, a state or at least a "principality" *(Fürstentum)* integrated through *sankin kōtai* into the bakufu-and-han system—the *bakuhan taisei*. At Kyoto the imperial court represented a kind of vestigial source of sacral legitimacy, like the Holy Roman Empire. The whole system was politically suited to function as part of the feudal order. It reflected a structural predisposition to maintain a distinct set of separate political units, and it kept the "continent" (the realm of Japan) safe from outside interference. But it also held the component domestic units, the han, in approximate equilibrium. We are perhaps entitled to doubt that Prince Metternich could have improved upon it.

Levers of Change

Into the beautifully articulated Tokugawa world order came a series of debilitating challenges during the nineteenth century. These challenges issued from within and without. They proved unrelenting and finally undid the feudal system with its delicate power balance. Whether they *caused* the Meiji Restoration after the collapse of the Tokugawa bakufu will always remain a matter for definition and debate; undeniably their conjunction in midcentury represents a meaningful coincidence. It was a concatenation of forces too difficult for the systems of Tokugawa Japanese behavior to contain or neutralize.

Treatments of change in Tokugawa Japan, both Japanese and Western, tend to concentrate on economic change more than on other matters. This is a defensible approach in view of the vast range of innovation throughout the economy, but it does ignore philosophical and ideological departures that also have a bearing on the Meiji Restoration. Yet among the levers of change, several are properly called economic.

First, the population stabilized at about thirty million from 1720 all the way to 1850. This population stability was concurrent with increased productivity in all sectors of the economy. The result was that some Japanese got immensely richer, of necessity, because total wealth accelerated upward while the number of mouths stayed roughly the same. In any system of distribution or redistribution of wealth, some people get poorer, but when the total product goes up, so does the economic welfare of a very large number if not a majority of the populace.

Second, cities that headquartered the many daimyo and their vassals burgeoned as merchants competed to provide services in exchange for money and privileges paid by the samurai status group. Other already large cities such as Osaka, Kyoto, and Nagasaki also grew in size and wealth. While these cities were never capitals of the bakufu, the Tokugawa contrived to control them all. Meanwhile its seat of power at Edo became the greatest urban center of all, a metropolis with a population approaching one million by 1800. But the castle towns of the larger daimyo also grew into sizable cities where commerce prospered.

Third, from about 1700 rural markets began to expand and diversify in various parts of the country. Forces were deliberately unleashed by han governments—often in response to alternate attendance–induced deficits—to start cash cropping and commercial farming as well as small-scale industries in order to build han revenues. Urban wealth had grown most among the merchant status group. Rural prosperity probably came most often to ambitious farmers who possessed the resources and the will to take risks and invest in new methods and new endeavors.

No one can cavil at the importance of these changes for the future of Japan following the Meiji Restoration. In English their most persuasive exponent is Thomas C. Smith, and his work sustains an overwhelming argument that, lacking such changes, the transformation of Japan after 1868 would have gone nowhere.[11]

In contrast to economic explanations, efforts to suggest that changes in other aspects of life also spurred change after the restoration used to meet with minimal success. There is no exemplar for the notion that sufficient change occurred in the political system to herald anything but confusion and potential chaos. Discussions of Tokugawa culture often point to the diffusion or entropic redistribution of cultural creativity both geographically and sociologically, but cultural change has only just begun to be put forward as a necessary precondition for subsequent changes that took place in the Meiji era. Social stratification patterns changed during the Tokugawa period, but the contention that urban merchants gained so much wealth that they became the wave of the future has not stood the test of scholarly research. The demarche into the new cultural history comes from Harry Harootunian in his chapter for *The Cambridge History of Japan*'s volume on the nineteenth century.[12] He sets forth an argument that culture depends neither upon the economic "substructure" nor (as older theories would have it) upon political structures as they change. Rather culture itself helps to determine the flow of politics and the economy. Indeed, culture becomes a creative metaphor for the intellectual sources of social change that have been given credit for driving the great modification that finally overtook Tokugawa Japan. Harootunian points to the "polyphonic discourses" that accompany changes in later Tokugawa thought; he calls attention to the fact that "the operation of mediations" intervening between society and culture is responsible for these changes, not some abstract conception of priority resulting from the "reflection" of base changes in "superstructural" arenas such as culture (as we are told in the usual version).[13]

It is to the intellectual sphere that one must turn for announcement of the generation of changes that were ultimately to mark the period after the Meiji Restoration. These new ideas usually came from the minds of samurai, and the question therefore arises, What happened to Tokugawa intellectual history that made reformers out of obedient servants in a fundamentally feudal hierarchy? We have this question from Harootunian as well as from other writers, such as Tetsuo Najita, who has shown that merchants decisively shared in the creative elaboration of discourses that originated in the samurai worldview.[14]

The simplest answer to the question lies in the writings of late Tokugawa thinkers, and it seems the best answer to sketch here: it is that perceived reality no longer accorded with the canons of Confucian thought, and concerned thinkers therefore sought other doctrines that would better conform to their perceptions. This Kantian sort of answer is perhaps too pat to do justice to the widespread effort to understand reality, an effort that drew impetus from the very Confucian teachings that were to come under scrutiny and attack; for Confucianism encouraged curiosity and "the investigation of things" *(kakubutsu kyūri)*. But Confucian doctrines were found inadequate long before American and European ships began to prowl Japanese seacoasts in hopes of bringing to pass the second opening.

Domestic Japanese conditions prompted thoughtful scholars to abandon the orthodoxy of the bakufu and most of the han. Only a minority of commentators on public affairs reached toward radical changes in discourse that would match the radical discontinuities observable in society. But those who did deserve attention.

First, the pioneers who studied things Western challenged orthodoxy, though sometimes only in oblique or tangential ways. The so-called *rangakusha* and *yōgakusha,* "Dutch scholars" and "specialists in Western studies," made their presence felt out of all proportion to their minuscule numbers. Many of them worked for the bakufu itself, or for their own han governments. They did not begin by seeking change; rather, they sought to understand the Western nations and the sources of strength that were propelling Western ships across the world's oceans. By the time of *bakumatsu, yōgaku* functioned as an important voice calling for planned change in Japanese institutions.[15]

Second, action-oriented samurai who were disenchanted with the passivity of Confucianism, its contemplative side which was touched by Zen Buddhism, looked for more active traditions through which to express their ideas. Often such people took the mantle of *jitsugaku,* "practical studies." *Jitsugaku* implied action instead of words, but it also connoted the unhappiness of those who had "real talent" *(jitsuzai)* that they could not use, because their relatively low samurai rank excluded them from posts of authority. *Jitsugaku* rivaled and was often coupled with *yōgaku* in the slogans and programs of *bakumatsu* youth.

Finally, a core of "nativists" *(kokugakusha,* often misleadingly rendered as scholars of "national learning") emerged to launch a furious condemnation of Confucianism as an alien—that is, Chinese—and outdated language of discourse. To these people the problems of the entire Tokugawa period, reaching back to early in the seventeenth century, had to be viewed in uniquely Japanese terms. China was not the enemy so much as *Chinese*—the alien tradition whose language, and therefore linguistic code, could no longer articulate Japanese concerns.[16] Joining their own message to that of some Confucian scholars who can be styled "classicists" (the *kogakuha*) because they wanted to express their ideas in the uncluttered concepts of original Confucianism, the nativists ultimately did much to politicize domestic intellectual trends. Both the nativists and the classicists were seeking simple concepts to serve as "verbal icons" against the status quo. The Japanese tradition, for the nativists, and ancient Chinese thought, for the classicists, thus supplied linguistic protocols that could express indignation, condemnation, and dissatisfaction.

The nativists have recently enjoyed a bright burst of exploration by Peter Nosco (for the eighteenth century) and Harry Harootunian (for the nineteenth).[17] Nativist endeavors are cloaked by the occasional opacity of their writing, but their purpose seems clear enough. They raised ideas indigenous to Japan to a new height, and they used their teaching to aid ordinary people in conducting their lives and running their villages.

The texts of these thinkers often seem arcane, but that may be attributable to our insensitivity to their referents and contexts. There is reason to suggest that their doctrines prepared the ground for radical political change and had as much to do with the events of *bakumatsu* as those of any other writers, including thinkers from the Confucian historical school in the Tokugawa-branch han of Mito. *Kokugaku* and *kogaku* both stand as intellectual levers of change.[18]

The Realm as a Normative Concept

These manifestations of change within Japan coincided with the arrival of foreigners who were bent on reopening the country to outside contact. The holistic conception of the realm *(tenka)* was threatened, and the Meiji Restoration signaled its downfall. Thereafter the realm had to be replaced by the state; more technically it was the nation-state concept, borrowed from the West where it originated, that finally supplanted the realm.

But the substitution was unequal. The state as a system of power might be more authoritarian but never could attain the moral authority of the realm. Embracing rituals as well as rights, symbols of culture as well as those of power, the realm combined state and society into a wider entity, one that encompassed all Japanese as well as all of their physical environment.[19]

When twentieth-century Japanese "ultranationalists" championed the *kokutai,* they were nostalgically harking back to the notion of the realm. Its function was central and it was "religious" in character, so it is appropriate to the sense of metaphor to follow George Elison in translating *kokutai* not as "national polity" but as "the mystical body of Japan." [20] As a self-regulating total entity, the realm rested on a political base that was intimately related to its legitimating symbols. The Japanese creation myths, including the triumphal accession of Jinmu Tennō, had authorized the Tokugawa bakufu to rule as *primus inter pares* of all the secular powers. But the myths by no means demanded a centralized nation-state, so when they were used in order to rationalize the creation of such a state, they lost some of their force because they were subjected to the scrutiny of the political center stage onto which they had been thrust.

How the transition from realm to state occurred during the short period known as *bakumatsu* is the subject of the remainder of this study. As we proceed we may recall that the suprapolitical connotations of the realm as "all under heaven" were never lost, and that historical actors were themselves embedded in a cultural matrix that was at least as important as the political drama in which they were playing. To restore the emperor was seen by more than one group of political actors as a way to redeem the realm, to make it whole again, and so the realm was the appropriate form of organization from the viewpoint of most informed Japanese.[21] But the nation-state was the particular political form that won out in the Meiji settlement. Even now the realm remains a treasured ideal from the past, one that again may prove important for Japan's future.

Chapter Four

Plotting Bakumatsu History:
A Fourfold Narrative

The French Revolution as commonly conceived never took place.
—Claude Lévi-Strauss

Flashy words seem to be necessary to characterize the course of events that marked Japan in the decade and a half from Perry's arrival in 1853 to the Meiji Restoration of 1868. Students of the period disagree on many things but universally hold that *bakumatsu* Japan witnessed a whirlwind of memorable events happening one right after another. In this chapter I shall reevaluate this process of events using a new approach intended to highlight the onset of large-scale political and social change. The basis of the approach lies in analyzing the multiple "plots," or story lines, that historical agents (human actors) experienced during the final years of the old regime, in this case, that is, of Tokugawa rule. Long-lived as it was, lasting from 1600 to 1868, the Tokugawa period appears to retain its synchronic unity across the centuries. But the era ended with the country in profound disarray. Considering all this confusion, those who study *bakumatsu* Japan have never been content with just one plot, just a single "arc" of narrative reconstruction.

Motives and Narratives in Writing History

Instead of focusing on samurai heroes and villains who contested the foreign incursion into Japan, this chapter will identify four groups of actors during the *bakumatsu* years. It will present each of these groups according to the motives and experiences of the members. It will point to the interactions between the four narrative structures, the plots or *mythoi,* but it will do so without trying to homogenize them into a unitary historiographical line. This is a method that accepts the inevitable prefiguration of the historian's field but seeks nevertheless to convey the perceived intentions of differing groups of historical actors.

Bakumatsu Japan was above all a diversified era. In a time famous for its disorders, many and different voices echoed around the land. Chaos beckoned where order had for so long prevailed. The impulses expressed by the Japanese of the *bakumatsu* years emanated from a multiplicity of motives. To be sure, real people do not play out "story lines" or experience "generic plots." They live in the here and now and try to make the best of it. Historians, however, have no choice but to look backward; they must construct narratives that try to decode the random data handed on from the past, data that include evidence about the aspirations of historical actors. So it is the point of this chapter to explore the differential roles of four interacting groups on the eve of the Meiji Restoration.

Let us begin by noting that historians have allowed that the era was diverse but have been unsure about how to deal with this diversity. In a passage notable for capturing the surface contradictions of a time of confusion, George Sansom once declared that in *bakumatsu* Japan "a fantastic ethos prevail[ed] throughout the land." He goes on to list the seeming paradoxes that beset the analyst who would retrospectively make sense of the era:

> The domestic politics of this period were described by more than one contemporary writer in works with such titles as *Yumemonogatari,* or *Story of a Dream.* That, though not so intended, was a fitting description of the plots and counterplots, the quarrels and arguments, the confusion between names and things, the misunderstandings and bewilderments which characterize this uneasy epoch. It is full of episodes that seem not to belong to waking life, but have the plausible inconsequence, the unearthly logic, of events in a dream.[1]

If this means Sansom had trouble explaining what happened between Perry's arrival and the restoration, then he is surely right, but why does the confusion of the era lead to confused explanations? True, as the bakufu comes closer to the end of its time in power, the historian looking back finds it correspondingly difficult to formulate a coherent narrative. The chronology gets "hot," as Lévi-Strauss would say, as stunning events follow one another with dizzying speed.[2] The result is a period heavy with names and dates but hard for the historian to convert into a clear-cut unitary narrative.

The confusion over how to present an explanation of this period stems perhaps from the irregular and even extraordinary quality of life at the time. Victor Turner characterizes such periods as "liminal," arguing that reason and logic rarely govern the course of events in these historical watersheds. Instead, myth works its way to the fore, appealing to the psychological need for stability and deep-seated truth—deep truth, more compelling than the superficial and perhaps transitory facts of existence, truth shared by elites and masses alike. "Myths treat of origins but derive from transitions," writes Turner. "Myths relate how one state of affairs became another. . . ; how chaos became cosmos."[3] Myths reassure people when events threaten the viability of the social or political order; for myth promises recurrence, the return of fundamental virtues and heroic action, as Nietzsche and Mircea Eliade were always pointing out.

No liminal period in world history is more rife with myth and the quest for redemption than *bakumatsu* Japan. There are numberless accounts of what happened, concurring in a skeletal outline of facts and events but not in what those facts and events mean. Although the chronology is not seriously in doubt, there are many schools of interpretation. Social scientists disagree about the "revolutionary" character of the Meiji Restoration. Writers who judge the restoration a failure, or simply deem it deficient, usually deny that it amounted to a revolution. Others who applaud the experiments of the restoration's leaders take refuge in a thesis that their revolution was made from above, by an oligarchy, yet it did wonders for Japan and therefore deserves high praise.[4]

A working historian confronted with the multifarious versions of how the *bakumatsu* period proceeded and the Meiji Restoration came to happen must despair about what any retrospective observer can really know. We were not there and cannot "objectively" decide the worth of every competing piece of documentary evidence. Whether we can draw any valid conclusions, and thereby proceed to a clear explanation, is a challenging question. The issue boils down to one of faith, or simply one of ideology, in which a historian emphasizes an explanatory pattern based on the sort of evidence that seems most appealing—ideas, demographic data, political actions, or whatever. The facts of *bakumatsu* history are not really in dispute; the issue arises rather over how one strings them together to produce an explanation. In recent years social science models among Western scholars and the economic determinism that tends to prevail among the Japanese have stimulated an effective search for "new" factual information (previously unknown or frankly forgotten data) to add to our working knowledge, but they have muddied the issue of what the restoration finally signifies.

The search for another way to explain the *bakumatsu* years and the restoration tends to draw a historian back to first principles—really, to the principals themselves, the actors who took part in the many dramas of *bakumatsu* Japan. Collingwood pointed the way by identifying the objective thus: the historian must remember, he wrote, that an action is "the unity of the outside and inside of an event," that is, of its exterior happenings and its interior "ideas"; so the historian's "main task is to think himself into this action, to discern the thought of its agent." [5] Kenneth Burke, meanwhile, was cautioning readers that those who would understand human motivation must bear in mind "a pentad of key terms": act, scene, agent, agency, and purpose.[6] The purpose of this chapter is to go back and reconstruct the history of *bakumatsu* Japan according to the intentions and perceptions of the "agents"—the groups of actors who participated in the stories that go with the era.

But this formulation raises the question, how many dramas? The Greeks (and the indefatigable H. W. Fowler) would remind us that no "drama" can have more than a single protagonist.[7] Yet reality intervenes in the harmony of artistic design. So the necessarily simultaneous occurrence of many small histories within the larger history of *bakumatsu* Japan allows us the license to speak of several protagonists, several dramas. By a further leap into the admittedly arbitrary realm of assigning literary plots to the aspirations of historical actors, we may choose to assign a name to the kind of story that each of the several groups lived through. Once we have done this, the crazy quilt of seeming paradoxes and bewildering turns of action that bothered George Sansom may be less troublesome, and we can patch together some sort of order in the process of producing explanatory patterns.

It is a commonplace that people have to make sense of events by construing them in story form. "We tell ourselves stories in order to live," observes the contemporary critic Joan Didion. "We interpret what we see, select the most workable of the multiple choices. We live entirely . . . by the imposition of a narrative line upon disparate images, by the 'ideas' with which we have learned to freeze the shifting phantasmagoria which is our actual experience."[8] The people of *bakumatsu* Japan had to make some sense of their life situations if for no other reason than the very novelty of much of what they faced. Excited and confused, their existence altered by forces that seemed to them inscrutable, they experienced different stories depending on the attitudes they brought to their rapidly changing world.

And no one of these groups experienced the same Meiji Restoration that any of the others did. Different motives and different perceptions yielded different results, ranging from defeat and frustration to success and jubilation. Lévi-Strauss, referring to another world-historical context long viewed as liminal, that of the French Revolution, puts the point boldly:

> When one proposes to write a history of the French Revolution one knows (or ought to know) that it cannot, simultaneously and under the same heading, be that of the Jacobin and that of the aristocrat. *Ex hypothesi,* their respective totalizations . . . are equally true. One must therefore . . . give up the attempt to find in history a totalization of the set of partial totalizations; or alternatively one must recognize them all as equally real: but only to discover that the French Revolution as commonly conceived never took place.[9]

Lévi-Strauss regards recorded history as a batch of "fraudulent outlines" whose only peculiar characteristic is chronology: the important thing is the temporal order (sequence) in which events occur. "Dates may not be the whole of history . . . but they are its *sine qua non,* for history's entire originality and distinctive nature lie in apprehending the relation between *before* and *after.*" Some historical reconstructions are loaded with dates, representing eras about which the historian feels that "the pressure of history" is high. Such histories, as noted, feature "hot" chronologies, while others are cool or cold by comparison. The presence or absence of dates will depend on what and whom the historian plans to emphasize—

whose "story" is being told.[10] As a result, no history of the French Revolution could ever give an "adequate" account of what happened, only a narrative that is chronologically correct, yet contextually truncated. Some things would have to be left out, because the total historical field in question holds the potential for an infinite number of events and stories. So it was with Japan. Many restorations occurred, not just one: many different experiences of the events of *bakumatsu* Japan took place, despite the fact that we routinely speak of "the Meiji Restoration" as if it were a uniform process.

Most people have written restoration history from the point of view of the winners, those hardy dreamers who lived out their passionate ambitions imbued with myths about Japan and its destiny.[11] But the winners were hardly alone in living so close to myth. Turner has pointed out that by its nature "liminality [is] a period of structural impoverishment and symbolic enrichment" when people take stock of their cultural inventory and seize upon myths that relate to life crises and milieux outside of normal rules and procedures.[12] For this period I propose to use a quaternary scheme that identifies four sets of actors—four "protagonists"—who lived four separate story arcs requiring four orientations toward the world along with four different ideological and political outlooks.[13] This scheme excludes some groups and lumps individuals willy-nilly for purposes of clarity. But the danger of oversimplification from conducting this exercise seems minimal compared to the advantage of looking at the restoration through the lenses of a well-delineated set of groups.

A full elaboration of the method proposed in this chapter would require a book in "thick description," the phrase that Clifford Geertz borrowed from Gilbert Ryle to characterize an ethnography that reveals multiple layers of meaning in behavior as it is viewed in cultural context.[14] That sort of thorough elaboration will not be our task here because I need to concentrate on the method and the perspective it offers.

By the terms of this method, the protagonists of the several dramas on the eve of the Meiji Restoration divide into four groups, each with its own story arc: (1) the Western diplomats and traders; (2) the bakufu and its allies, even when they disagreed, so that this "one" group perforce includes both the imperial court and the daimyo of those large han that did act; (3) the people, i.e., the bearers of popular millennial and other "religious" movements; and (4) those who called themselves imperial loyalists, who finally did "seize the jewel" that was the Meiji emperor and made the restoration in his name. Adapting from the analysis of literary plots by Northrop Frye, we may say that the foreigners sought reconciliation, on their own terms, and lived the story line of *comedy*. Not that theirs was a funny story, it just ended the right way from their standpoint, since it managed to reintegrate a disordered Japan and made stable trade relations possible again. The other narrative forms include *irony* on the part of the bakufu and leading han, *tragedy* for the popular movements that were suppressed and redirected after the restoration, and *romance* or adventure for the self-proclaimed patriots who quested after and finally found the grail that betokened success.[15]

Now, these four "agents" or groups of historical actors perceived and explained their own actions and intentions very differently, in conformity with their disparate views of the "scene of action" and the discrete purposes that animated them. This is not a formal psychological judgment, but one based on cognition and perception. The question of how we define cognition and perception arises here, but I am using them in a nontechnical manner with no intent to stray into formal psychology. Both cognition and perception signify awareness or discernment but also the process by which someone becomes aware or discerning; what is involved is knowledge, and the way knowledge is acquired. Geertz might say that their worldviews conflicted, that the four groups of actors construed sheer reality in quite different and basically incompatible ways.[16]

It will give us a handle for comparing these four groups if we separate them on the basis of their perception of reality—whether they saw reality in an *integrated* or a *dispersed* way. Let me summarize the juxtaposition of integration or dispersion as opposed tendencies among competing social groups in a tabular display, where the protagonists appear on the left-hand side:

Western envoys	Integrative
Bakufu and daimyo	Dispersive
Popular revivalists	Integrative
Imperial loyalists	Dispersive

All four groups of actors sought national unity and a revival of Japan's stability. On this point they concurred, but on others they did not, specifically on their cognitive attitude towards social action: depending on whether a particular group saw its basic welfare as residing in itself alone, or in the ethnic collectivity of Japan, they may be said to be either *integrative* or *dispersive* in orientation.[17]

Western Envoys and the Drive for Stability

Foreign diplomats who came to Japan as representatives of their governments knew that the Japanese were no match militarily for the force of arms and technological sophistication that had come to characterize the European great powers and the United States. Yet the Japanese did seem an uncommonly volatile lot, forever subject to shifts of mood despite their discreet external behavior. The foreign traders who followed the diplomats when the commercial treaties went into effect felt much the same way.

What these foreigners wanted was to be able to deal with Japan unfettered by concern about personal security or the ramifications of internal Japanese political turmoil. Theirs was the start of a mission of deliverance: the best of them—the American consul, Townsend Harris; the English minister, Harry Parkes; and the French minister, Léon Roches—hoped to induce the Tokugawa bakufu to bring the country into the community of civilized nations and end the "barbarism" of ancient ways, which heretofore had kept Japan in feudal bondage. Ethnocentrists to the core, they found nothing in Japanese culture to arrest their faith in civilization and progress. They wondered how the Japanese would ever be qualified to pursue these twin muses of an emerging nineteenth-century Western social gospel.

When in 1853 the officials of the bakufu had looked with disfavor on Commodore Perry's assertion that Japan must abandon its long seclusion, he threatened them with the possibility of destroying Edo, which had a huge and vulnerable population of more than a million. Perry's return in 1854 resulted in the hurried signing of the Treaty of Kanagawa, binding Japan and the United States in ties of "perfect peace and amity."

Subsequent dealings with Japan also featured heavy reliance on forcible persuasion. In 1862 several samurai serving the daimyo of

Satsuma murdered an English merchant by the name of Richardson. Lacking progress on the issue, the British in the summer of 1863 punished Satsuma with a naval bombardment of its capital, Kagoshima.[18] Four Western powers—the United States, Britain, France, and the Netherlands—sent a joint flotilla to Chōshū in the summer of 1864. This small navy bombarded the port Shimonoseki to punish Chōshū authorities who had given orders to fire on Western shipping in a vain effort literally "to repel the barbarians" after the imperial court at Kyoto had proclaimed June 25, 1863, as the date when foreign trade must cease and foreigners must leave Japan.

Parkes and Roches took to forging alliances rather than bombing ports as the strategy of choice for treating with the Japanese. Roches made overtures to the Tokugawa bakufu; France even loaned money to Edo for military improvements.[19] The British hedged but decided to cast their lot with Satsuma and Chōshū, the two southwestern han that finally ended the bakufu's dominion over Japan. Most likely the outcome was unchanged by great-power intervention, though no one should doubt its importance: the Westerners made themselves felt.

Algernon Bertram Mitford served as a diplomat in Japan from 1866 to 1870. In 1867–68 "Bertie" Mitford worked for Parkes in the English legation. Later named Baron Redesdale, Mitford brought to his work an aristocrat's disdain for the ordinary. He disliked the newly opened trading port of Yokohama as a sailor's town, not typically Japanese, and he took pleasure in traveling to Kyoto where he could work with the samurai who ran the new Meiji government. Mitford's recollections attest to the preoccupation of the foreigners with maintaining law and order as they addressed affairs in Japan. This becomes especially clear at moments after they had been attacked by antiforeign loyalists.

On February 4, 1868, for example, Mitford was present when a number of foreign diplomats came under attack by a Japanese force commanded by a samurai from Okayama. This man, Taki Zensaburō, not surprisingly was ordered to kill himself by committing *harakiri* as punishment for launching the assault on the foreigners.[20] Mitford's fellow British diplomat Ernest Satow also indicates how important it was to the foreigners that the Japanese public should understand that antiforeign behavior was punishable by death. "The countrymen of this Bizen man [Taki Zensaburō] told us that they considered the sentence a just and beneficial one."[21]

By 1868 the foreigners had constructed their own version of what was going on, one punctuated by bloodletting. Five decades later when they wrote their memoirs, Satow and Mitford recalled the violence and death that marked the early postrestoration scene. In particular, they both wrote of three attacks by loyalists upon foreigners within the first few weeks after the January 3 coup in Kyoto. One of these was the Okayama force's shooting of an American sailor and subsequent assault on other foreigners at random. The second attack took place at Sakai on March 8, when a group of Tosa samurai assaulted the crew of a French vessel. This episode ended up costing eleven French lives and an equal number of the Tosa attackers, who were "allowed" to execute themselves by *harakiri*.[22]

The third of these three attacks was one that Mitford and Satow personally experienced. It is the one that caused them the most chagrin. It involved an attack in Kyoto on their chief, Harry Parkes, the British minister, and on his entourage while they were all en route to visit the emperor on March 23. As Satow ironically observes, "It was now our turn to suffer an assault at the hands of the fanatics of patriotism, from which our constant advocacy of the rights of the sovereign afforded us no protection."[23] Mitford recounts that "two Ronin armed with naked swords sprang out and began slashing and hacking in the maddest fury. . . . Satow had a narrow escape. . . . I saw the murderer coming at me [and] wrenched the bleeding sword out of his grip." After this close call, Parkes turned to him and said, "Sensation diplomacy this, Mitford." "It certainly was," adds Mitford.[24]

Mitford thought that a slaughter of foreigners was narrowly averted on February 4 when the Okayama troops had gotten out of hand at Kobe: "We had avoided the Scylla of Osaka [and] had steered into the Charybdis of Hiogo [Kobe], where we were . . . to undergo an experience which, by the merest luck, did not end in a general massacre of the whole of the Foreign Representatives, together with numbers of Consuls and subjects of various nations."[25] Satow concurred and called for swift retribution after the manner of the forced *harakiri* of the Sakai attackers: "As regards the case of the Tosa men at Sakai, no punishment was ever more righteously inflicted. These Japanese massacred a boat's crew of inoffensive and unarmed [French]men." [26]

By displaying military superiority over their Japanese hosts, the foreigners not only underscored their presence but also tipped their hand. Whether French or English, pro- or anti-bakufu, the Westerners considered Japan a small piece in the puzzle of the world's balance of power. The games they played were ideologically conservative in the extreme, and no wonder; their purpose was always to protect their own advantage. Sometimes they betrayed their extreme conservatism. This happened, for example, when the attack on Parkes at Kyoto moved Mitford to explain that it "was irrational and to us unintelligible; but the Jo-i [*jōi* or antiforeign forces] were animated by the spirit of a priest of Ise." [27] To assure themselves of success, the foreigners needed to preserve the status quo. As the French saw it, this meant continued bakufu hegemony over Japan. Through British eyes the revival of stability could better be accomplished by new leaders from Satsuma and Chōshū. Stability, however, remained the coin of the realm for all of the foreigners. A Japan in chaos was too troublesome a market into which to export and sell foreign goods.

It is sometimes forgotten just how chaotic the restoration really was as a process. Battles were fought and soldiers died in 1868 before the palace coup of January 3 could start to serve as the principal shaping event of modern Japanese history. "We began to feel that the dogs of war were loose," allowed Mitford.[28] Meiji forces commanded by imperial loyalists had to contend with active resistance from armies loyal to the shogun. Edo and other places, especially in northeastern Japan, stayed aloof from events in Kyoto and Osaka. Their ultimate fall may have stemmed as much from Tokugawa Yoshinobu's reluctance to take on "the emperor's army" as from the skill or success of the new forces. Even so, the foreigners could see that the old order was changing. Mitford commented on the hogdepodge of forces assembled to try to help the shogun: "They looked like the hobgoblins of a nightmare." [29]

It is not surprising that we seem to require more than one "plot" to lend verisimilitude to the way we represent the motives of those who acted during the *bakumatsu* period. The common people have received less attention than their many expressions of concern would indicate they deserve; the experience of the foreigners has also been inadequately represented in the past. Before we look at them, however, we need to turn to the Tokugawa *bakuhan* system and its pillars: these people are well known to historians, although the approach used here will show them in a new light.

Bakufu and Daimyo: Irony of the Establishment

On one key point—the protection of stability—the Westerners agreed with the officials of the Tokugawa bakufu and most of the major daimyo—or at least they did until 1866. Both the foreigners and the Japanese leaders approached events from a standpoint of situational congruence: these two groups were quite willing to live with the status quo if only they could revive it.[30] However they might tamper, neither the foreigners nor the bakufu and daimyo wanted to forgo Japan's essential stability.

While the Westerners were intent on securing Japan as a stable trading partner under duress, Japanese authorities worried more about internal stability and its requisite political order. Bakufu officials and leading daimyo shared a common concern with the status quo, and they made policies designed to maintain it. An occasional maverick like Ii Naosuke, lord of Hikone and the great elder *(tairō)* of the bakufu from mid-1858 until he was assassinated in March 1860, aimed to turn back the clock and use tyranny to revive a status quo ante that had become impossible to defend. But frankly all Japanese leaders favored the existing political configuration. Their notions of situational congruence varied from domain to domain, and within the chambers and councils of the bakufu where lesser officials ambitious for power concocted schemes for maximizing the bakufu's authority. Situational congruence was to remain its own reward, a fit objective for politicians to pursue, and one fully sanctioned by a Confucian hierarchical political order.

It is true that some Japanese leaders labored mightily to change the political system. They displayed real energy and conviction in doing so, and this very disposition toward change sets them apart from the foreigners, who were anxious not to disturb the status quo because they wanted to perpetuate their trade advantage. Bakufu and han officials played opposing forces off one another to disperse threats and resolve disputes through subsumption of the conflicting parties into the overall context. But the more they worked at this strategy, the harder it became to keep things in any kind of order.

The best of these Japanese officials were what we might call "liberal" because of their desire to spread around the benefits and the authority they held, thereby hoping to co-opt potential opponents into an effective consensus while the bakufu was still ensconced at its head. Abe Masahiro had tried this tack while he was chair of the bakufu's Council of Elders *(rōjū)* from 1845 to 1855, and his successor, Hotta Masayoshi, followed the same course until Ii Naosuke forcibly intervened in 1858. After Ii was murdered at the hands of samurai whose feudal leaders he had treated harshly during his so-called Ansei Purge of 1858–59, new bakufu leaders resumed a policy of temporizing, consulting, and inviting both the court and the daimyo to combine in new tactical arrangements that begged the question of full and systemic reform. This was the political strategy known as *kōbu gattai*—"union of court and camp" (Kyoto and Edo) in a grand alliance to reestablish stability.

The twin geniuses of this whole "liberal" approach in *bakumatsu* Japan were Matsudaira Shungaku and Tokugawa Yoshinobu, well-known leaders who were respectively the daimyo of Fukui and the daimyo of Hitotsubashi. Both were close relatives of the original line of shoguns. In 1857–58 these two joined forces to create a small alliance of influential daimyo together with bakufu and court officials who tried to secure the shogunal succession for Tokugawa Yoshinobu, born the seventh son of Mito's former daimyo Tokugawa Nariaki and qualified by status within the family to succeed if the main line failed to produce a shogun. This was a crucial moment in Japanese history, and it involved a full-fledged campaign among the court nobles in Kyoto to lobby for Tokugawa Yoshinobu's candidacy. But the opportunity passed unrealized when Ii Naosuke's "Ansei Purge" blocked this stratagem. They had to await another opportunity.

Their opportunity came in 1862. Tokugawa Yoshinobu was named the shogun's guardian *(kōken)* and Matsudaira Shungaku received the new bakufu post of "political executive" *(seiji sōsai)*. These two seasoned and popular political figures now attempted at one and the same time to rebuild feudal morale and to strengthen the bakufu. They relaxed the feudal obligation of alternate attendance *(sankin kōtai)* that required the daimyo to shuttle periodically between Edo and their own domains. Thereby they succeeded in saving money for the fiscally pressed daimyo at home, but this economy measure backfired politically as Edo was turned into a partially depopulated city beset by economic recession. The samurai component of the city's population, numbering almost half of Edo's million-plus residents, by and large left and went home or elsewhere in search of reform. The problem of an economically diminished Edo shortly led to an unsuccessful attempt to rehabilitate alternate attendance.[31]

By the beginning of 1867, however, Tokugawa Yoshinobu finally assumed the mantle of shogun (the last shogun, as it turned out) and set out to cooperate with ambitious middle officials to maintain the bakufu's supremacy, even while acknowledging daimyo claims to feudal autonomy. The apex of this policy was reached in the fall of 1867, when the bakufu announced the new policy of *taisei hōkan,* which would formally return governing power to the imperial court. According to this plan devised by Tosa han, the shogun would step down and join all other feudal lords in a new participatory system based on a council that would "advise" the imperial court on actual policy formulation. The Tokugawa house would remain in control of feudal allocation of economic resources, with its landholdings undiminished.

The conciliar scheme might have worked if Satsuma and Chōshū had gone along. Instead, acting through the old imperial court at Kyoto, they intervened in January 1868 to restore the Meiji emperor on their own imperial loyalist terms. In a fickle age, however, liberal reformers are always ripe candidates for an unhappy end. Ample resources and a political culture well disposed to compromise are the sine qua non of liberal politics, but *bakumatsu* Japan was running short of both. Beset by external troubles and pressed to adopt sometimes mutually exclusive domestic policies, the bakufu and those daimyo who cooperated with it were confronting a dilemma whose only remedy appeared to be the use of force. The liberals did not want to compel their detractors to support the status quo, yet they were quite willing to divide and conquer: they would discriminate against feudal lords who were recalcitrant, even though the ultimate support of all the daimyo was necessary for the success of the liberal line. Plainly they required consensus, but their own policy of working back and forth to accentuate the weaknesses of their rivals hampered them in getting it. Against heavy odds they made a valiant effort, though it was one they might as well have given up as hopeless.

The problem of the liberals is nicely illustrated by a statement attributed to Tokugawa Yoshinobu in 1863, when the British crisis with Satsuma over Richardson's murder reached a climax. Not a thing that is going to happen, he wrote to the Council of Elders, can do any good for the bakufu. If hostilities should break out between Britain and Satsuma, then "victory for the English would be a disgrace for the country, victory for Satsuma a blow to the bakufu's prestige." [32] For the bakufu this brought a classic dilemma: to intervene in Satsuma's internal affairs would invite accusations of disrespect for feudal proprieties, yet to ignore Britain's demand for retribution would show weakness to the foreigners.

Nothing could capture the liberal dilemma more clearly. Because the han were outside the bakufu, the bakufu could not punish Satsuma for killing the hapless Richardson. But because Satsuma was a part of the Japanese political system, it appeared to the bakufu that Japan could only lose if Satsuma were injured by the British, and Japan's loss was necessarily also the bakufu's. The bakufu was *primus inter pares* in the feudal order and the source of authority to which all foreigners looked as they tried to wrench Japan into the international system that they were erecting around the world.

How could such a dilemma be resolved? The same problem recurred when the bakufu twice tried to punish Chōshū for practicing radical policies that infuriated some foreigners and some Japanese—and coincidentally challenging bakufu authority. First in 1864 in response to the imperial court's wishes, then again in 1866, the bakufu mobilized troops and mounted punitive expeditions against Chōshū. In 1866 the forces supporting the bakufu actually were repulsed, causing great embarrassment for the whole political system because it ultimately depended on bakufu military supremacy within Japan. Yet far from calming the fears of other daimyo, this pair of assaults on Chōshū sparked the greater fear among the daimyo that if the bakufu had dared to move in this fashion against Chōshū, might it not soon attempt to make their own feudal autonomy an anachronism?

Satsuma therefore came to rethink the cozy relationship it had cultivated with the bakufu. Early in 1866 Satsuma decided instead to make common cause with Chōshū in a secret alliance whose existence eventually made possible the coup d'état of January 1868—the Meiji Restoration in its classic form. All the complexities of this political situation were familiar to the bakufu, whose officials possessed the greatest stock of knowledge and understanding in Japan about the outside world; they had even established schools and offices for analyzing the sources of Western military, political, and economic strength *(yōgaku)*. Despite bakufu expertise about internal as well as external affairs, the 1860s were to witness a massive outburst of simplistic yet powerful emotional distress at the condition of the country. This outburst finally cost the bakufu its hegemony.

The Hopes and Fears of Common People

The great simplifiers had taken the field. It was a time when the many complex truths would be ignored while everyone concentrated on the presence of noble motives and heroic deeds. As one author remarks apropos of the Irish revolutionaries of 1916, "The agents must be great simplifiers if they are to rise to the purity of heart that is to hate one thing";[33] or to love one thing, such as the cause of imperial loyalism in Japan. Nor was this simplification confined to the samurai elite or to purely partisan politics.

The common people made up the bulk of Japan's population of some thirty-five million, and as a disaggregated mass they came to stand on grounds just as situationally transcendent as those of the most dedicated anti-bakufu imperial loyalist samurai. But the common people were not disaggregated, nor any sort of unitary collectivity. Some commoners felt little or nothing in direct response to the troubled times; their lives continued more or less without change. Others, however, found themselves searching for new ways to cope with the perverse present, for novel forms of behavior that might afford the hope of a better future.

Some of these millions of people decided to follow new religious muses. Roads filled with pilgrims mark this period as they had in certain earlier decades, but the pilgrimages of the 1860s—to sites such as the sun goddess's Grand Shrine at Ise in central Japan—were redolent of the fears of a populace in flux. It was a time when new sects came into being, old faiths were abandoned, and all sorts of social movements burst into flower. Uncertain people look for answers in untypical conduct, and *bakumatsu* Japan became a laboratory for popular pessimism, anxiety, and yearning.

Ultimately it was a time of *yonaoshi,* a millennial urge to re-make the world. These movements for "world renewal" varied from rural and urban uprisings to the fanatical pursuit of new or refurbished deities. Religious sects such as Tenrikyō and Konkōkyō claimed thousands of believers. Carnival behavior often accompanied the pilgrimages, or else arose spontaneously. By the second half of 1867, when two years of bad harvests finally gave way to marginal improvement, a circus atmosphere came to pervade the streets of major cities. At that point the *ee ja nai ka* commotions coincided with the events attending the death of the bakufu and the "restoration" of the emperor as ruler of all Japan.

For purposes of this chapter, let us take the example of just one religious sect, Tenrikyō, which the Japanese historian of religion Murakami Shigeyoshi calls "the representative entity among popular religions established during the *bakumatsu* and Restoration era."[34] Founded in 1838 by Nakayama Miki, wife of a prosperous merchant-farmer in a central Japanese village located between the metropolises of Osaka and Kyoto, Tenrikyō stressed "heavenly wisdom" *(tenri)* as embodied in a benevolent creator god, Tenri Ōnomikoto. A happy family life, amelioration of financial woes, and community togetherness became hallmarks of the new sect. Nakayama Miki, who had found her calling in the midst of a faith-healing episode, was the earthly mediator between humans and Tenri Ōnomikoto.

Tenrikyō differed profoundly from existing Buddhist sects as well as from the Confucian ideological orientation of the samurai elite. It differed in its monotheism, its founding by a charismatic personality, its appeal to the rural poor and impoverished urbanites, its emphasis on family and the individual regardless of sex or social status, its message of universal salvation through faith, and even in its eschatological anticipation of the attainment of millenarian *yonaoshi* in this world.[35] Thousands of pilgrims descended on the new town of Tenri that sprang up around Nakayama's rural home, and the location itself became Tenrikyō's *jiba* (place of places), the font of creation where humankind and this world as we know it were supposed to have originated.

It is hard to speculate about the actual number of followers Tenrikyō managed to attract, but contemporary observers and retrospective commentators agree that the community of the faithful grew rapidly during the 1860s. Not only did the new religion promise a final and total change for the better here on earth, it also aided its community in the interim by providing loans and jobs to many who were hard hit by the economic difficulties of *bakumatsu* Japan. The sect served as a kind of credit union and employment-security agency for its neediest converts. Some of the new religious movements were first known as *kō* or *kōsha*, terms that denote a mutual financial association for community benefit.[36] Tenrikyō thus attended to both spiritual and mundane requirements among its faithful, and the religion grew as did the ranks of the poor and needy.

Nakayama Miki seems to have welcomed the Meiji Restoration as the advent of the millennium.[37] She had witnessed *okagemairi,* "pilgrimages of thanksgiving," through central Japan ever since the massive migration of 1830 when she was a young adult. The carnivals that came along in late 1867, with their watchword *ee ja nai ka,* struck Nakayama as millennial portents.[38] Yet the fate of Tenrikyō, of its founder and followers, while hardly tragic in the literal sense, was literally "pathetic" when compared to their expectations. After 1868 the new government turned on Tenrikyō with a vengeance, denied Nakayama's hope of heaven on earth, and eventually forced the sect to register as a heterodox variant of Shinto, a status it had to abide until the era of religious freedom that came with the American occupation after World War II.[39] The triumph of the millennium had failed. Tenrikyō was never the only target, since Meiji authorities viewed all of the new religious movements with disfavor. It was the same for mass movements of any stripe, whether religious, as in the pilgrimages, or economic, as in the rural uprisings, or political, as in the later push for liberty and civil rights *(jiyū minken).*

Ee ja nai ka celebrations in the cities also wound down after the new government came to power in January of 1868. *Ee ja nai ka* is the topic of chapter 6. The preliminary survey given here will summarize points that support the idea that a seemingly "random" phenomenon like the *ee ja nai ka* carnivals must be analyzed if we are to grasp what the general public was undergoing at this time of crisis and change. This peculiar phenomenon, in which the urban masses behaved in an "antinomian" manner by flouting prevailing mores and expressing contempt for existing institutions of law and order, appeared on the scene late in the summer of 1867 and totally ceased by the following spring. Often likened to unplanned carnivals, the celebrations began near Nagoya, then spread both east and west, right across Japan's widest belt of urban population density.

Ee ja nai ka dancing started after pieces of paper *(ofuda)* bearing the names of Shinto deities dropped out of the sky on surprised—and "charmed"—urban crowds. Launched by persons unknown, these religious talismans were distributed far too widely and spontaneously to have resulted from a political plot, even though the city crowds did appear to favor the anti-bakufu forces over the representatives of the old regime. Those who received these tokens of good fortune from on high quickly congregated to share their good luck by feasting with relatives and friends, and above all to stage dancing and singing parties that ran on through day and night and clogged the major districts of major Japanese cities.

Ee ja nai ka (why not! or right on!) was the phrase that closed each verse in the improvised songs to which the merrymakers danced. Usually without overt political meaning, these verses were sometimes directed against usurious rice and sake merchants or others whom the crowds disliked. Other verses might ridicule the foreigners, whose trade policies had disrupted local commercial routines near the port cities where overseas trade was beginning. But *ee ja nai ka* itself is simply a linking stanza; it was a way to assure the crowd that the jollity of the moment would keep right on going as new songs were sung and more fun was had by one and all.

Specialists on *ee ja nai ka* acknowledge its importance in perpetuating the mood of *yonaoshi* yearning that marked the pilgrimages, the rise of new religions, and the bitter rural and urban riots of the mid-1860s. Itō Tadao, for instance, writes that *ee ja nai ka* was inseparably bound up with the hope of *yonaoshi* felt by the people at large in their disgust with the old order. Every form of protest is different, and *ee ja nai ka* suited the modest amelioration of common people's lives that came two-thirds of the way through the decade of the 1860s. Itō points out that the number of rural uprisings actually declined from a Tokugawa-period record high of 106 in 1866 to just 34 in 1867—the year of the *ee ja nai ka* celebrations—before climbing again to a new peak of 108 in 1868.[40]

A brief look at the city of Kyoto will show how divisive the *ee ja nai ka* frenzies could be at a crucial moment in Japanese political history. The old capital was beset in late 1867 not only by the intrigues that would result in the imperial restoration, but also by the residue of real economic hardship. White rice that indexed at 304.6 in 1865 jumped nearly threefold to an index price of 1147.6 for 1867. Soy sauce was up 150 percent during the same two years and sake almost 200 percent, while miso (bean paste) tripled in price.[41] Then in the tenth month of 1867, "popular *ee ja nai ka* . . . appeared as a storm of . . . mass hysteria."[42] More than sixty sites all over Kyoto witnessed continuous *ee ja nai ka* dancing. Such demonstrations almost all occurred in commercial neighborhoods, many of them in the city's congested subcenters—Gion, Pontochō, and major north-south arteries such as Teramachi and Horikawa as well as east-west avenues like Sanjō and Gojō. The celebrations in Kyoto went right on and only ceased after the new government took over the city in 1868.[43]

These efforts to defy public norms and mold new realities are tantamount to political acts of violence against the old regime. This is so whether or not the commoners involved were subjectively trying to attack the status quo. All of these new mass phenomena involved acts of radical desperation committed by people whose worldview transcended the existing situation in Japan. The effect, they hoped, would be to realign their conception of the world with the cultural ethos through which they experienced reality. For worldview and ethos were out of alignment in the *bakumatsu* travails.[44]

Imperial Loyalists: Adventure and Romance

Popular participation in disorders, pilgrimages, and carnivals was deeply unsettling to all samurai and all political leaders, whether of the old regime or the new one that was forming. Such leaders did not see the people as a constructive force, and in the general Confucian frame of ideological perception these various examples of popular discontent were tainted; they were viewed as improper and dangerous. Uprisings in the countryside and city crowds or mobs conveyed a sense of unsettled lives and political malaise. Such happenings disquieted the imperial loyalists just as they did the bakufu and daimyo.[45] In principle one could try to argue a causal link between the rise of chiliastic behavior among commoners and increased militancy on the part of the loyalist samurai, but there is little evidence to confirm a connection. What is so is that the loyalists at last concluded that the bakufu and its attendant systems were bankrupt, and this conclusion emerged at the very time when the *ee ja nai ka* carnivalers were making nonsense out of the downtown streets of Kyoto as well as other cities and towns, in the autumn of 1867.

Sentiment for imperial loyalism had arisen earlier in quite a different context. The core of the ideology of imperial loyalism is the idea of *sonnō jōi*, which Maruyama Masao has called the final "form of pre-nationalism" in Japan: it was a self-congratulatory hierarchical ideology propping up the feudal system, and in its emphasis on the institution of the *tennō* it did contain the seeds of a transfeudal breakout but was unable in the end to get past feudalism's "last historical iron barrier."[46] The xenophobic impulse to drive off foreigners *(jōi)* had been a part of Japanese coastal defense schemes for many decades prior to 1868. That kind of cultural togetherness could be expressed better, however, by reverence for the emperor *(sonnō)* as a symbol of all Japanese. Bringing the two phrases together was largely the work of political thinkers from the Tokugawa collateral domain of Mito.[47] The motive for most of those who brandished the slogan *sonnō jōi* during the *bakumatsu* period was their desire to change Japan in order to right society's wrongs, even if they did couple their internal concerns with recalcitrance toward outside intruders.

The *sonnō jōi* impulse thus originated among samurai who were willing to court anarchy if necessary to accomplish their objectives. These were figures altogether different from the cautious officials of the bakufu and han. Many of them suffered from an acute sense of status deprivation: they were part of the elite, yet their circumstances were straitened, and they could not depend on office-holding to advance themselves. When they looked at the world they saw a black-and-white reality that badly wanted changing. They also thought they perceived a moral imperative that needed to be expressed in the form of courageous action against those samurai who used their high status to sit above the fray, preventing able but lowly samurai from rising to the top. Their appreciation of politics was tempered by a highly formal view of society, community, and the world as a congeries of dispersed idiographic entities. In chaos they quested for redemption, not for order. Their overriding motive was to make Japan a proper place by relieving distress; another modest one was to pacify the country, since that too was consistent with the redeemer's role.

A profile of the loyalists must allow for a variety of motives that nevertheless finally coalesced into a situationally transcendent impulse. Some samurai turned old grudges into the stuff of new power relations. Some sought simple self-gratification. Others sympathized with the plight of poor commoners, while still others championed the cause of Japan against the ravages of foreign intervention. All these motives fed into the stream that flooded the political ground of the 1860s. All these motives channeled into a disposition not only to overthrow the bakufu, but also to make a new Japan, a nation that could better deal with its domestic and international troubles. Not all the loyalist samurai were simplifiers, but they did share a sense of adventure that moved them to try various kinds of change, from the political coup to more tedious if no less novel attempts to seize the power of the realm. Some of them surely acted from selfish rather than altruistic motives, since fear and greed and naked ambition were bound to join patriotism and redemption as motives of behavior in such complex and convoluted situations. But at root the impulse was one of idealism.

Nobody personifies the profile of a prerestoration imperial loyalist better than Yoshida Shōin. He is the perfect incarnation of *bakumatsu* idealism. Maruyama Masao says that it was he who radicalized the *sonnō jōi* tradition, taking it to the point of renouncing the feudal *bakuhan* system.[48] Born in 1830, Yoshida grew up in Chōshū, far from Japan's political center. He was man of avid curiosity and revealed it in every episode that made his reputation. In 1854, for instance, came his stunning attempt to catch a ride on one of Commodore Perry's steam frigates to see the world. As punishment for his daring he might have lost his head, but luckily for him the bakufu only sentenced him to spend time in jail. (In 1859 he was in fact beheaded during the Ansei Purge.) Though a prodigious scholar, Yoshida uncompromisingly divided the world into black and white, right and wrong. He never suppressed his sense of adventure, and a strain of melancholy afflicted him, well suited to the personality of a wide-eyed romantic. Perry's records indicate that Yoshida (along with a single accomplice) waxed poetic despite being thrown in a cage at Shimoda when his stowaway attempt failed. Beside his cage he left a placard for the Americans to see and translate, and they reported part of what it said as follows:

> When a hero fails in his purpose, his acts are then regarded as those of a villain and a robber. In public we have been seized and pinioned and caged. . . . We wished to make the circuit of the five great continents. This was our hearts' desire for a long time. Suddenly our plans are defeated. . . . Weeping, we seem as fools; laughing, as rogues. Alas! for us; silent we can only be.[49]

This kind of cant inspired no less than Robert Louis Stevenson to write a sketch of Yoshida in the English popular press, praising his irrepressible idealism. Since the turn of the century, foreigners have often viewed him as the quintessential model of an imperial loyalist, and his strict ideals keep him popular today both at home and abroad.[50]

What characterizes all the imperial loyalists is their impatience. There lay one source of their essential disaffection from the old regime. From the idealistic rebel Yoshida Shōin to the manic heroes of the mid-Sixties, they aimed to disperse all of the other forces in order to attain their own ends. The leaders of the Meiji government were cut from this same cloth. Requiring the cachet of a new movement to propel them, they sought to mobilize the ancient myths of Japan on their side. As they appropriated the old legends, they let loose powerful levers of change, more potent than underlying patterns of institutional change that can be measured and charted through the long duration of the Tokugawa era. When it fell to the loyalists in their hour of triumph to keep the realm intact, they found it hard to do. The genie rarely goes back in the bottle.

The struggle that culminated in the Meiji Restoration consumed many of the imperial loyalists, victims of bakufu or han justice or targets of zealots known as *shishi* within their own ranks.[51] Yet those who survived the struggles ended up inheriting the realm. It was not easy, however, to reimpose order amid such chaos. Although the survivors managed to restore order, they paid a high price to do so. They mortgaged the future of Japan to their own ability to imagine a program of reconstruction. As simplifiers themselves, even the best of them were disinclined to be generous. They came down hard on internal dissent because they distrusted the very diversity whose seeds they had helped to sow, and they were fearful of proposed solutions that involved compromise. They did not long countenance the residues of other situationally transcendent forces, such as the followers of Tenrikyō or the makers of rural uprisings.

It is these common people who took part in the religions, rebellions, and demonstrations that other treatments of *bakumatsu* have often overlooked. Their pilgrimages, cult behavior, and carnivals do not lend themselves to the kind of causal explanation that historians usually offer. Documentation is scanty and incomplete, much of it irregular in type. The letters, memoranda, and state papers prepared by the well-educated leaders of this era do not accord much space to the doings of the masses, whose foibles and expressions of concern went substantially unrecorded. It is hard to establish connections among revivalist and millenarian movements, or to insert manifestations of popular distress into a straightforward narrative focusing on the politics of reform, exclusion, and imperial loyalism in Japan. The popular phenomena erupted at a time when rural riots were on the increase in the mid-1860s, but that appears to be coincidental, or simply epiphenomenal, as if troubled times just naturally spawn public anxieties or generate an outbreak of the symptoms of social unrest.

This public outcry over the state of the world, like the enthusiasm for *yonaoshi*, is a constituent element of the history of *bakumatsu* Japan. We ignore these phenomena at the risk of constructing an inadequate and irresponsible account of what happened. The masses who were there for the turmoil of the 1860s made up the lion's share of Japan's population at the time. Theirs were powerful expressions that color the period's history and give it depth. In the arrangement of historical actors for this chapter, therefore, "the people" have occupied a key place.

A Matrix of Motivational Determinants

In this chapter a fourfold narrative based on the motives of different groups of actors has replaced other possible organizing devices for conveying what happened in *bakumatsu* Japan. What are the advantages of the method outlined here? Are there disadvantages that offset the method? Difficulty in assembling a persuasive body of supporting evidence weakens the force of any argument that bases itself on motivation, and some of the actors dealt with here—the "people," for instance—never speak with just one voice or in unambiguous terms. *Ee ja nai ka* sounds simple but is scarcely univocal. Evidentiary limitations, however, do not render the claims of the argument invalid. Such claims will indefinitely remain hypothetical, or logical only on the basis of "abduction," to use the term preferred by Charles S. Peirce.[52]

Among the advantages of the history of motives are its novelty and its capacity to discriminate among multiple lines of plot development. The motivational model bypasses both Marxist and modernization approaches to Meiji Restoration history. Unlike the evolutionary theory that underlies both of those approaches, which assumes the march of progress from a state of barbarism to one of utopia, the method used here treats and also represents the punctuated equilibria that mark the "hot" chronology of *bakumatsu* Japan.

From this perspective it is obvious how unlikely any particular outcome was. Every new turn of events surprised the actors. Plans and blueprints had no practical utility. These people were obliged to act on an ad hoc basis, and their improvisations followed no fixed program, only the deeper cultural and class inclinations that prefigured their attitudes and guided their actions. Recognizing the diversity of perception and motive, the method proposed here leads towards a new interpretation of the history of Japan from 1850 to 1870. Such an interpretation must acknowledge the place of all sorts of impulses that historians tend to relegate to epiphenomenal status. Our examples have included the rise of new religious followings, the outbreak of angry riots in cities and villages, and even the sudden release of popular energy through carnivals in the streets. Normally wary of myth, historians interested in this approach need to recognize claims of inspiration from mythic sources like the ones that arose from the timely recuperation of the Japanese imperial institution and its liminal utility in politics.

These sweeping trends take on importance as a result of the application to historical problems and data of concepts developed by ethnography, religious studies, literary criticism, and other disciplines. The integration of these trends into a set of four overlapping stories goes further than do the usual political accounts to explain the pace and timing of the changes that marked the Meiji

Restoration. The new leaders after 1868 not only had to build a central government; they also felt obliged to suppress potential challenges to their authority appearing in the form of violent episodes and antinomian trends.

The approach offered in this chapter tries to play down the historian's old favorite explanatory scheme—the one based on cause and effect. Instead, in order to compensate for the lack of causal statements to anchor the narrative, I have used multiple and overlapping stories as a means of heightening the narrative force of this account. We see that the actors onstage in *bakumatsu* Japan—as groups—experienced at least four story arcs or "generic plots," each one affected by the playing out of the other three, yet analytically recountable as an independent story.[53] Conflict among the four groups identified here arose from their differing values and worldviews, which were put at risk in *bakumatsu* Japan within the crisis atmosphere that had come to prevail. As perceptions of the world differed and sharpened among the four groups, the values that animated their behavior abruptly began to contribute to shifting alliances and conflicting motives.

The grid shown here, "A Matrix of Motivational Determinants," identifies much of the intellectual parentage of this study in capsule form.[54] Readers will note that the matrix sets forth the four groups of actors without suggesting that this foursome exhausts all possible groups that might be identified, but I would hold that these four, through their clashing perceptions and responses in regard to their world and one another, convey the sense of a more vivid and conflict-laden Meiji Restoration than we may conventionally find.

The elements of *motive* in the matrix exceed those of *plot* in both number and sophistication. Plot elements come from the model supplied by Northrop Frye and reworked by Hayden White in the context of modern European historiography. Important as the story lines are, the motives of *bakumatsu* historical actors assume greater importance for this study, since conflict in motivation led to behavior changes that set the stage for the drama of the restoration itself.

The matrix indicates that the motives ascribed to *bakumatsu* actors flow from at least two levels of conscious thought about the world. One is the explanatory and ideological orientation of the four groups. (But it may flow as well from deeper levels involving

ELEMENTS OF PLOT AND MOTIVE AMONG BAKUMATSU ACTORS

A Matrix of Motivational Determinants

	PLOT *Story Line*[a]	EXPLANATION *Cognitive Strategy*[b]	IDEOLOGY *Political Orientation*[c]	TROPE *Rhetorical Prefiguration*[d]
Western envoys	comedy *anagnorisis* spring	organicist integrative	conservative situational congruence	synecdoche integration representation
Bakufu and daimyo	satire/irony *sparagmos* winter	contextualist dispersive	liberal situational congruence	irony negation dialectic
Popular revivalists	tragedy *pathos* autumn	mechanist integrative	radical situational transcendence	metonymy reduction contiguity
Imperial loyalists	romance adventure *agon* summer	formist/idiographic dispersive	anarchist situational transcendence	metaphor identity continuity

[a]Northrop Frye, *Anatomy of Criticism: Four Essays* (Princeton, 1957). [b]Stephen C. Pepper, *World Hypotheses: A Study in Evidence* (Berkeley, 1942). [c]Karl Mannheim, *Ideology and Utopia: An Introduction to the Sociology of Knowledge* (New York, n.d.). [d]Hayden V. White, *Metahistory: The Historical Imagination in Nineteenth-Century Europe* (Baltimore, 1973).

preconscious rhetorical configuration of the world by means of "tropes.") The other level is that of perceived plot, or story line. In short, while an actor's motive may arise in part from plot, other factors such as cognition, ideology, and tropological prefiguration of the historian's discursive field may be held to exist separately from plot. All of these elements help to determine the motive(s) of any given group of actors.[55] This matrix, despite referring to motivation and perception, does not issue from the discipline of psychology but is drawn chiefly from Hayden White's analysis of nineteenth-century European historical and philosophical texts. The sources White uses for his scheme of rhetorical prefiguration in the writing of European history supply most of the elements of plot and motive that are mentioned in the matrix. These sources derive from literary criticism (Northrop Frye), metaphysical philosophy (Stephen Pepper), and sociology of knowledge (Karl Mannheim).

Eclectic and flexible, the matrix should lend itself to uses that cross temporal and cultural boundaries. Readers will recognize that the intellectual ease of its transference from place to place, or from time to time, does not prove the scheme's "veracity" as a means of characterizing human group behavior. Rather it is a heuristic device whose application to Japan brings Japanese history into a dialogical relationship with analogous ways of accounting for Western historical behavior. Whether it is a valid approach no one can know: we use the tools that scholarship has placed before us in our own time, and most of these emanate from the Western tradition that has lately overspread the world. Besides, as a heuristic device it does seem to work, in the sense that its interrelated stories are consistent with the restoration's known outcomes.

It is the way in which this matrix works that persuades me of its utility. Its workings also govern the choice and development of topics in the next three chapters. The matrix allows for four groups of actors whose "narrative" experience, worldview, and ideology are separate and distinct. Overlapping among the four groups does not diminish their differences, although it suggests reasons for the temporary alliances or affinities of purpose that sprang up between some of the groups. The matrix further suggests a "logic of position" in the effort to explain popular participation in the events leading to the restoration. The role of the public has looked either epiphenomenal or extraneous to many scholars, but the popular movements allowed for an interactive capacity that has to be there if the other three groups of actors are to be comprehended. In other words, for three of the groups to have acted as they did without the impact of popular revivalists is analytically illogical: their motives (and their actions) are more easily understood in light of the common people's conduct. The matrix thus works to suggest a necessary fit among the four principal groups of actors in *bakumatsu* Japan.

We have seen that the foreign diplomats and traders interpreted the significance of events according to a cognitive strategy accompanying deeply conservative ideological convictions and a desire to stabilize Japan by any and all means. Theirs was, in Frye's terms, a comedic plot, because its avowed goal was stability and its archetypal theme was reconciliation *(anagnorisis)*.[56] The story flows from the worldview, and perhaps also from the deep structure of rhetorical prefiguration as conceived by White. The Western envoys were dedicated to the virtue of an integrated Japan, as suggested by the tropological predilection of synecdoche, through which the mind substitutes a part for the whole (or vice versa) as a way to apprehend the situation.[57] For them a part (Edo or the bakufu, or Satsuma and Chōshū) served in place of the entirety of Japan.

Proceeding to the three Japanese groups that acted during the *bakumatsu* period, we find other models of group attitudes and behavior. Bakufu officials and leading daimyo found themselves caught in an untenable situation. It was a situation which they were nevertheless committed, by faith rather than by tradition, not to modify. Theirs was a "cold" story, one fraught with the unpleasant turns of irony that connote dedication to a righteous but a losing cause. They foredoomed themselves to a manipulation of the context without trying to change the substance. The archetypal theme of *sparagmos*—confusion and frustration—marks their effort to preserve the existing order. Their belief in it drove them to accept the status quo, and that belief finally leaves them, like the Western envoys, committed to what Karl Mannheim called situational congruence.

By contrast, both the millenarian forces of popular revivalism and the imperial loyalists came to oppose the very premises of the status quo. They finally rejected the *bakuhan* feudal system. They shared a mighty disaffection for the conditions of this world, committing themselves instead to situationally transcendent programs. Their beliefs led them in the direction of overcoming (by destroying) the status quo. For many who labored on behalf of these two groups, overthrow of the existing order took on a self-sufficient cast, as if surmounting the bastions of power and privilege could ipso facto produce a resolution of Japan's problems.

Beyond their shared situational transcendence, however, these two groups proved unlikely allies. Indeed, the transcendent world-view that underlay a temporary convergence of their interests covered over differences that were too great to reconcile. The cognitive strategy of the imperial loyalists was idiographic and self-important to the point of dismissing other concerns.[58] They were ideologically exempt from guilt and preoccupied with fulfilling their own destiny. They had an "anarchist" bent, in Mannheim's sense, that blinded them to the claims for continuity made on behalf of the existing order.[59]

The ideological orientation and explanatory proclivities of the popular revivalists were opposed to those of the imperial loyalists. By a mechanistic reduction of reality to a plot that was simple ("radical," in its root sense), the popular forces awaited a reintegration of the Japanese realm, a healing and relieving outcome. The generosity of their simple faith is reflected in a predilection to rely on the trope of metonymy, the substituting of a name for a complex reality or set of phenomena, or of a quantity for a quality.[60] The story they ultimately lived, though it was one they assuredly did not seek, was tragic. It led them from temporary triumphs to disaster and suppression as a result of their own flaws and the power of their antagonists. The archetypal theme of *pathos* in the plot is not contrived but is, literally, "pathetic": catastrophe befalls them.[61]

The contrast between this autumnal tale and the summer adventure of romance that was lived by the imperial loyalists could not be sharper, despite the deaths of a considerable number of the leading loyalists before they could work through the "plots" they were experiencing. Their consciousness prefigured by metaphor, they put one thing in terms of another. They even rationalized treason as duty to a higher authority—to the "emperor" rather than to the traditional political overlord, the shogun of the Tokugawa bakufu. The loyalists instinctively saw themselves as the real carriers of tradition and as champions of the true Japanese spirit. What happened to them in the Meiji Restoration was a triumph of the arche-typal theme of *agon,* a struggle for survival against evil, and the prize—the whole realm of Japan—was theirs to master. Their quest was crowned with success: the loyalists empowered themselves to make a newer world, while the popular movements could only chase after one.

Reconsidering the History of Motives

Even if we acknowledge the matrix as versatile, it may excite antag-onism. Some will object that it is too Western in derivation to fit the Japanese context. The names of its several authors are all well known in modern European thought. But should this objection bar the door to a cross-cultural methodology? Western as they origi-nally were, the elements of the matrix, when applied to Japan, en-able insights that affect some of the oldest questions asked about the Meiji Restoration. Such questions include why the bakufu re-formers failed when they controlled so much information, why the popular movements enjoyed apparent success but were then throt-tled, and why the imperial loyalists rode roughshod over the guard-ians of Japan's established order as well as over the common people who rioted or celebrated. For each of these questions of cause and effect, the matrix suggests possible answers that have been touched on here.

But the matrix cannot yield definitive answers to these ques-tions of cause and effect. It is a means of illustrating coincident and contingent situations. It does have an inherent logic of its own. Fol-lowing the usage of the authors whose work makes it possible, the matrix suggests a natural affinity between certain plots and certain explanatory modes, between explanation and certain ideological orientations, and between all three of these and a specific tropolog-ical prefiguration of the historical field, a predisposition to see events in a certain way. The four groups of actors fit together sensi-bly; their collisions in real historical events arose from conflicting values and worldviews as outlined in the matrix.

Of course, the Meiji Restoration cannot be diagrammed like a computer's circuitry, nor did it happen inexorably according to a blueprint. But the groups protrayed in the matrix all had a part in it. The part each group took validates the interpretation that arises from a consideration of the parts taken by all of the other groups. Logically persuasive, the matrix is historically suggestive. Thus it can add to our understanding of *bakumatsu* history.

Cautionary problems remain for the history of motives. This explanatory model involves a high degree of formalism and assumes a cross-cultural similarity of motivation. In this day and age there is, to be sure, an unusual degree of contact and fertilization across the borders of distant and presumably "different" cultures. We can make allowance for ideological variables different from those of western Europe or the United States. Yet who will ever know whether we can posit a universal human set of cognitive attitudes?

This whole book is conceptually grounded in Hayden White's Eurocentric doctrine of formal rhetorical determinism, with its assertion of linguistic deep structures, or poetics, as preconscious figurative forces in deciding how history will be perceived and language deployed to convey historical narratives and meanings. In his book *Metahistory* White employs Northrop Frye's literary analysis of plot structures *(mythoi)*, Stephen Pepper's philosophical typology of explanatory strategies, and Karl Mannheim's sociological dichotomy of situational congruence and situational transcendence. The Japanese who study such things are well aware of these approaches to social critique, but could we ever describe the approach used here as "universally valid"? Is it valid for Japan? Finally, can we transmogrify a *historiographical* scheme for decoding the linguistic and rhetorical preferences of European writers of history into a pattern of political behavior assigned to multiple occupants of the actual *historical* field of nineteenth-century Japan?

Still, the effort to apply this model may be useful. For too long a sort of acquired historicism (it is not innate) has moved historians to write smooth narratives and paint conveniently well-ordered and congruous pictures of events that took place in the past. To go beyond this, we need to look back to the principals themselves for evidence about the conflicts they actually faced. Taking this tack should expedite our attempt to "present" the *present* they experienced rather than a *past* which we reconstruct; for they lived through dilemmas that we can do nothing but represent—since we cannot relive them. This is a historiographical refinement that carries the potential for making the past more like the present with its brute contingency and relentless overdetermination. In the present we ourselves have no way to benefit by hindsight, though we can, if we wish, think historically and draw analogies with past behavior. Thus we as agents always have to act in an open-ended arena wherein we discern multiple causes at work in our lives as well as the diverse directions that (uncertain) future action may take. That is what those who lived through the Meiji Restoration had to do in their own time.

Chapter Five

Pursuing the Millennium in Bakumatsu Japan

The essence of millenarianism, the hope of a complete and radical change in the world . . . , [appears] in all revolutionary movements of whatever kind.
—E. J. Hobsbawm

And I saw a new heaven and a new earth.
—Revelation 21:1

Great events in world history do not merely leave traces. They erupt onto the scene as stunning transformations generated out of the existing structures of society. So it is with the Meiji Restoration of 1868. The date is too confining, the concept of restoration too narrow, to comprehend so vast a transformation.

Analysts of the restoration have been preoccupied with the issue of the character of the transition from bakufu to imperial rule, from a late feudal military system based on land tenure and agrarian production and headed by the Tokugawa bakufu at Edo to a monarchical early national state governed by a "sovereign emperor." Whether they praise or condemn its outcome, restoration scholars usually dwell on the relative ease of transition, the smooth and bloodless calm with which the new regime came to power and began to act. In explanation of this smooth transition they point to the docility of the Japanese people, their traditional habits of discipline, or to the frustration of the forces of bourgeois revolution.

But in the wake of the Meiji Restoration, Japan changed in four decades from an insular society into a world power. The magnitude of the restoration's consequences drives us to seek a more satisfying answer than docility or discipline to the conundrum of Japan's apparently easy passage from a feudal polity to a new nation. The *bakumatsu* years had witnessed the release of great energies that did not simply dissipate when the symbolic authority of the Japanese imperial house was invoked as a means of unifying the country. George Sansom was right to note the mystery: "From this welter of contradictions a solution presently emerges, nobody can say exactly how or why. Things and ideas cease their demented gyrations and fall into their appointed place." But Sansom was wrong to draw the analogy of a dream, as if waking up could dispel the confusion: "The dream is over, and the country is united under one leadership." [1]

The temptation to rest with easy answers perhaps arises from the rational cause-and-effect procedures of narrative reconstruction through which historians of sharply differing ideological persuasions look at the Meiji Restoration. They see the Meiji leaders engaged in Machiavellian politics, and they know that many discontented people were roaming the land, stirring up rural as well as urban turmoil. The resolution of struggles among the samurai elite, and the suppression of political countermovements, made the new government's tasks look deceptively simple.

Apocalypse and Artifice at Liminal Moments

What is missing is attention to the much more dynamic manifestations of the popular anxiety that permeated the very atmosphere of the tumultuous *bakumatsu* years. Throughout the country during the mid-1860s, throngs of pilgrims congregated at religious sites, especially the complex of shrines at Ise in central Japan, where the regalia and mystique of the imperial house's mythical past resided. Public pilgrimages to sacred places like the Grand Shrine of Ise were periodic features of Japanese history since the late sixteenth century. [2] What changed in the 1860s was the intensity and the random quality of the pilgrims, whose behavior verged on the hysterical. [3]

The last mammoth convergence of pilgrims upon Ise had taken place in 1830, but the Sixties brought an explosion of new or revitalized religious sects onto the scene in central Japan, along with ordinary as well as extraordinary crowds of pilgrims. Farmer uprisings *(hyakushō ikki)* grew in number until the peak year of 1866, displaying utopian *(yonaoshi)* features that were unique in this decade.[4] Meanwhile, urban carnivals competed for public notice with riots, burnings, and trashings; revelers and rioters made a shambles of many a downtown area as they danced and sang about a better life to come. Victor Turner calls pilgrimages and related communal movements "liminal phenomena," associated with revival, or sometimes with rejection, of the existing order: "A limen is . . . a 'threshold.' A pilgrimage center, from the standpoint of the believing actor, also represents a threshold, a place and moment 'in and out of time,' and such an actor . . . hopes to have there direct experience of the sacred, or supernatural order."[5]

Such are the signs and tokens of millenarianism. Yet they tend to be neglected in the explanatory strategies of historians and social scientists. Western theorists of millenarian behavior are partly to blame for this omission, because some of them have argued that Buddhist theology is passive and cyclical in nature and therefore precludes the coming of the millennium even if salvation can be accessible in another life.[6]

Millenarianism, as used in this chapter, follows the sensitive treatment given the topic by the sociologist Yonina Talmon. At the most fundamental level, she defines "millenarian" as an attribute that is "typologically [applied] to characterize religious movements that expect imminent, total, ultimate, this-worldly, collective salvation."[7] Another definition applicable to the usage in this chapter is Peter Worsley's. He uses the term *millenarian* "to describe those movements in which there is an expectation of, and preparation for, the coming of a period of supernatural bliss. . . . The term . . . includes both those movements which anticipate that the millennium will occur solely as a result of supernatural intervention, and those which envisage that the action of human beings will be necessary." Worsley adds a pointed reminder:

> Millenarian beliefs have recurred again and again throughout history . . . precisely because they make such a strong appeal to the oppressed, the disinherited and the wretched. They therefore form an integral part of that stream of thought which refused to accept the rule of a superordinate class, or of a foreign power, or some combination of both, as in Taiping China. This anti-authoritarian attitude is expressed . . .

through the rejection of the ideology of the ruling authority. . . . Millenarian doctrines often become openly revolutionary and lead to violent conflict between rulers and ruled.[8]

The revolutionary potential of the Japanese social fabric may
be inferred from a study of the millenarian combination of conservative and innovative impulses that culminated in the Meiji Restoration. Looking not at the origins or development of Japanese millenarian phenomena, but rather at their eruption into the ambience of
foreign and domestic strife during the 1850s and 1860s, I will argue
that the bakufu reformers and the fanatic imperial restorers whose
activities helped make way for the new regime must be viewed in
coincidence with many hundreds of thousands of rural as well as
urban people whose millennial aspirations expressed their anxiety
about their own future and Japan's. The samurai elite and the popular movements were simultaneously groping for a new and stable
order in Japan.

Millenarian movements partake of both historical and mythical
time, accepting history as linear but believing that divine intervention will somehow bring a halt to an intolerable present and restore
political and social well-being. Yonina Talmon refers to millenarian
movements as both revolutionary and traditional: yearning for a
lost past, they await a novel future.[9]

In the context of the Tokugawa social hierarchy, millenarian
pressure from "lower" status groups may have emboldened unhappy elements within the samurai elite, and it may have diminished the effectiveness of the gradualist reforms pursued by the Tokugawa bakufu and its allies among the great han. The survivors—
those *shishi* or "zealots" who had to build the new order—may not
all have been fanatics, but they did inherit the millenarian ardor of
their fallen comrades who had glorified mythic Japanese tradition
and called for a return of political power to the emperor. The Meiji
leaders thus found it expedient as well as legitimate to manipulate
the imperial symbol while they worked to construct a new order
that would be at once revolutionary and traditional because of the
transformed nativism *(kokugaku)* on which it was based. If the revolutionary component in this mixture was muted because traditional values played so large a part, it was nonetheless present. It
was also a constant threat to erupt again among unstable or ambitious groups within the populace.

It is true, of course, that strong and visionary leadership came to the fore from among elements of the samurai status group; without such leadership Japan might have foundered in the effort to deal with challenges both at home and abroad.[10] It is also evident that long-term social change in city and countryside had prepared Japanese people from many walks of life to assume new roles suitable for rapid industrialization. But these conditions of elite readiness and widespread distribution of skills, including literacy, among the populace do not suffice to account for Japan's abrupt transformation into a new nation.

Turning outside of Japan, efforts to identify the Western powers as catalysts of change in Japan only compound the problem. Causal attribution to the foreigners has the effect of mistaking the catalyst of many confused reactions for the producer of one vast "national" response to crisis. If anything, the external threat heightened internal tensions, reduced the political system's normal capacity to cope with dissension, and led to a stalemate in politics just when social and economic change was quickening. The chaotic situation yielded what Conrad Totman has characterized as a "systemic crisis" precipitated by the Western "imperialist intrusion" of the 1850s and 1860s, and by the novel demands placed upon the bakufu by Japanese who were anxious to respond to this intrusion.[11] But the West deserves neither credit nor blame for "causing" a powerful centralized system to constitute itself out of a social and political structure in disarray: it was the disarray—not the new regime and its actions—that stemmed from the Western intrusion into Japan.

Why should any part of the ruling samurai status group have pursued radical political reorganization and put its own position at risk?[12] What was it that so alarmed some Japanese leaders that they experimented with drastic new policies, even though they fastidiously clothed them in the raiment of tradition? One answer is that millenarianism on a wide scale affected both popular consciousness and the samurai sense of propriety, chipping away at the authority of the Tokugawa *bakuhan* system. The profusion of millenarian manifestations helps to explain the slide from anti-bakufu hostility among some of the samurai to revolutionary action initiated by the Meiji government employing "traditional" ideas reworked for the new purposes of Japan as a nation.

Popular millenarianism had to frighten all samurai. But the ones whose own ideas made them receptive to substantive change were able to alter their programs to accommodate a modicum of popular aspirations; at the same time, they could still keep the lid on revolutionary violence. Some of the more radically disaffected samurai who were influenced by the thinking of the late Mito school of historiography fit this pattern.[13] Acts that the Japanese feared the imperialists might commit, acts whose very possibility inspired millenarian dreams of redemption and utopia, would demand quick responses. This situation prevented the popular movements from gaining either the time or the space needed to organize altogether novel policy initiatives. Japan's reconstruction by means of transforming extant sociopolitical mechanisms was more important than laying master plans for a new society. Yet the result might have seemed to be the same, so sharp were the Meiji state's departures from past practice. Its mixture of revolutionary energy and traditional values met the requirements of the situation. As the new state built up its authority, not only popular ambitions but also the objectives of the samurai themselves were sacrificed in the name of national unity and industrial development. Thus the old elite was obliged to transform itself as well as the country as a whole, but it did so in accord with the latent potentialities that were generated within the matrix of Tokugawa society.

No one can find it surprising that the years from the melodrama of Commodore Perry's arrival in 1853–54 to the consummation of political reorganization in 1868–71 witnessed an explosion of millennial hopes and dreams among Japan's common people. The times were already in transition: to underscore the temporal notion of "threshold" as used by Victor Turner, we may say that a liminal period of uncertain duration had come to Japan—a "margin in time," if you will, when old and new commingled.[14] Folkways and politics both suffered from disturbances of routine, and stirrings of patriotic concern affected people far and wide, high and low. Cities underwent calamitous changes, fortuitous as in the great Edo fire of 1855, and disingenuous as in Edo's depopulation after the bakufu's 1862 edict relaxing alternate attendance obligations on the part of the daimyo. Economic competition sparked by the coming of foreign trade disrupted local industries and regional commercial networks. The price of rice to consumers in the cities increased sevenfold between 1863 and 1867.[15] The movement of farmers from place to place unsettled a populace that was not accustomed to dealing with outsiders. A paradigm of a way of life was in danger of decomposing; while most responses fell within accepted norms, there were some that did not.

The frightened, the frustrated and humiliated, and the economically deprived and distressed segments of Japanese society entertained millennial hopes for respite from their plight. They dreamed of a renewal of peace and tranquillity. These phrases with differing emphases resonate through both elite and popular tracts for the times. Not a few thinkers found it convenient to predict utopian solutions in order to remedy present difficulties. Others, like the anonymous Osaka physician who chronicled the turbulence of the age in *Ukiyo no arisama* (The way it is in the Floating World), chose to record the events that animated people's anxieties without much comment on how such anxieties might be relieved.[16] For disenchanted elements within the samurai elite, as well as for the general public, various beliefs arose about the ways in which a new dispensation might be revealed.

Millennial Dreams as Models of Social Action

Tradition suffuses millenarian movements as surely as utopia colors all revolutionary programs, and relief from deprivation stands as a ubiquitous millenarian goal.[17] Its achievement may come about in various ways, sometimes involving the public at large, sometimes only the true believers, sometimes just the activist few. The agent of millenarian dreams may be a prophet or a messiah.

Consider, for example, the astounding role of Amakusa Shirō Tokisada, a veritable masculine and Japanese version of Joan of Arc in the so-called Shimabara Rebellion of 1637–38.[18] His Christian banner, tattered but intact, was one of the few relics (and few rebels, for that matter) to survive the savage Tokugawa destruction of the rising of this economically deprived provincial community of embattled converts to Catholicism, stuck in a forsaken corner of western Kyushu, not far from Nagasaki. Though he and the thirty-seven thousand people he led could not prevail over the vast military expedition that the bakufu deployed against them, Tokisada revealed millennial hopes of redemption in an impossible situation and is remembered as a tragic hero in the annals of Japanese history. This is so even though the faith he died for was alien to Japan, a fact that George Elison remarks when he writes, "Tokisada [was] spiritually twice beyond the pale"—in the eyes of Rome, a "new Christian" (that is, a former heathen) and also a chiliast.[19] Indeed, Tokisada was doubly antinomian too in the eyes of Edo—convert to an alien religion and rebel against the established social order.

More often, however, the agent of millennial dreams is a collective entity. Mid–nineteenth-century Japanese conceptions about relief may be found in phenomena ranging from the rise of new religions and cult behavior to mob outbursts and mass pilgrimages along the roads and carnivals in the city streets. These phenomena fit into types of active and passive millenarian behavior that could serve as models for others to follow. Such action models provoked countermeasures designed to exploit, contain, or combat them. Historians should join specialists in religious studies to study these phenomena and work them into the explanatory modes that are used in treating this period.

In the countryside the millenarian aspirations of farming communities appeared as efforts to reorganize and improve agriculture. Increasingly, too, there were pilgrimages of thanksgiving (*okagemairi* or *nukemairi*) to local, regional, and "national" cultural and religious centers, such as the Grand Shrine at Ise. The foremost nativist scholar Motoori Norinaga, who lived from 1730 to 1801, was so impressed by the huge numbers he found recorded in the documents he was studying that he left his own account of the coming of throngs of pilgrims who had arrived at Ise in 1705, when 3,620,000 people are said to have visited the shrine complex in one fifty-day period.[20] Averaging more than seventy-two thousand a day, such a concentration of pilgrims was heavy, yet it was expected. When the 1860s arrived, however, pilgrimages of such a magnitude were unexpected.

Pilgrims nevertheless also clogged the roads in the years preceding the Meiji Restoration. Central Japan, as access and egress for Ise and the site of the rise of many new religious movements, was particularly affected. But riots, ostensibly concerning economic issues, also marked the *bakumatsu* years. Food prices climbed, tax collection became more arbitrary, and local market relations sometimes fell into a disheveled state. The number of peasant uprisings dramatically increased in the decade before 1868, reaching a high point in 1866, when some 106 outbreaks qualify as *hyakushō ikki*.[21] A millenarian content infused these 1866 risings as their leaders called for a utopian kind of *yonaoshi*.[22] Only at their peril could bakufu and han authorities overlook such uprisings, yet it proved impossible to suppress them altogether, and they went on happening even after the restoration. Despite the prevalence of destruction over construction as a goal of such outbursts, and despite the importance of frustration as a factor in triggering them, they did afford opportunities to vent the tensions within a community, and they became "causes" with which to identify in opposition to the existing order.

In the cities, violent demonstrations (*uchikowashi* or *yakiharai*) were directed against rice merchants, sake dealers, pawnbrokers, landlords, and others who were seen as exploiters of the urban poor. Even the less violent but strictly antinomian behavior of city crowds as the old order ended in 1867 and early 1868 struck fear into the authorities, perplexed the foreign observers, and maintained a basis for destabilization that prompted the adoption of firm new political policies after the Meiji government took power. The appearance of carnivalers in the streets on the eve of the restoration, shouting crude rhymes that closed with the catch phrase *ee ja nai ka* and engaging in transvestite and other hysterical forms of behavior, led to summary suppression once the restoration had occurred.

The crucial significance of these *ee ja nai ka* outbursts has not received adequate attention, and this phenomenon is the topic of chapter 6. Occurring in urban areas that the bakufu had to control at the very time when its political authority was unraveling, the orgiastic *ee ja nai ka* festivities created a difficult situation for politicians who were trying in vain to return Japan to some sort of stability under the bakufu's auspices. Yasumaru Yoshio goes as far as to say that the *ee ja nai ka* frenzies "had the effect of temporarily paralyzing the bakufu's system of rule," and that they amounted to a "gusher" of popular millennial aspirations coincidentally spouting forth right in the "central region [where the] *bakumatsu* political wars" were being waged.[23]

The rabble and the hoi polloi found unwilling allies among samurai who had become enraged by the bakufu's tolerance of foreign intervention in the affairs of Japan. Cut off from the realities of high-level politics and international negotiations, samurai agitators began to call for a crusade of ethnic redemption against outsiders. The nativist impulse for such feelings, justified earlier on a rational basis by Confucian precepts holding that things must bear their right names and people assume their proper relationships, finally shifted into Japanese nationalism, a supradomainal, trans-feudal political creed requiring new forms of organization and renewed traditional institutions that would raise Japan's reputation in the eyes of a predatory world. To save the country's honor became an unwittingly revolutionary goal—and a decisively millenarian one.

Salvation Sects: Tenrikyō and Konkōkyō

Organized religion in the usual sense was not a wellspring of popular activity during the *bakumatsu* period. But deviations from existing religious practices were so numerous that the early and middle nineteenth century became one of the most vibrant eras in the history of religion in Japan.[24] Numerous sects sprang up and prospered, their creativity adequate to propel them into the twentieth century and to perpetuate them even today. Two among them illustrate the whole phenomenon of religious revivalism in a particularly apt way. Tenrikyō, formally founded in 1838, is the prototypical "new religion" of the nineteenth century. Its rise and the articulation of its doctrines might serve as a type case for the eruption of a millenarian religion. Konkōkyō, formally launched twenty-one years later in 1859, emphasizes inner peace and individuality, but it too bears the mark of a call for salvation and typifies the utopian visions of the *bakumatsu* period.[25] Both sects also embodied the need for a reintegrated community that so many ordinary people of this era seem to have felt.

Konkōkyō's founder was Kawate Bunjirō (1814–83), a farmer who lived in a rural area near the city of Okayama to the west of the Osaka region. In midlife Kawate underwent a series of personal disasters to rival Job: "Three of his children died; the community was ravaged by a smallpox plague; he lost all his cattle; and . . . in 1855 he was afflicted by a severe throat ailment from which it appeared he would not recover."[26] But Kawate came out of these doldrums, and he did so—a pious man—by coming to terms with a magical demon called Konjin, a mountain deity thought to personify evil. Kawate had assumed that Konjin was the source of all his troubles. Now he changed his mind and reinterpreted Konjin as a benevolent spirit capable of ending human sorrow and of promoting natural harmony. He eventually renamed the deity Tenchi Kanenokami, "Spirit uniting heaven and earth," and produced a canon based on belief in Konjin.[27] For himself he took the name Ikigami Konkō Daijin, the "great living god of harmonious light." For the rest of his life he elaborated the doctrines of his quietistic faith and built a substantial church with its headquarters in the small town near Okayama where he grew up.[28]

Tenrikyō does not draw on preexisting spirits like Konjin. Instead its founder, Nakayama Miki (1798–1887), articulated a new theology of divine grace and communal love, which she believed would lead to the collective salvation of the faithful. Both Tenrikyō and Konkōkyō are monotheistic, placing their faith, respectively, in Tenri Ōnomikoto, the "supreme deity of heavenly reason," and Tenchi Kanenokami. Both religions had a charismatic founder who assumed the status of a living god. Both appealed to farmers in economically advanced parts of central Japan where the problems of late Tokugawa Japan gave rise to economic dislocations both before and after the intrusion of foreign goods. And both offered salvation and peace in the here and now, a better life through immersion in a new community of believers. These are standard attributes of millennial cults.[29] Tenrikyō was more successful than Konkōkyō in attracting a mass following. Founded in the heart of the Yamato plain east of Osaka and south of Kyoto, the new faith claimed many thousands of adherents. Great celebrations were arranged at the founder's farm, which was believed to be the very spot where human beings and the world as we know it were created. The *jiba* (place of places) is the holiest site known to the faithful.[30]

Tenrikyō pronounced its own universal validity. It was available to save the souls of all people everywhere, and the legacy of this feature of its origin has made it a potent missionary force in many parts of the world today. It continues to grow and prosper in Japan as well. Originally, of course, Tenrikyō was a new faith through which only Japanese could be saved. The "world" was itself Japanese, and according to the logic of this standpoint Tenrikyō was "universally" valid—for Japanese, who were the occupants of the realm-world. Founder Nakayama Miki was the wife of a middling and not impecunious farmer. She discovered powers of spirit possession *(kamigakari)* within herself (to her amazement) while attending a ceremony performed by a faith healer whom she had engaged to treat the illness of her own eldest son.[31] Thus inspirited at the age of forty in 1838, Nakayama was prepared to assert her own divinity as "parent" *(oyasama)* of an entire system of faith for the rural poor and discontent. Very quickly she attracted a huge crowd of believers who were interested in both the possibility of salvation and the socially redemptive value of the new community of the faithful.

One author writes that Tenrikyō "was the representative entity" among the newly established religions and could hold its own in the recruitment of followers with the major Buddhist salvation sect, Jōdo Shin, the "true pure land," with its twin temples in Kyoto, the Nishi Honganji and Higashi Honganji.[32] The actual number of Tenri adherents is difficult to estimate, but its appeal went beyond the farming villages to embrace the urban poor, who soon flocked to the founder's headquarters during times of pilgrimage. These new pilgrims constituted a burden added to the numbers of older groups of pilgrims headed for the Grand Shrine at Ise.[33] Tenrikyō was not alone in building a new religious center, and central Japan was the core of such activities. The predictable outcome was ever increasing traffic and confusion on the roads connecting the major cities in the middle of Japan's main island, Honshu.

The rites and rituals of Tenrikyō were codified, and the sect grew all through the period up to the Meiji Restoration. A city— Tenri—sprang up around the farm of the founder, and the faith soon became a potent force in society.[34] Militant, determined, and pious, Tenrikyō also stressed love, tolerance, and humility. These opposed traits worked through a kind of synergy to attract followers, but the emphasis on individual peace of spirit kept Tenrikyō away from direct confrontation with civil authorities. Yet it is no accident that the subsequent history of Tenrikyō is studded with conflict. The Japanese creation myths were not the cosmogonic stories in favor at Tenri, and political leaders of the bakufu and han offered no message of hope that could affect the followers of the doctrines of Heavenly Reason.[35]

The beliefs popularized by Nakayama centered on family life

and personality development. Togetherness, socialization, and good health receive much attention. An overtone of equality between the sexes conflicted with the Confucian paternalism that dominated Japanese ideology in the Tokugawa period, and it was this same Confucian orthodoxy that was purposely promoted after the Meiji Restoration to restore order in society. As pillar and "parent" for the faithful, Nakayama Miki herself embodied the possibility of female eruption into prominence in a society whose outward forms were under male control by way of hereditary ascription. The challenge of Tenrikyō surpassed stratification issues involving the four Confucian status groups. It also went beyond questions of merit and achievement versus heredity and ascription. Women and children became the objects of Tenri beliefs and practices, and the participation of families was the criterion for organizing followers. All these departures from the norm—charismatic originator, sex-blind recruitment, elaboration of a new religious canon based on strict monotheism, and the fervor of the faithful after conversion—clashed with accepted practices and threatened to undermine social mores.

In the inside circle of those who made the Meiji Restoration, there was no place for Konkō Daijin, let alone the *oyasama* Nakayama. Their salvation doctrines and new views of community did look ahead to a supposedly millennial event, and the restoration seemed to be that event. Nakayama Miki is said to have entertained the expectation that the new Meiji leaders would prove to be the salvation of all Japanese.[36] But the government soon turned on the representatives and followers of the new religions: they found their ardor both unwelcome and unsuited to the Meiji settlement. In origin their vitality and spirit ran parallel to the gestation of Japanese patriotism and the streak of xenophobia that marked the *bakumatsu* years. In action their organizational strength, the size of their congregations, their similarity to financial self-help associations among the faithful, and their new communal beliefs posed a threat to the new government.[37] Both Konkōkyō and Tenrikyō found it hard going after 1870. They were finally registered and closeted away as variant forms of Shinto—"sect Shinto"—a status they could not escape until the years of reform that followed World War II. The Meiji leaders rejected them just as surely as had the bakufu and han authorities whom they had always distrusted.

The Millenarian Conversion of Samurai Nativism

Most accounts of bakufu and han politics during these years stress the vacillations and indecision of policymakers. We need not be so patronizing. Faced by unprecedented problems from abroad and a cacophony of demands at home, the leaders responded in various ways to meet constantly changing circumstances. These responses were neither good nor bad—just effective or ineffective. More often than not they showed greater knowledge and willingness to make changes than critics recognized or would have favored. Caught in the vortex, obliged to make decisions, the reform-minded bureaucrats who prepared bakufu policies in Edo adopted programs intended to change Japan, but the inevitable confrontations of the age rendered this kind of gradualism both unattractive and unattainable. The time constraints were too tight; they demanded quick fixes. The fate that befell the establishment was a function of routine processes overtaken by the imperatives of catastrophic events. No matter how affirmative the responses were meant to be, their authors could not get them off the ground against the storms that assaulted Japan's leaders at every turn. Catastrophe outpaced the bureaucracy's ability to act. Erosion of authority, in part a consequence of popular discontent, added to the dilemma by diminishing the system's capacity to dispense even-handed justice and efficient services.

Two examples will illustrate this general problem. In 1858 and again in 1866, the bakufu had the authority as well as the will to take the initiative and reform the political system in order to build an effective national response to the imperialist intrusion. A new shogun, preferably Tokugawa Yoshinobu, son of the former daimyo of the Tokugawa collateral han of Mito, could have revived a sense of unity in 1858 and turned "open country" (*kaikoku*) into a positive policy for Japan instead of the tactical retreat that Edo strongman Ii Naosuke made of it when he seized control of the bakufu at midyear. Success, however, was out of the question because of the confusion and sense of crisis that gripped the bakufu. The rest of the country was unprepared to go ahead with a forward strategy, preferring to reinforce traditional practices by limiting the de facto extent of the open-country policy that was accorded to the American consul, Townsend Harris, as an inescapable concession.

Rather than an opportunity, Ii Naosuke viewed the opened country as a temporary diversion to be corrected when Japan was stronger. That day never came. In 1860 Ii was murdered, and bakufu authority declined.[38]

In 1866 Tokugawa Yoshinobu actually did become shogun. Although it turned out that he was to be not only the fifteenth but also the last of the Tokugawa shoguns, he began vigorously enough by approving a series of measures designed to industrialize Japan and arm it with French assistance. But by 1866 opposition to bakufu authority had spread across much of the country, fanned by flames of popular unrest and uprisings. Seeking a symbolically deeper and more effective remedy than technological innovation, leaders and followers alike looked to the old imperial house in Kyoto. Satsuma and Chōshū seized the palace on January 3, 1868, "restored" the youthful emperor Mutsuhito to political power, and eliminated the "conciliar restoration" that Yoshinobu and his allies offered them in the autumn of 1867. The new government soon eliminated the bakufu as well. With it went all the baggage that was the *bakuhan* system, consigned to history by 1871, a relic incapable of coping with current problems.

What the establishment might have accomplished in 1858, in other words, it could not do at all by 1866, despite the fact that the same political elite groups were jockeying for power within the bakufu and in Japan generally during the critical turning points that occurred in these key years. The difference lay not merely in the intensification of imperialist pressures on Japan; it was mainly a matter of the rise of popular agitation, whose auguries were too dire to allow for the perpetuation of the status quo. By 1868 a transformation was well under way.

The charge that *shishi* zealots among the samurai co-opted popular revolutionary energy and turned it against the existing regime, only to suppress it after the restoration, has found influential exponents.[39] It is not an inaccurate interpretation, only an incomplete one. Also incomplete is the argument that nativism, deriving from an extended revival of interest in Japanese literature and myth, became the engine of the Meiji Restoration. The emperor's role did change from that of a backstage legitimating principle for the *bakuhan* system to one of an onstage actor (a "principal") in whose person all political authority came to coalesce.[40]

From mythical times the imperial line had served Japanese political needs. As a presumed direct descendant of Japan's divine
founding heroes, the emperor occupied a unique position in the
troubled political firmament of the mid–nineteenth century. The position of the throne was all the more compelling because the times
demanded new options, and the recycling of the emperor as a "principal of politics" (rather than a principle) came to be seen as an
attractive alternative to the old arrangement with the shogun and
his bureaucrats in command. Nativist ideas did inhere in the throne.
These ideas did encourage malcontents to promote the far more demanding idea of political restoration. To the extent that popular
unrest set the stage for the Meiji Restoration, the new leaders did
benefit by the expenditure of energies beyond those of their own
making.[41]

But Japanese millenarianism combined historic time and
mythic time. It embraced traditional virtues like reverence for the
imperial house while simultaneously evincing a strong revolutionary potential in its own right. Popular millenarianism both frightened and inspired the more daring among those samurai who were
willing to act in search of a simple solution to Japan's midcentury
crisis. People as different as the Chōshū activists Kusaka Genzui and
Takasugi Shinsaku (both pupils of Yoshida Shōin) and the Shinto
priest's son Maki Izumi all determined at one time or another to
undertake drastic action in order to bring their hopes to fruition.[42]
Many thousands of confused samurai faced similar dilemmas of
conscience. As their fervor became more and more politicized, so
was their nativism metamorphosed to a revolutionary nationalism.

This is a powerful combination, one that enabled the Meiji Restoration to take the path it did. Yonina Talmon's scrupulous reca-
pitulation of the features of millenarianism lays stress on "its com-
posite, 'intermediate' nature":

> It combines components which are seemingly mutually exclu-
> sive: it is historical as well as mythical, religious as well as
> political, and, most significant, it is future-oriented as well as
> past-oriented. It is precisely this [amalgam] of a radical revo-
> lutionary position with traditionalism that accounts for the
> widespread appeal of [millenarianism] and turns it into such
> a potent agent of change.[43]

Only a profound concern about popular discontent and a determination to act rather than reflect could have energized the forces that won out in the restoration. Only their revolutionary zeal suggests a rationale for the thoroughgoing quality of subsequent reforms. But they had too lately come from status elitism, and from a nativistic impulse to redeem Japan, for them to turn their eyes to the satisfaction of inchoate popular urges. Their plans focused instead on Japan's macroscopic needs, perceived through the particular prism of their own background and training, hence very heavily political. The fate of the millenarians became less important than the political need to suppress millenarianism.

Chapter Six

What the Hell! Ee ja nai ka Dancing as a Form of Protest

Some play can be very serious indeed.

—Johan Huizinga

But a storm is blowing from paradise.

—Walter Benjamin

Historians like to cite the Meiji Restoration of 1868 as the critical event that launched Japan on a deliberate course of political, economic, and social change leading to the creation of the Japanese Empire. Lost in the calculus of elite behavior during the "imperial restoration" is the question of popular participation. To what extent did the public at large respond to the general crisis that gripped Japan during the 1860s? Given the absence of revolutionary mobs, and the lack of an articulate set of papers, a *Federalist*, advocating a program of reform on the part of the common people, interpreters have had trouble developing a rationale of popular involvement in the restoration. Yet there are all kinds of signs indicating that public agitation set the stage for this key episode in world history. In this chapter I will survey the problem of the dancing demonstrations known by the catch phrase *ee ja nai ka* and try to suggest ways of appreciating this irregular phenomenon at the heart of restoration history.

Falling Charms and Dancing Parties

No stranger dimension attaches to the history of the Meiji Restoration than the *ofudafuri,* the mysterious descent from empty skies of countless thousands of paper talismans, and the wild dancing parties they inspired in cities, towns, and villages late in the year 1867.[1] These lucky charms *(ofuda)*, like pennies from heaven, became a pretext for hysterical dancing and orgiastic behavior across a wide band of Japan's most densely populated geographic heartland, from Hiroshima in the west, back in an easterly direction to Nagoya and on toward Yokohama, and from Kyoto south to Awaji Island in the Inland Sea and Tokushima in Awa Province on the island of Shikoku. The legends on the paper charms showed that they represented a host of Shinto shrines and Buddhist temples; most often they carried the name of the Grand Shrine of Ise, dedicated to the sun goddess Amaterasu and the pantheon of *kami* celebrated in the Japanese creation myth.

Picture if you will the spectacle of thousands and thousands of people dancing and singing in the streets of a downtown urban center. Dressed up in their holiday finest, they present a lively and colorful feast to the eye. Food and drink abound, and the merrymakers pass them around freely. On close scrutiny it appears that many of the men have put on women's kimono, while some of the women masquerade as men. Young and old trade styles of dress and behavior in an orgy of cross-dressing. Revelers surge through the streets and alleyways, all the while accompanied by the rhythm of percussion—drums and gongs, chimes and whistles. On occasion the dancers enter a house or restaurant, compelling the occupants to join in their revelry. From among the festive crowds as they sing and chant, a constant refrain echoes: "Ee ja nai ka, ee ja nai ka." The phrase denotes both closure and transition. About what has already happened, "Wasn't that great?" rhetorically asks the refrain. "Right on! Go for it!" follows the rhetorical implication, and the singing and dancing begin anew.

The notion of "pennies from heaven" expresses only a state of mind, but reports circulated about all sorts of falling objects, some of them valuable, as in the case of coins. Reports tell not only of paper amulets but also of masks, stones, and many other objects coming out of the sky. Various kinds of sacred objects, from stone or metal or earthenware images to wooden grave-tablets, are supposed to have showered down upon the landscape during those ominous days. Even human hands and feet, heads, and whole bodies fell from the sky, if we are to believe some accounts.[2] People are said to have turned into foxes.[3] Those favored by such startling visita-

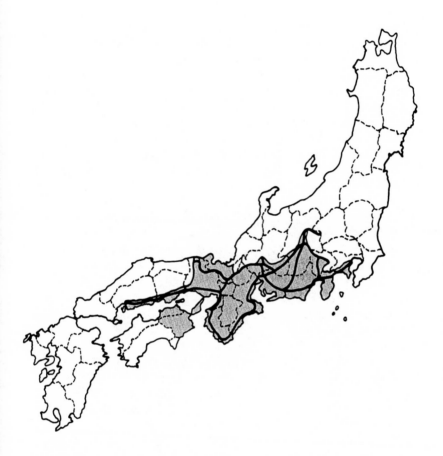

Area of *ee ja nai ka* distribution. From Takagi Shunsuke, *Ee ja nai ka* (Tokyo: Kyōikusha, 1979), p. 24.

tions from on high were not only the poor, but what we would regard as the middle class. They eagerly received the *ofuda* and whatever else fell on them, rushing to share the good news with neighbors and relatives. A community sense of celebration ensued. Sake, fish, and rice cakes were freely passed around. Music and percussion sounded. Servants got the week off and started visiting one party after another.[4] The drudgery of everyday life fell from the shoulders of people as they relieved their anxieties through food and drink, song and dance.

The tale of the falling talismans and rowdy dancing does not lead to obvious answers or spring from sources easy to explain. Conspiracy theories about the political origins of the flying scraps of paper, for example, fail to meet ordinary logical tests; nor is the evidence to support them persuasive. The amulets fell from the sky in large quantities over a vast area. Maybe some of the people on whom the *ofuda* fell went berserk because they were in fact ill. People did show some inclination to read these signs from the skies as political auguries. Maybe the *ofuda* came to symbolize the chaotic state Japan had reached by the summer of 1867. Or maybe the revelers who staged parties and sang and danced in places where the amulets dropped had no other motive than to release their daily cares in the abandon of the moment. Shouting slogans, chanting rude verses, the singers ended all their songs with that single rhetorical line, "Ee ja nai ka."[5]

Translating *ee ja nai ka* poses a problem. The most straightforward translation is simply "Why not?" In the dancers' syntax this phrase functioned as a rhetorical negative, put as a question and employed for effect: "Isn't it so?" or "So, no?" But there is more involved. As a colloquialism used in singing and chanting, *ee ja nai ka* not only connoted more than it stated, it also took on a wide range of varying oral forms. Verse endings like "ii ja nai ka," "ei ja nai ka," "yoi ja nai ka," and "e ya nai ka" have led some to suggest "Isn't it good?" or "That's right!" to render the meaning. Such translations do catch the substance of the thing, for the dancers certainly were having a fine time. But the spirit of what they were doing carries a touch of the blasphemous: "What the hell!" evokes it nicely. When it is preceded by salacious comments (as often happened), it even conveys the feeling of the rougher recent expletive "No more bullshit!" And it has a progressive connotation:

the dancers wanted to "go right on" having a good time. They also meant to put up a bold front to the authorities whose rules they normally observed. *Ee ja nai ka* was a defiant semiotic incantation "thick" with the possibility of multiple layers of meaning. It was a collective protocol exhorting the crowd to carry on with its frolic.

The year 1867 climaxed a decade of troubled politics inside Japan, and between Japan and the outside world. Food riots and rent riots and farm uprisings had reached a peak in 1866, when historians record 106 *hyakushō ikki* and 35 urban *uchikowashi*.[6] The shogun as head of the Tokugawa bakufu decided to resign and try to rebuild his government along conciliar lines, keeping himself at the top of the new council but incorporating many powerful daimyo whom the bakufu had traditionally relegated to an exterior status. The conciliar plan came to nought at the turn of 1868, when a covey of new leaders from Chōshū and Satsuma seized the imperial palace in Kyoto, proclaimed the "restoration" of the sixteen-year-old emperor Mutsuhito, and set the stage for Japan's dazzling leap to international prominence by 1900.

Consider again the dramatis personae of the age. (1) As we have seen, the foreigners were bent on reconciliation. They would do anything necessary to promote the return of stability and order to Japan so that trade and diplomacy might continue unabated. (2) The shogun and his allies used every device at their disposal, but in the end they suffered the ironic fate of seeing their dispersive effort to divide and conquer weaken their capacity to fight and leave them powerless. (3) Meanwhile, under the banner of *sonnō jōi* (revere the emperor and repel the barbarians), a group of outside daimyo and their samurai quested after the romantic dream of a new Japan that would be both orderly and secure: fulfilled, as it were, in relation to Japanese history and values. (4) And everywhere among ordinary people there was commotion. Their only certainty was that their world was in disarray. They found themselves fearful but also hopeful about a fast-changing environment where economy and polity both seemed out of phase, and foreigners had moved in on the very livelihoods of some Japanese. It was a bad time for predictions but an exciting time to be alive, and many commoners turned to new religious sects or new forms of collective behavior that might lead to redemption.

Ee ja nai ka arrived on the scene like a shower but soon threatened to become a deluge. "Then in the autumn of 1867," as E. H. Norman gracefully phrased it, "like a tropical storm a frenzy descended upon the people."[7] It was a slogan for the common run of humanity, not for the samurai elite with its high political concerns. It came to involve hundreds of thousands of ordinary people who from the seventh month of 1867 until the fourth month of 1868, from the fall of the year through the following spring, gave vent to a variety of emotions through the carnivals that followed.

A sound analysis requires that we consider these public manifestations of concern by the populace. We should not dismiss them as epiphenomenal products of a disordered age, the detritus cast off by a dying polity. Though the *ee ja nai ka* frenzies may have "reflected" Japan's political malaise in 1867, it can also be argued that they contributed to that malaise. The rioters belong to a category of public disturbance that had a long history in Tokugawa Japan, but never before had this sort of thing taken so clearly antinomian a turn.[8] The genus of this type of public disturbance is usually called *okagemairi*, a "pilgrimage of thanksgiving," and its several species include actual pilgrimages to places like the Grand Shrine of Ise. Other species are the irruptions of religious fervor that involved faith healing, salvation, joy, and the founding of new cults and sects. There are also the economic disturbances, such as *hyakushō ikki* and *uchikowashi,* which are often classed together with *okagemairi* phenomena. *Ee ja nai ka* was the last of these deviant (or defiant) behaviors to appear on the scene, the only one triggered by objects falling from on high, and the happiest and most festive of a set of popular vehicles for releasing tension among large groups in the population.

The hysteria was probably less important than the uncertainty it implied, the disnomy it revealed. The demonstrators longed for security rooted in solid and stable ways of doing things.[9] In this regard it may be that *ee ja nai ka* was not so remote in motivation from the pilgrimages, which also produced large crowds if not such unruly ones. But *okagemairi*—despite the breaking of ordinary taboos against promiscuity and despite the loose behavior that accompanied them—were carefully orchestrated manifestations of people's need for mobility, even if they were striving for a new and stronger sense of community. *Ee ja nai ka* was spontaneous orgiastic and sometimes destructive behavior, less ritualistic and less formal, harder for the authorities to predict and cope with than *oka-gemairi.*

I shall argue in this chapter that *ee ja nai ka* was actually a form of protest against the old order; that the dancing and singing crowds heralded a major political change as surely as the silent masses who bowed low at the sight of the "restored" emperor's entourage en route to Tokyo in 1869; and that sudden orgiastic conduct such as *ee ja nai ka* may be viewed in conflictual terms as a show of dissatisfaction comparable to that which animated major peasant uprisings and urban disturbances when they hit a peak the year before, in 1866. After poor harvests in both 1865 and 1866, the abundant yields of 1867 may well have induced a celebratory mood when persons unknown propelled lucky charms down onto a surprised and relieved populace.[10] But the response of the crowds, their dancing and carousing, discloses a consciousness of change, of challenge to old values, of certainty only that tomorrow would differ from today. Theirs was a kind of interior monologue proceeding rhythmically alongside the better-known political events of late 1867. It is the sort of phenomenon that characterizes millenarian movements. They aimed to achieve *yonaoshi*—"world renewal," the Japanese version of social transformation, as it were.

The sense that time would stop and all evils be cleansed away, the binding of the mythical to the typical, the immediate desire for deliverance—these elements are all present. So is an orientation towards the future utopia to come, rather than a harking back to some golden age in the past. Regarding sequence, *ee ja nai ka* seems to have gone through two distinct but overlapping phases. The first phase, sparked in Mikawa Province near Nagoya in the seventh or eighth month of 1867, witnessed that odd but defining occurrence which in time was passively received by people living as far apart as Hiroshima and Edo, and almost everywhere in between: *ofuda,* the pieces of paper from shrines and temples that so anomalously floated down like snowflakes out of the summer sky. This phase involved the widest geographical area and featured the *ofudafuri* phenomenon, something that a majority of Japanese experienced in late 1867.[11]

The second phase of *ee ja nai ka* began when the public actively responded to the falling amulets with community get-togethers that soon turned into extended parties. This did not happen everywhere, but it characterized most places where *ofudafuri* occurred. A carnival atmosphere permeated these revels and prolonged them through days and nights and whole weeks of drinking, feasting, carousing, and above all dancing. The crowds of people who thronged together in cities and towns became a tangible sign of the disarray gripping Japan at this moment of rupture in politics. There were, of course, local issues, and personal ones, that caught up the merrymakers. They often vented their frustrations on usurious merchants and landlords by carrying their dancing orgies right through the houses of the wealthy, stomping on the straw mats, smashing the paper screens, throwing mattresses into the streets, and stealing crockery, dish cupboards, and anything else they could carry off, as if it were all communal property anyway. One author argues that in the terms of social psychology, *ee ja nai ka* furnished an opportunity for ordinary people to compel the rich and powerful among them to do their bidding, even to entertain them. On this analysis the lower strata "intentionally" used the commotion set up by falling *ofuda* to induce merchants and local officials to provide food and drink and participate in the festivities that resulted.[12]

Paralysis of Central Space

How could all this happen? Japan is (we think we know) a controlled society, its people disciplined and restrained, perhaps even docile. Surely it was all a plot. To explore the political character of *ee ja nai ka* we need to address three questions—those concerning paralysis, conspiracy, and xenophobia. To start with, many historians agree that the carnivals had the effect of paralyzing the authorities in major cities during the weeks that preceded the restoration. Yasumaru Yoshio, for example, asserts that *ee ja nai ka* "paralyzed" Japan's urban centers, the very space that was the object of the hot political contest between the bakufu and its rivals. Inoue Kiyoshi says that *ee ja nai ka* "completely paralyzed the bakufu's military and police functions" in the affected areas.[13]

By itself this paralysis probably did little to impede troop movements or political machinations. But bakufu and han administrators were sure to be sorely pressed to cope with the crowds that jammed the middle of many large cities. In Kyoto, as we shall see, official orders to cease dancing fell on deaf ears. On the other hand, *ee ja nai ka* seems not to have deterred the bakufu's enemies. In some places the crowds came right out and expressed support for Chōshū because of its anti-bakufu stand.[14] Plenty of verses survive to remind us that Chōshū's stock was soaring in public admiration even as the bakufu's standing plummeted. The rhythmic stanzas praise Chōshū and mock the bakufu, usually in symbolic terms:

> Nishi kara chōchō ga tonde kite,
> Kōbe no hama ni kane nuite,
> Ei ja nai ka, ei ja nai ka![15]

Here a play on words empowers the singers to invoke the homonym *chōchō* (butterflies!) to stand for Chōshū: the verse says that butterflies came flying in from the west and attracted money to Kobe harbor. Such parodies of political economy were widespread and are well documented.

Some sort of paralysis did occur, however limited it would have proved to be for stopping armies. But what about the matter of conspiracy? To what extent was *ee ja nai ka* the result of deliberate planning and execution by elements hostile to the Tokugawa *bakuhan* system? Say, for example, that a conspiracy was hatched by Satsuma and Chōshū forces grown bold at the stalemate that Chōshū achieved in its second military confrontation with the bakufu, in 1866. In the *bakuhan* system, only the bakufu should have come out on top in such a confrontation with a han, so the standoff that resulted was a kind of triumph for Chōshū. If not Satsuma or Chōshū, perhaps it was the agents of the Kyoto courtiers who created this ruckus. Fukuchi Gen'ichirō, a Meiji journalist who had served as a minor bakufu official, speculated in an 1894 book of *bakumatsu* recollections that "Kyoto people may have agitated the popular mind" and inspired *ee ja nai ka*.[16]

But evidence to counter any sort of conspiracy theory is compelling. Certainly both the scope and the longevity of the *ofudafuri* falling-charm episodes and *ee ja nai ka* carnivals raise doubts about the thesis that a political plot underlay them.[17] The *ofuda* mysteriously appeared, to be sure, but they kept on falling month after month across a swath of the most densely populated area of Japan, on the Pacific coast side. Sasaki Junnosuke writes that even the anti-bakufu activists could never have created an artificial scenario so amenable to their purposes that identical falling charms would be found (as they were) by persons as far apart as a farmer in the Tango peninsula north of Kyoto, a landlord's manservant near Kobe, and a Buddhist monk in Nagoya.[18]

There are random bits of evidence that point to the involvement of loyalist agents in the showering of paper charms that set off the *ee ja nai ka* carnivals. In spring 1868 the pro-bakufu *Chūgai shin-bun* in Edo carried an item about a *rōnin* who was detained by bak-ufu police and found to be in possession of several thousand amu-lets from an unnamed Shinto shrine.[19] We may assume that this man was about to salt the clouds over some eastern city with these talis-mans as a way to agitate the local citizenry. Contrast this, however, with another case in which three woodworkers in Shizuoka were found guilty of raining *ofuda* down onto ninety-four houses.[20] Yet this sort of instrumental use of *ee ja nai ka* tells us nothing about its genesis. The two cases happened well after the first spontaneous carnivals. Among recent *ee ja nai ka* scholars, no one advocates a conspiracy thesis.

Foreign Views of ee ja nai ka

Xenophobia is a third area of political concern. If *ee ja nai ka* did not paralyze the bakufu's military forces and did not grow out of a conspiracy against the bakufu, did it instead arise from hostility to foreigners and foreign impact on Japan? All indicators suggest that *ee ja nai ka* was a genuine popular movement. To demonstrate that its roots lay in xenophobia, therefore, we would have to establish that it was consciously directed against foreigners. Antiforeign out-bursts did indeed occur in the course of the *ee ja nai ka* festivities, but they were rare and do not appear to have exerted a definitive influence on events.

Itō Tadao for one holds that these outbursts might have turned an existing "consciousness of ethnic crisis" into full-blown xeno-phobia.[21] At the station town of Fujisawa, clubs were waved and stones thrown at a pair of foreigners on horseback, who wisely enough fled.[22] At Numazu Station a woodblock print turned up among the falling objects with the motto "Ijin taiji," "Exterminate the aliens!"[23] Then there is a famous verse that originated in Awa Province:

Nipponkoku e wa kami ga furu,
Tōjin yashiki nya ishi ga furu,
Ee ja nai ka, ee ja nai ka![24]

This oft-repeated refrain promises that "The gods will descend to Japan, / While rocks will fall on the foreigners in their residencies." But most of the evidence suggests that domestic problems rather than foreign ones were the focus of *ee ja nai ka* concern. Harvests, happiness, and heaven on earth were the millenarian objects of *ee ja nai ka* versification, and the crowds rarely attacked anybody, although certainly there were forays against the property of sake dealers, rice merchants, and landlords who were thought to be gouging the public. The first part of the same verse quoted just above also reminds us of the domestic provenance of most of the revelers' concerns:

Sari totewa, osoroshii toshi, uchiwasure,
Kami no okage de odori, e ja nai ka,
Nipponkoku no yonaori wa ee ja nai ka,
Hōnen odori wa medetai.

To paraphrase this passage: But, then, it was a frightfully bad year (1866) and is best forgotten. Thanks to the *kami* we shall dance, right? Right. Right on! Remaking the world of Japan is right, too, no? Yes. Go for it! Congratulations are due on the good fortune of a bountiful harvest this year, so let's dance on it.

Georges Lefebvre remarks that contemporaries found the Great Fear of 1789 in France "a total mystery." [25] Foreigners in Japan were unlikely to do any better when confronted with the *ee ja nai ka* dancing frenzies. For Algernon Bertram Mitford it was a timeless wonder of the sort that is never repeated: "Thousands and thousands of happy fanatics were dancing along the streets . . . shouting till they must have been hoarse, 'I ja nai ka, i ja nai ka!' . . . It was a weird and wonderful sight, such as, maybe, will never be seen again." [26] Mitford's colleague in the British foreign service, Ernest Satow, tells of twice encountering throngs of revelers in Osaka during a mid-December 1867 visit that the two of them made to the city. They had gone there and to Kobe to work out the details of the forthcoming entry of both ports into the international trade system mandated by the unequal treaties. Treating familiarly with people on both sides of the Japanese political fence, and straddling it with some people, they paid a visit to a high bakufu appointee (Shibata Takenaka) one afternoon and the next day spent several hours with a Satsuma agent (Yoshii Tomozane). Two days later they consulted at length with a major figure (Gotō Shōjirō) from Tosa, another interested feudal domain. On two evenings during their visit to Osaka they found their bodyguard cautiously steering them through a dense mass of *ee ja nai ka* dancers. Satow notes that "some difficulty was experienced in making our way through the crowds of people in flaming red garments dancing and shouting the refrain *ii ja nai ka*." Despite much jostling, however, "the crowd did not offer any rudeness to us, and let us pass without hindrance."

> Crowds of people in holiday garb, dancing and singing "Ii ja nai ka, ii ja nai ka" (isn't it good), houses decorated with rice-cakes in all colours, oranges, little bags, straw and flowers. The dresses worn were chiefly red crape, a few blue and purple. Many of the dancers carried red lanterns on their heads. The pretext for these rejoicings was a shower of pieces of paper, bearing the names of the two gods of Ise, alleged to have taken place recently.[27]

Their difficulty in finding a restaurant moved Satow to comment on what happened at one house when they tried to enter for dinner.

> A herd of young men and boys trooped in, shouting and danc- ing, and tossing about in their midst a palanquin occupied by a fat doll clad in the most gorgeous robes. All the feasters in the house came out to meet them, one cannot say at the doors, *for in Japan there are no doors,* but on the thresholds in which the sliding screens run that divide the different parts of a house. After a violent united dance executed by all present, the troop disappeared again.[28]

Satow expressed amazement at the size and energy of the crowds, who he imagined were all out there celebrating the immi- nent opening of their city to foreign trade. "We found the whole population occupied with festivities in honour of the approaching opening of the city to foreign trade." [29] His official host had told him that the people were happy because Osaka and Kobe were about to become treaty ports! Disingenuous as the authorities may have been on this issue, it does appear that Satow was right in sensing little overt hostility from the Osaka crowds. They apparently intended no harm to the diplomatic party.

Urban ee ja nai ka *in Kyoto*

If ever a place was central to the consciousness of nearly everybody in society, that place was the city of Kyoto in 1867–68. The politics of an entire era focused on Japan's ancient cultural capital. *Ee ja nai ka* in Kyoto has received considerable attention because the city had just recently begun an economic recovery.[30] Inflation's ravages started to abate as the summer harvest of 1867 proved to be abundant.[31] The Kyoto public also knew that their city was rife with agents acting out the many political dramas of a divisive time. Chōshū and Satsuma had concluded their secret anti-bakufu alliance a year earlier. The bakufu's second expedition against Chōshū, directed from nearby Osaka Castle, had failed in 1866 and was terminated. But its economic effects lingered, and bakufu forces remained in the Kansai area until summer 1867.

The new shogun and the new emperor were both in Kyoto when autumn came in 1867. Tokugawa Yoshinobu occupied Nijō Castle with some of his advisers, while Mutsuhito stayed out of harm's way, in the eye of the hurricane, at the imperial palace. During the tenth month, a series of abrupt political moves took place. The shogun suggested a plan (on 10/14) that would return administrative authority to the emperor. He resigned his office as shogun, but the court declined his offer. Meanwhile, the conflict of opinion had already become public knowledge throughout the city. Kyoto people generally were cognizant of what was going on. A pawnbroker and community leader in Shijō Ōmiya, Takagi Zaichū, indicates in his diary that he knew within twenty-four hours what the shogun had proposed upon visiting the palace on 10/14. Takagi says that in the next two weeks talismans began falling all over Kyoto.[32]

In the meantime Iwakura Tomomi, the influential politician and court noble who was active in the radical movement to restore the emperor, made a diary entry that includes the phrase "assistance from heaven" *(tenjo)* to characterize the falling talismans and resulting carnivals. There is nothing else to suggest that a political connection existed, but it is clear that he did think highly of the impact of *ee ja nai ka:* "A great and mysterious event" occurred in the old capital, intones Iwakura, during the tenth month of 1867, when "religious talismans came fluttering down out of the empty sky." People jubilantly accepted these signs from above and staged drinking sprees and celebrations. Women dressed like men, men like women, and all ages were active. Everyone danced and sang and pounded drums. Iwakura repeats some of the standard *ee ja nai ka* verses and concludes that the popular craze in the streets lasted long enough to be useful to the forces that were trying to make an imperial restoration.[33]

Ofuda may have fallen on Kyoto as early as the eighth month, although that seems unlikely. The amulets proliferated in the tenth month, and so did the *ee ja nai ka* celebrations.[34] Pawnbroker Takagi Zaichū first saw them on 10/22, and thereafter they appeared regularly.[35] Of course, Kyoto had handled crowds and annual celebrations for centuries. It continues to do so today, as huge masses of people gather to observe the city's festivals. But the eleventh month of 1867 brought behavior that differed from ritual patterns. The crowds danced around the clock. They clogged the centers of city life, all but paralyzing commercial neighborhoods such as Teramachi, Pontochō, and Gion in the middle of town. Lewd and drunken behavior resulted in frequent riots. Vandalism and pillage and arson were rampant.

To combat such conduct the two Kyoto city magistrates issued a prohibition on 11/13 against *ee ja nai ka* dancing. Their order had no appreciable effect. Two days later, at a downtown restaurant on the west side of Kawaramachi between Sanjō and Shijō, bakufu hirelings murdered the respected Tosa political agents Sakamoto Ryōma and Nakaoka Shintarō. Further inflamed, the people danced on while agitators fueled the fires of political conflagration. Again on 11/25 the city magistrates tried to proscribe the *ee ja nai ka* festivities.[36] Then on 12/9 (January 3, 1868, by the Western calendar) the final and formal imperial restoration was proclaimed, the one that has stuck in historical memory.

On 12/10 the common man Takagi Zaichū confided to his diary that "an unprecedented upheaval" *(kokon tairan)* was in progress, creating "great confusion all over the city." At this very moment, according to Iwakura Tomomi, the *ee ja nai ka* demonstrations in

Kyoto all of a sudden ceased.[37] The shogun soon repaired to Osaka Castle, bereft of his office, while his two Kyoto magistrates had theirs abolished.

A fair suspicion lingers that the Kyoto demonstrations arose from avarice rather than political enthusiasm or popular millennialism. Unlike other cities, the amulets in Kyoto contained a high proportion of salutations from Daikokuten and Ebisu, deities representing wealth, and some merchant houses appear to have manufactured their own *ofuda* as advertising stunts. A contemporary map showing the distribution of *ee ja nai ka* activities marks sixty-one points of concentration, virtually all of them commercial centers.[38]

But then Kyoto was after all a commercial city. The merchants who took advantage of *ee ja nai ka* for promotional purposes no more deserve credit for starting it or keeping it going than do the assassins and provocateurs. The authors of the Kyoto municipal history conclude that *ee ja nai ka* activities grew out of deep-seated distress and antinomian behavior in the city. "Popular *ee ja nai ka* activity, with no warning, suddenly . . . erupted as a storm of mass tumult. . . . As a phenomenon, this can be apprehended as mass hysteria. But when examined closely, it becomes clear that this was popular activity which shook society itself to its very roots, rejecting the forms, values, and ethical norms of the people's own everyday life." [39]

Rural ee ja nai ka *in Harima*

In the Kansai area the countryside as well as the cities became involved in *ee ja nai ka*. Some of the river villages on the upper Kakogawa in Harima Province, not far from Kobe, experienced the dancing parties. In the reconstruction offered by Kinugasa Yasuki, the characteristics of rural *ee ja nai ka* differ little from those of the cities, although typically they seem to have lasted a shorter time. Kinugasa regards the local *ee ja nai ka* outbursts as displaced forms of peasant uprisings, probably shaped by the economic needs of individual communities. He quotes from the diary of a village headman who was an oil merchant in Funamachimura. He witnessed everything from the mass *okagemairi* of 1830 to the *ee ja nai ka* celebrations of early 1868. Along the Kakogawa the pilgrimages to

Ise had given way to local dancing festivals called *okageodori*. Fairly violent dancing was involved, and in Osaka such behavior was strictly proscribed, but the rural authorities usually tolerated it. Sometimes punishments were levied on the dancers. Though all ages were represented, young people predominated. In at least one part of Harima numerous dancers were punished for their *okageodori* activities; almost all of those who were punished were teenagers.[40]

When *ee ja nai ka* came to Harima, the imperial restoration of January 1868 had already occurred.[41] In some of the river villages, uprisings broke out and were forcibly put down by troops dispatched by the magistrate, an officer of the old regime. In the villages of Kita and Funamachi the conditions for such uprisings were also ripe, but Kinugasa finds that intravillage mediation contained the discontent and led to *ee ja nai ka* celebrations instead of rebellion.

The oilman's diary does note that special demands were made and heeded. For example, year-end bills were deferred, coming due instead on the last day of the new year's first month. This part of Harima was advanced in its economic diversification. By-employments were common in some of the villages. Kinugasa speculates that the people in those villages averted outright rebellion in order to keep their jobs and to insure that the local cotton-fabric-processing business could continue operating. To Kinugasa, *ee ja nai ka* appears to carry forward the tabooed tradition of the *okageodori* dancing orgies.[42] The behavior of the villagers was violent and utopian, but it seems to have fallen short of becoming millenarian.[43]

So where shall we situate *ee ja nai ka* physically in the history of the Meiji Restoration? There is no question that it was an urban phenomenon despite the spillover effect that touched the countryside. *Ee ja nai ka* was a form of spontaneous carnival behavior that took place where people live and work, in their own neighborhoods, and that makes it something of the sort that happens in cities. Considerable "exurban" participation also occurred through pilgrimages to municipal shrines.[44] Recent studies also stress the "suburban" connection: *ee ja nai ka* was transmitted through the *shukuba*, station towns such as those along the Tōkaidō that Andō Hiroshige made famous in his woodblock prints, towns where travelers congregated and told of popular fashions and trends.[45] It seems likely that *ee ja nai ka* had a more limited impact on rural communities, where both custom and the occasional use of force as well as harsh penalties tended to keep the merrymakers subdued.

As suddenly as the commotions began, so too they stopped, early in 1868, when the new government had asserted control over central Japan and most of the rest of the country. Thereafter we hear no more about *ee ja nai ka* celebrations. They occurred at times and places that were important for the political transition, occupying the attention of the authorities, who were trying to govern the central space of the realm and to defend it from samurai zealots. So *ee ja nai ka* has only a synchronistic and coincidental relationship to political authority and its troubles. Yet we cannot leave it out of what happened, for it gave texture and meaning to the events of 1867–68.

A Historiographical Question

How have the Japanese people responded to the challenges of the last century? This deceptively simple question is present in every attempt to study Japan's model event, the Meiji Restoration. How does *ee ja nai ka* fit into a Japanese matrix of transformative or revolutionary behavior?

Even a brief survey will indicate that *ee ja nai ka* has excited an odd mix of assessments from Japanese historians. In 1931, for example, Tsuchiya Takao announced in *Chūō kōron* that *ee ja nai ka* was merely "the nonsense attendant on restoration history." [46] Tsuchiya, a pillar of the Rōnō school of interpretation, viewed the whole restoration process as an incomplete bourgeois revolution. Hani Gorō—working from the rival Kōza school's viewpoint that the restoration's revolutionary promise was subverted by Japan's backwardness, resulting in the trough of "absolutism"—took the opposite tack: he said in 1933 that *ee ja nai ka* was a real disruption that had "paralyzed" some of Japan's central space just as the restoration was starting. [47] Following Hani's lead in 1951 was the Kyoto University historian Inoue Kiyoshi, while Tōyama Shigeki, his chief rival within the dominant Kōza camp after 1945, held that *ee ja nai ka* was purely epiphenomenal. Tōyama did come to agree that *ee ja nai ka* paralyzed much of Japan's geographic center, but he continued to treat it as trivial even in 1968, after he had revised his own version of the absolutism thesis in order to argue that Japan became a kind of colonial dependency during *bakumatsu,* its fate determined by the context of imperialism.[48]

During the 1970s the first thorough postwar studies of *ee ja nai ka* appeared. In that decade the Japanese began to salvage the analysis of "consciousness" *(ishiki)*—especially "popular consciousness"—from the theoretical morass that the Marxist historiographical formula of absolutism had made out of Meiji Restoration studies.

Then a decade ago Sasaki Junnosuke proposed a stage theory of *ee ja nai ka.* He asserted its ultimate politicality within a pattern of escalating urban and suburban violence under the rubric of *yonaoshi.* According to Sasaki, all *yonaoshi* movements arose from the urge of smallholders to protect their property and thereby avoid falling into the landless "semiproletariat" stratum. The first stage of *ee ja nai ka* started in the sixth month of 1867 and involved only harvest dances. An actual "movement" began with the second stage, which involved falling charms but no wild dancing and carousing, and lasted halfway through the ninth month. At this point stage three started, and the *ee ja nai ka* movement became a *yonaoshi* phenomenon typified by violence and obscenity among the dancers. Poor peasants from nearby villages began to take part. But it is Sasaki's fourth stage, from the middle of the tenth month, that adds a "political character" to *ee ja nai ka,* chiefly in the Kansai area around Kyoto and Osaka. This fourth and final stage went on through the first month of the new year. Sasaki observes that in Kyoto and Osaka the tenth month of 1867 witnessed the launching of a frankly political *ee ja nai ka* movement, stemming from the shogun's offer to return formal administrative authority to the imperial court.[49]

The record of the Meiji Restoration as written in the West discloses a modicum of popular activity. *Ee ja nai ka* was the motto for a style of behavior so far off the beaten track that most Western writers on late Tokugawa history take little or no note of it. To be sure, E. H. Norman was different. He spoke of it with interest, whereas most accounts tend to skirt it. In Conrad Totman's *Collapse of the Tokugawa Bakufu,* for example, *ee ja nai ka* appears as a matter of no consequence. And it is treated as apolitical by William Beasley's *Meiji Restoration.*[50] By contrast Norman paid serious attention to *ee ja nai ka* in his effort to establish what happened to the people's aspirations in the course of the restoration. He regarded the dancing orgies as hysterical manifestations of popular discontent with feudalism. He viewed the pilgrimages and carnivals as linked phenomena growing out of the despair of the oppressed masses. But even for Norman *ee ja nai ka* constituted epiphenomenal and basically flawed behavior; it was "a 'mock' revolt, a perversion of the people's resistance to an oppressive regime," a largely harmless if symbolically fascinating indicator of mass distress. He summarily labeled it "mass hysteria," calling the dancers "choreomaniacs" and likening their behavior to St. Vitus' dance in medieval Europe.[51]

Yet the popular problematic manages to live on. Much recent work on both sides of the Pacific seeks to examine the historical personality of the Japanese public. Popular programs that articulate an explicit "revolutionary" purpose may be rare, but a universal sense of anomie is seen to pervade *bakumatsu* Japan. We are told that by 1867, when *ee ja nai ka* appeared on the scene, this anomie had succeeded in expressing itself even in the absence of the kind of formal opposition that marked the 1866 uprisings, the so-called *yonaoshi ikki*, or the earlier rural disturbances known as *murakata sōdō* as well as the "trashings and burnings" (*uchikowashi* and *yakiharai*) that occurred in the cities.

A Revolutionary Situation?

But the evidently apolitical character of *ee ja nai ka* does not signify that the demonstrations were unimportant, just different from the coincident activity of samurai rebels and others who inclined to more direct action. It was hard for samurai to express discontent, formally or informally, without incurring severe punishment. There were conventions that allowed for speaking out, though these forms were limited and the ground rules strict. Known as *shoshi ōgi*, "private opinionizing" by samurai, such speaking out, when it happened at all, was not governed by one's status as a samurai.[52] It was much more likely to occur after the failure of the second bakufu campaign against Chōshū, in mid-1866, when the tenuous grasp of the old order was apparent to all, and the gathering troubles of the system elicited a steady stream of complaints.

The historian Shibahara Takuji frankly calls the bakufu's 1866

Chōshū fiasco the turning point that doomed it. This was the institutional failure that precipitated rural and urban disorder and brought into being what Shibahara calls a "revolutionary situation" *(kakumeiteki jōsei)*.

Here is Shibahara on the matter:[53] A revolutionary situation involves the possibility of the "total systemic transformation of society" *(zentaiseiteki na shakai no henkaku)*. It arises in political circumstances in which "the conflict between action and reaction, between revolution and counterrevolution," reaches a climax. The people press their rulers for radical change, no longer content with the gradualism of reforms and improvements. The mass base of such pressure begins to alarm all sectors of the political elite. The entire elite is forced to conclude that it can no longer maintain order and that things as they are have become untenable. Dissent within the elite intensifies, fragmenting it, and a political counterelite plots its own course to save the realm from chaos. This political infighting ignites further popular discontent, and the ultimate crisis develops. All samurai come to share the discontent felt by commoners, and even those samurai who were committed to the old regime find themselves appalled by its injustices and incompetence.

Another historian, Tanaka Akira, cites an arresting bill of complaints left at a bakufu office in the Koishikawa ward of Edo sometime during the eighth month of 1866. This was just after the military effort to suppress the Chōshū activists had collapsed. This is a damning statement of the bakufu's multiple defects and a call to correct them through far-reaching social reform. It is a daring document, really a "manifesto," and it deserves the frequent attention that Tanaka gives it.[54]

The authors of the Koishikawa manifesto said their names were Ōkawabe Chikara and Takeda Shūunsai. The former grandly identified himself as "governor general of the welfare of [Japan's] sixty-six provinces"; the latter was said to be Ōkawabe's "deputy." They began by castigating the bakufu, questioning the morale of the people it governed, and warning that weakness invited aliens to prey upon Japan.

> Recently bakufu authority has declined, and the daimyo do not follow its orders but are encouraged into sectionalism. The Chōshū traitors grow ever stronger while the commodity

prices grow ever dearer, and the impoverishment of all the people is grave and may lead to their destruction by wealthy families. In this situation it is inevitable that the realm [*tenka*] will come to a massive rebellion and our country will be expropriated by foreigners. That the late bakufu struggle with the Chōshū traitors was futile is probably due chiefly to that province's common people, who were all of one mind and one will and were willing to lay down their lives. If it had been Edo, would the metropolitan populace really have coped with the government's problems, or not?[55]

"It is lamentable," the authors go on, "that the bakufu still temporizes" and does not undertake the needed reform measures. Reaffirming their loyalty as samurai, the two writers urge the bakufu to raise an army of righteousness "to annihilate Satsuma and Chōshū and other insubordinate daimyo" and "to nurture all the people of the realm."

Next in the manifesto comes a set of twelve proposals that amount to a radical program for the social reformation of Japan. Jobs shall be protected, poverty wiped out, usury stopped, crime eradicated. Prices shall come down to save samurai from the catastrophe faced by fixed-income people inundated by inflation. Education must be improved so that "truly able and virtuous persons" *(saitoku sugureru mono)* may assume important office despite their poverty of wealth or status. In a climax worthy of the later Meiji oligarchs, the two authors predict the outcome of all these desired reforms. "Our hope is that [such changes] will make a naturally good government, cause foreign trade to flourish, enrich the country and strengthen the military [*fukoku kyōhei*], and turn Japan [*Nipponkoku*] into the world's foremost benevolent country [*sekai daiichi no zenkoku*]."[56]

These two concerned samurai were not calling on the shogun to quit. They were, however, issuing demands in the form of recommendations, and these demands were ones that the bakufu could no longer meet. Their expectations, like those of the commoners who sang and danced while chaos threatened to envelop them, had gone beyond the point of possible return.

What was taking shape here was a binocular expression of deep concern as seen both by ordinary people from their perspective and by samurai conspirators from theirs. The congruence between these groups was coincidental, yet meaningful for the history of Japan. And the specific outcome was different and more visionary than the straightforward coup d'état that brought the collapse of the Tokugawa system. The Meiji Restoration was that outcome. It met the need of the conspirators to break down the system, and it fulfilled the dream of the millenarians for a world made pure and perfect. In the restoration new leaders came forth who in effect "sublated" popular energy into the dialectic of their own transformational goals. Not lost or betrayed in the process, the popular groups that lodged protests in various forms during the 1860s were "elevated" (a process denoted by the concept of *Aufhebung*) and brought into the particular resolution that the Meiji leaders were able to frame for Japan's problems.

Therefore I would argue that such protests were "sublated." In Hegelian dialectics, *aufheben* (to sublate; Japanese *yōkisuru*) means to negate or cancel something but also to preserve and elevate it as part of a resultant synthesis. The concept of sublation befits this argument that the Meiji Restoration eliminated but also absorbed the popular energy that was let loose amidst the conflicting tensions of the *bakumatsu* era. Indeed, "eliminate" seems inaccurate, since the process of sublation retains the force that seems to have been eliminated by transmuting its form, and it stays there with the potential to reappear.

In contrast to the Marxist writers who had complained that Meiji leaders sucked lower-class energies into their struggle against the bakufu only to abandon them once in power, I would hold that various forms of popular consciousness went hand in hand with the new government's proclivity to move further than the bakufu in the direction of deliberately transforming Japan from above. As part of a coincidental synchronic dialectic, popular consciousness never really got lost; it reasserted itself from time to time after the restoration. The new leaders had to take account of such expressions of concern. However unlike their original motives, these two groups of historical actors were voicing similar notes of distress. The Charter Oath of the Meiji government, issued in April 1868, refers to "all classes, high and low," and it bids to bring the people into the governing process.[57] By the same token, however, the congruence that made a "misalliance" between commoners and samurai had to dissolve. It was a false congruence for the long term, forged as it was between incompatible groups.

Whatever its scope, *ee ja nai ka* obviously indicates disnomy—uncertainty and anomie. The values and qualities that command assent in society came under challenge in the 1860s, and features reflecting this sort of uncertainty ran through popular beliefs and attitudes. Different from peasant uprisings with local and urgent aims, different also from a pilgrimage with its rituals and conventions, *ee ja nai ka* only in part reflected discontent. The phenomenon was as spontaneous as the *ofudafuri* falling-charm episodes that triggered it. The most disturbing feature of all this for the samurai elite—both of the bakufu and of the imperial loyalist han—must have been the disnomic tendency running through it, the happy-go-lucky, devil-may-care attitude of the dancers who expected *yonaoshi* to arrive with the dawn. If the carousers seemed to identify with Satsuma and Chōshū in the political wars, that was only natural in the circumstances. Like Satsuma and Chōshū they aimed to do away with the old order and its antiquated and inadequate forms. Both the rebels and the revelers were anxious to redeem the spate of troubles that had plagued the realm.

After 1868 the Meiji leaders could not long endure the millennial dreams of the street crowds, any more than they could tolerate new religious sects like Tenrikyō and Konkōkyō. Pilgrims and urban malcontents had to be suppressed much like rebellious farmers if the politicians were to restore order to a united nation. Bred to an elite role they had no reason to share, the new proconsuls marched Japan down a straight but narrow path. Their interest ran to putting down the signs of a living popular consciousness, and later, in the early 1880s, they did so forcibly to crush outright rebellions at places like Fukushima, Kabasan, and Chichibu.[58]

Ee ja nai ka the Movie

In 1981 the popular director Imamura Shōhei brought out a film about *ee ja nai ka*. Employing the vast facilities of Shōchiku Studios and his own tested resources as a maker of action movies on anthropological themes using garish and risqué subject matter, Imamura made an exciting picture that won prizes for cinematic excellence. Drawn on a sprawling tapestry and splashed with color, it features a knot of Dickensian characters who enliven the narrative with their life stories during the key prerestoration years of 1866 and 1867. Foreign adventurers as well as Japanese villains (and a few heroes) rush headlong through the film. Director Imamura sees the common people as a force, but a force uncertain of its direction. At the beginning of the movie we are told that the imperial loyalists and the shogun's supporters have clashed and that a "hundred factions" in between are clamoring for a profit into the bargain; that "beneath" all this tawdry commotion are the people—"heedless, unmindful, frivolous, [but] strong." [59]

The film has some of that quality of idealistic fervor that is typical of Japanese movies, but with a difference. The main motive of the characters in this motion picture frankly seems to be greed. The odd faithful figure will make his point and live according to a strict code, but most of the characters run back and forth from one kind of hedonistic get-rich-quick scheme to another. The bakufu for its part seemingly can survive only through a strategy of buying up everything and everyone in sight. Satsuma and Chōshū are also portrayed as selfish forces, in league with rich British merchants like Thomas Glover of Nagasaki and anxious to feather their own nests at the cost of the public interest.

There is a refreshing verisimilitude in this effort to portray the great events of history in a human light, to display base as well as noble motives, and more of the former than the latter. No doubt fortunes were made on the spur of the moment in *bakumatsu* Japan, and surely this happened irrespective of the "nobler" requirements of duty and loyalty: Imamura reveals these as sentimental values— quaint and dated notions rather than guiding lights in his swift-paced, action-packed scenario.

At the end the *ee ja nai ka* dancers are carried away by the noise of their own mad rhetoric. After desultory presentations of the "yonaoshi can-can" and other forms of amusement, they take to dancing in the city streets; at last the crowd decides to head downtown, towards Nihonbashi. "Ee ja nai ka, ee ja nai ka!" they chant, heedless of the consequences of their snakelike dancing through the streets of Edo. Bakufu troops stand their ground and fire on the dancers; some of them are killed. The demonstrations end inconclusively, and only one thing is clear: the people have acted, but their action is finally pointless, for they have no purpose. As the movie closes we have no idea what will come next. Yet we can be sure that the energy they have displayed is on the minds of all the many characters who occupy the film. Everyone knows the old world has collapsed. We may assume that the Meiji Restoration is on the way.

A few errors of fact enter into the film, probably with the full knowledge of the director. No real historical figure is depicted in action. Some actual persons are referred to in the screenplay, such as Thomas Glover, Saigō Takamori of Satsuma, and also the last shogun, Tokugawa Yoshinobu (who is called an idiot by some of the bakufu's own samurai). In representing the genesis of *ee ja nai ka*, Imamura has the amulets start to fall on Kyoto at cherry blossom time, but this is wrong since *ofudafuri* actually began very late in the summer and not at all in the spring of the year 1867. In Kyoto there were no *ofuda* before October and few of them until the end of November.

The most puzzling thing is the director's decision to stage the climactic confrontation between bakufu troops and the *ee ja nai ka* dancers at Ryōgoku Bridge in Edo. That scenario seems to satisfy plot and cinematic needs, but it has no evident basis in reality. To be sure, people in Edo came to congregate in response to falling talismans of many types, but the reality is that large-scale *ee ja nai ka* dancing demonstrations did not take place there. In late 1867 the shogun's capital did experience frequent *ofudafuri* episodes, as noted by Minami Kazuo, who has studied the social history of Edo on the eve of the restoration. The incidence of falling amulets is easy to establish and to date, and the phenomenon ran on for at least two to three weeks very late in the year. Riots and demonstrations, however, did not follow in their wake.

Why this should be so tests Minami's ingenuity as a historian. He suggests that only in Edo, of all the places where *ofuda* fell, was order so strictly maintained that the *ee ja nai ka* demonstrations were interdicted. He concludes that the wild dancing that typically accompanied *ofudafuri*, at least as it happened in Nagoya and other cities to the west of Edo, simply was not allowed to materialize in the seat of the Tokugawa bakufu.[60] Whether this was due to stringent police oversight or to the discipline of an enterprising populace is open to debate. Minami for his part attributes the absence of demonstrations to the "strong this-worldly, profit-seeking tendency" of Edoite commoners.[61]

Films are fantasy. They exaggerate for effect and have no obligation to be faithful to the past. Invariably they tell us more about the time when they were made than the time they purport to represent. (To be sure, this is true of all efforts to represent a different age and place.) In Imamura Shōhei's *Ee ja nai ka,* popular energy is a powerful force. Even without a coherent program for change, the people turn out to be nobler by far than the greedy merchants and the seedy aristocrats who pass for samurai in the *bakumatsu* period. Imamura's last point (ironically expressed in the movie by one of the greediest merchants) is that a world of change is a cruel world. That seems to be an ineluctable (and perhaps ubiquitous) conclusion arising out of revolutionary situations. France during the Great Revolution was not the only society driven by cruelty as well as by principled action. The Meiji Restoration had its share of "fear and ambition," and of greed as well.[62]

Maybe it was the world of postwar Japan that Imamura Shōhei was thinking of when he made the movie in 1981. Postwar Japan has been a tense place of suppressed (or repressed) action. Conflict is everywhere subordinated to the requirements of a surface calm. Even Japan's own people seem not to be aware whether much in the way of protest and violence has marked the postwar scene. The political troubles of 1960 and more recent years seem to be blips on an otherwise vacant screen. In the 1970s, when farmers in Chiba violently resisted the construction and then the operation of Narita International Airport east of Tokyo, most Japanese were not all that concerned. Nor are they today when Narita is expanding. Imamura is reminding them that the general public is always a force for social change, whether or not it points in such a direction. This is a lesson that may be fantasy but sets up a resonance between current events and those of the 1860s. Imamura also puts a high valuation on the potential of play for effecting social change. Presumably he would agree with Huizinga's comment that "some play can be very serious indeed."[63]

The *ee ja nai ka* celebrations sounded the death knell, however festively, for the Tokugawa system, whose final collapse followed abruptly. This is not the way historians expect things to happen. As Thomas C. Smith has observed, "Great historical structures are not brought down until the popular beliefs and behavior supporting them are deeply eroded, and this necessarily long process is not always accompanied by the beating of ideological gongs." [64] Most of us would agree with the first half of this statement. But can we not agree also that the actual erosion of historical structures may sometimes be sudden? In taking the measure of such matters, we will do well to listen to all the ideological gongs that may be audible on the historian's soundscape. That includes the gongs and drums, and the chimes and whistles, of a semiotic gesture like *ee ja nai ka*.

Chapter Seven

Epilogue: The Crowd in the Meiji Restoration

Every act of world history was accompanied by a laughing chorus.

—Mikhail Bakhtin

Bakhtin's study of Rabelais teaches us that carnival behavior carries the potential for social transformation because it tends to level hierarchical distinctions.[1] At liminal moments in history when the old order is changing, carnivalization points to new outcomes that can result from a revolutionary situation. Such a moment came on the eve of the Meiji Restoration, in late 1867, when temple *ofuda* began falling across a wide band of east and central Japan. The mysterious appearance of these lucky charms led to the outbreaks of popular dancing and saturnalia that are identified with the catch phrase *ee ja nai ka*.

Shimazaki Tōson in his grand novel of the restoration, *Yoake-mae*, has the narrator assert the essential mystery of *ee ja nai ka:* "It had a certain savage power to disorder the civilized breast. . . . It intoxicated the senses of vast numbers of people."[2] But Tōson's epic romance came out in the early 1930s, more than six decades after 1868. A later literary text is not the place to seek evidence of social revolution; rather we look for signs that appeared at the time it was occurring. For Japan in 1867, consider this scene involving the eastern seaboard station town of Fujisawa.

A Funeral in Fujisawa

A late autumn haze covers the small town in the afternoon calm. It is the eleventh month of the third year of Keiō (1867). All day long people have been socializing in aggressive ways. Young and old consume cakes and sake; men and women appear cross-dressed. Music sounds, drums and koto and samisen. Revelers invade wealthy houses and levy provisions from their midst.

At last as dusk falls a silent procession leaves town with black flags flying. It is a mock funeral for the Tokugawa bakufu. More than a dozen marchers attend to their solemn progress. They are carrying a coffin, and the once great house of Tokugawa is now the subject of grim ridicule: "Nikkōsan Tōshōgū," proclaims a banner evoking the memory of Tokugawa Ieyasu, the founder and first shogun.[3]

All of it is farce, all in deadly earnest. These are the symbols of cultural transformation that greeted travelers in the fall of 1867 along the Tōkaidō, Japan's famed Eastern Sea Road. Fujisawa is the station town *(shukubamachi)* where this particular incident occurred, a compact community situated just west of Yokohama in Sagami Province (modern Kanagawa Prefecture). An 1864 census shows that 932 households were registered in Fujisawa and a grand total of 4,566 persons lived there.[4]

The funeral scene for the bakufu is a vivid visual image that we get from an *emakimono* (picture scroll) titled "Shinbutsu miei kōrin no keikyō" (The advent of images of the *kami* and buddhas). The scroll belongs to a family named Horiuchi and was for a long time the property of Horiuchi Tōhisa, the *bakumatsu*-era headman *(nanushi)* of Ōkubochō in Fujisawa. Tōhisa wrote the text *(kotobagaki)* that accompanies the illustrations, which are the work of his son, Ikunosuke. As it happens, Ikunosuke died young in 1871, so it would seem that this work was produced in close proximity to the actual events. Today the Horiuchi scroll containing Ikunosuke's *emaki* and Tōhisa's text resides in the Fujisawa City Archives. A century went by before it was introduced to the Japanese historical community in 1972.[5]

Descriptive sources abound for *ee ja nai ka,* some of them known for decades. For Awa Tokushima on Shikoku, *ee ja nai ka* material began appearing in folklore studies early in this century. The phenomenon there was treated as if it were an entertainment of the sort intended to appeal to tourists. For Kyoto the record of *ee ja nai ka* is fairly strong (as we saw in chapter 6). Major figures in the restoration movement as well as ordinary citizens commented favorably when paper amulets and other objects started falling in the tenth month of 1867, just as the shogun was proposing to "return" power to the imperial court. For Ise, the Grand Shrine was the source of many of the *ofuda* that triggered the *ee ja nai ka* dancing, and an Ise merchant's diary describes the celebrations there.[6]

But it was in the station towns on the main avenues of east-west communication that the political effect of *ee ja nai ka* was most pronounced. The text of the Horiuchi *emakimono* tells us that *ofuda* first fell in Fujisawa around 11/6.[7] The pictures show scenes of talismans falling, and the labels on them indicate that they emanated from Buddhist temples as well as Shinto shrines. The public is enjoying itself, and feasts and celebrations are under way.

Carnival or Festival?

A festive atmosphere prevails, and it is true that a sense of festivity suffuses the first six panels of the Horiuchi scroll. But the remaining four panels show that more was going on than festive behavior. For heuristic purposes I want to suggest drawing a line between festival and carnival. Festival is ritual—regular or repetitive communal behavior, acknowledged and sanctioned by the authorities, like church celebrations in Catholic Europe. Carnival is spontaneous and potentially hostile to those in power, substituting ridicule for rebellion but manifestly breaking with the status quo. Scenes of menace and dramatic parodies such as our mock funeral threaten all the comfortable social arrangements.[8]

The final four Horiuchi pictures disclose issues that are clearly political.[9] First there was the funeral itself, no easy matter in a stern hierarchical society. Second is the practice of coercing the affluent to share their wealth: partygoers appear in the scroll marching through the compounds of merchant homes, taking what they want, sharing with the poor, and obliging their social betters to join in the merrymaking. This form of social extortion has obvious political importance in small communities; it is a feature of *ee ja nai ka* that emerges from the Fujisawa scroll and was also observed elsewhere along the Tōkaidō.

Third on this list of political issues is the old question of xenophobia. In one scene we see two scruffy foreigners fleeing on horseback. Local residents stripped to the waist chase after them, throwing stones and waving sticks in gestures of attack. The text calls this scene a triumph of "the Japanese spirit" *(Yamatodamashii)*.[10] We do not have to contend (as Yano Yoshiko does[11]) that this drawing exemplifies a literal enactment of *jōi* political consciousness, but it does depict popular antipathy to foreigners. Such warnings give the lie to the recollection of British diplomat Ernest Satow, who says that in December 1867, when he asked Shibata Takenaka, governor of Hyōgo and a leading bakufu expert in foreign affairs, why people in Kobe were jamming the streets in ceaseless dancing, he was told that they were celebrating their city's imminent opening to overseas trade.[12]

On this question it seems that Satow was misinformed. "Alien" presence in Japan was one of many targets when *ee ja nai ka* dancers surged through the streets of cities and towns. Some of their chanted refrains referred to foreigners, and we can see foreigners in the Horiuchi scroll being chased off by good Japanese. Beyond serving as the butt of a joke, however, foreigners are largely immaterial in this genre of popular dissent. The emphasis is on domestic problems. We have seen that a modest revival of optimism ironically contributed to that emphasis. Things were still bad, but not as bad as they had been all through the year 1866. In 1867, inflation rates that had pushed the price of rice to an average of 6.7 times its 1863 price level, sake 6 times, and salt 7.3 times had come down across Japan from 1866 highs reached while the Tokugawa bakufu was conducting its second military expedition to punish Chōshū. A failure, the campaign dissolved and the troops disbanded. This issue was crucial in the Kansai, since the bakufu's expeditionary army had been headquartered in Osaka. Modest inflation relief, however, marked every site where *ee ja nai ka* carnivals broke out.[13] By late 1867 a mood of disorder prevailed, both in large central cities— Nagoya, Osaka, Kyoto—and in the suburban station towns on the Tōkaidō and other overland routes, as we have seen in the case of Fujisawa.

Transportation by land across Japan's uneven and hilly terrain had to proceed through the station towns, so they became key links in the communications chain of Tokugawa Japan. The station towns thus acted as synapses in Japan's neuroanatomy, transmitting messages from one place to another throughout the system of social cybernetics. Passersby included farmers and day laborers and the carriers of trade goods and supplies for the metropolises lying far off in either direction at the poles of the Tōkaidō—Sanjō Ōhashi in Kyoto at the western end, Nihonbashi in Edo on the east. Through these station towns also passed the functional equivalent of modern information professionals: samurai on their way to study world affairs or to hatch political conspiracies; headmen from other towns and villages; tax officials on business; and fleet couriers *(hayabi-kyaku)* who sped their messages all the way up or down the Tōkaidō in a mere three days. Most of all, Fujisawa was a place where culture was contested and modified. Collective social behavior was on display and subject to refinement there, crossing boundaries of class and region. It was happening especially there, in this nerve center at the heart of the bakufu's hegemonic system of control. Suddenly in the station towns the usual hierarchy of persons and values was put on hold. Spontaneous *ee ja nai ka* carnivals hinted at the demise of the massive interlocking feudal edifice that had dominated the realm since 1600.

Despite similarities to celebrations and pilgrimages, *ee ja nai ka* held a transformational quality that sets it apart. In its taunting way it was a form of conversation with the authorities; as such the historian must engage it. All history is a dialogue with the past, which is dead and cannot speak till we call it forth. Through texts we conduct a dialogue with the minds of past actors. When the texts are those of symbolic action, like the ones treated here, the conversation gains a dimension, becoming a kind of trialogue: the past (1) is coaxed to converse with the present by living historians (2), who in turn interact with the mindset of their time (3) in an interpretative contest whose outcome shapes the culture that we all share and struggle over.

These symbolic texts rarely get high billing in the narratives that offer to explain recent Japanese history. They do not play well as stories. They are synchronic episodes not easily convertible to a narrative plot. They look somehow irrational and seem detached from concrete reality, even though like all rituals they are built from everyday life and routinely partake of it.

I have argued that the public along the Tōkaidō harbored a potentially revolutionary intent on the eve of the Meiji Restoration; that this was not some feat of legerdemain by elements of the samurai elite acting out their own political fantasies; that *ee ja nai ka* carnivals revealed an urgency belying the notion of mere passive acceptance; and that to omit popular participation from restoration history serves no truthful scenario for characterizing the Japanese people's faculty for political action. If the argument has merit, then this comment by Charles Tilly applies to Japan even as it does to France: "There lies the most important teaching of popular collective action: it is not an epiphenomenon. It connects directly and solidly with the great political questions. By the actions that authorities call disorder, ordinary people fight injustice, challenge exploitation, and claim their own place in the structure of power." [14] *Ee ja nai ka* laid such a claim. Its menace to the authorities arose not from direct confrontation but from ridicule that challenged the dominant feudal ideology. The received social imaginary had become clouded. It is not reality that was at issue; rather the social perception of reality, the imaginary that people use to construct a civic map of order and value in society, was being contested.[15]

When the bakufu's founder could become the subject of a symbolic funeral in a seaboard town just a month after his lineal successor as shogun meekly offered to share power with the old imperial court; when obscure samurai leaving complaints at bakufu offices like the one at Koishikawa could chastise their leaders for incompetence; then the bonds of feudal ideological sway were coming unraveled. That is one message of spontaneous carnival—it respects neither hierarchy nor power but possesses the latent force to pave the way for a new order. If the Meiji government liked the idea of popular laughter no better than did the Tokugawa bakufu, that would help to explain why evidence of carnivalization at the close of the *bakumatsu* era has remained in the shadows, away from the surface of common historical narratives.

The historical irony about this situation is that the popular movements had expected the new regime to fulfill their millenarian dreams and bring about deliverance. In place of deliverance came suppression. So ended the misalliance of elite and commoners that arose in the course of a short-lived revolutionary situation. The *ee ja nai ka* carnivals would quietly expire in 1868, and the new government would try to erase its legacy from the public mind.

But that legacy no more disappeared than the motives that called it into being in the first place. Its ultimate significance comes in the calculus of Japan's transformation after 1868, not in the particular set of collisions and interactions that brought down the feudal system in 1867–68. The restoration came about against the grain of conventional historical explanation. No European model can account for it. Bourgeois revolution never fairly got started, yet the old regime failed to survive even though it did try to employ the strategy and tactics of reaction. After the restoration, Satsuma and Chōshū promptly suppressed popular discontent, yet that discontent had served to drive these very leaders to make a revolution. The Meiji Restoration may have been a sublative revolution, but it was a revolution nonetheless.

Despite being put down as a political force, the Japanese people played a role in giving the restoration its character. The "circumstantial picture" presented in this study suggests that without that role the victorious samurai would have made a more modest settlement, in line with their own particular set of motives.[16] The process may be likened to a centrifuge, or simply to a vicious circle. Once the system began to fly apart, the uncertainty among ordinary people crystallized into a disnomic irreverence for the status quo. The emperor, symbol and substance of protean Japanese mythology and the object of universal awareness if not exactly of veneration, could then enter the arena as the agent able to end the centrifugal disorder. The emperor could do more to break the headlong rush, could even unify Japan in a way never before contemplated.

Violence was done in *bakumatsu* Japan, in the name of the many righteous causes whose flags flew in those years. The result resembles the "great revolutions" of recent world history—the French, the Russian, the Chinese—in the sense that it appealed for a transvaluation of all values. It resembles them too in that its makers backed away from so utter and total a reevaluation in favor of redress, reaction, consolidation. But the Meiji Restoration rarely inhabits the abode of these great revolutions as they are reconstructed by scholars of social upheaval. Why? It was insufficiently sanguinary, or it failed to change the class base of existing power relations, or it was only a response to the stimulus of foreign intrusion upon Japan.

The historian Shibahara Takuji, as we have seen, regards the demise of the *bakuhan* system as an exemplary instance of the "total systemic transformation of society." It amounted to a progression of events that involved an ever-increasing loss of credibility on the part of the rulers. The process reflected total and systemic disorder, and its outcome, the Meiji Restoration, also had to be total and systemic. The popular dream of a world made new—*yonaoshi*—melded with the hopes of samurai patriots for a redeemed Japan, strengthened internally and therefore able to hold its own in the external arena. This vision of a double transformation for Japan, at home and abroad, succeeded the events of the restoration era and continued to occupy Japanese thinking through the late nineteenth century and into the early twentieth. It is a vision still likely to appeal to thoughtful Japanese today, after several wars won and one lost and the passage of five generations since 1868. Not merely as a symbol of empire, but also as a beacon of faith for all Japanese about the viability of their own world, the Meiji Restoration lives on as the model event in Japanese history.

We have also seen that the four sets of actors who took part in this historical process had a great deal at stake. They diverged one from another and came to pursue sometimes contradictory and incompatible strategies for dealing with Japan's problems. Of the four groups of agents analyzed in this book, two had no intention of changing the structures that operated in Tokugawa Japan, let alone the ideological systems underlying those structures. The foreigners wanted secure turf for carrying on trade. The bakufu and the larger daimyo aimed to preserve the existing order. The other two groups of agents had long been reluctant to try changing the status quo. Those samurai who started off demanding accountability from the bakufu and the han had hoped to see their own talents rewarded through the appointment of officials by merit, not by heredity, but they did not envision the end of the *bakuhan* system. The system was the political base of the very order sustaining the realm of Japan.

Finally, we have seen that *bakumatsu* Japan was a realm in disarray. Every one of these groups of agents meant to rectify the trouble, to end the disarray and bring about a return to normalcy. Every group therefore found itself at some time or other confronting a dilemma: whether to attack or defend the status quo; and whether to do either one of these as a means of effecting radical change, or as a means of achieving revival. No one could stand still and watch the realm erode away.

Such a construal of the fundamental paradox of *bakumatsu* Japan stresses the need to act that was felt by all of the groups we have identified. As we might expect, the actions they took follow from the character of the groups doing the acting. The foreigners used military hardware—advanced technology—to disrupt as little as possible but to carry out their disruptions in graphic fashion. This method seemed most likely to impress the Japanese with the gravity of the situation, but without obligating any party in Japan to withdraw support from the status quo. The bakufu and its friends were more selective, targeting opponents for eventual oblivion, while striving to insure bakufu control over the rites and powers of the realm. These situationally congruent actors were undone by forces that admittedly did not dispose of comparable military skill or equipment. Under volatile circumstances, new forces with new perceptions helped to initiate a general crisis in Japan. Popular discontent assumed new forms and came to pose a threat to the existing order. No less than a world made new, a millenarian dispensation to redeem the wrongs of the present, became the prime objective of rebels and sectarians alike. Meanwhile, the samurai who also sought to save Japan gradually shifted the focus of their attention from redeeming their honor against the foreign menace *(sonnō jōi)* to preserving the realm from the perfidies of the bakufu and han leaders whose stewardship looked bankrupt. The situationally transcendent forces prevailed.

Leaving aside the question of how any one group directly or causally affected the other groups, it is easy to see why so fluid a situation yielded new alignments and let the various groups move away from doing things as they originally intended. By 1865 the foreigners were ready to choose sides among samurai antagonists. The common people embraced religion, or carnival, in an effort to transcend the troubles of the present. The bakufu conceived new policies that flew in the face of traditional arrangements. The loyalist samurai began to act in ways that finally challenged the authorities to stand up and fight.

The stage was set for the Meiji Restoration.

Notes

┌─────────────────┐

Preface

1. R. G. Collingwood, *The Idea of History* (Oxford, 1946), pp. 234, 213.

2. Paul Ricoeur, "The Model of the Text: Meaningful Action Considered as a Text," *New Literary History 5* (1973–74): 103.

3. Edward Gibbon, *The History of the Decline and Fall of the Roman Empire* (Philadelphia, 1804–5), l:iv.

4. Carl L. Becker, *The Heavenly City of the Eighteenth-Century Philosophers* (New Haven, 1932), pp. 116–18. Cf. Gibbon on barbarism and religion, *Decline and Fall* 8:265.

Chapter One

1. Marx made this remark at the beginning of his 1852 pamphlet "The Eighteenth Brumaire of Louis Bonaparte" (in *The Marx-Engels Reader,* ed. Robert C. Tucker [New York, 1972], p. 437). People make history, Marx continued, but they must do it "under circumstances directly found, given and transmitted from the past."

2. For a summary and elucidation of recent trends and issues involved in the analysis of agency in causation, see Alex Callinicos, *Making History: Agency, Structure, and Change in Social Theory* (Ithaca, N.Y., 1988), esp. chaps. 1–2 and 5.

3. A vast and popular topic, the Meiji Restoration has stimulated all kinds of treatments. In English, three influential studies that emphasize nationalism (as a response to the Western intrusion) as the chief cause of the restoration are Albert M. Craig, *Chōshū in the Meiji Restoration* (Cambridge, Mass., 1961); William G. Beasley, *The Meiji Restoration* (Stanford, Calif., 1972); and Conrad D. Totman, *The Collapse of the Tokugawa Bakufu, 1862–1868* (Honolulu, 1980), where the author prefers "ethnicity" to nationalism but stresses its causal connection to the foreign problem. For a similar approach in Japanese, one that has exerted strong influence

on Western studies of Japan, see Sakata Yoshio, *Meiji ishin shi* (Tokyo, 1960).

4. Hayden White, "The Value of Narrativity in the Representation of Reality" (1980), in *The Content of the Form: Narrative Discourse and Historical Representation* (Baltimore, 1987), p. 25.

5. Some analysts inveigh against "perspective" and other terms that imply relativism and may on that account impede the quest for truth in scholarship. But every historical actor, like every historian, has a "standpoint," both in space and in time, and presumably has a perspective based on the context of that standpoint as well. See, e.g., E. D. Hirsch, *The Aims of Interpretation* (Chicago, 1976), pp. 36–49.

6. See, e.g., *Mythology,* comp. Yves Bonnefoy (2 vols.; Chicago, 1991); Wendy Doniger O'Flaherty, *Other Peoples' Myths: The Cave of Echoes* (New York, 1988). See also such earlier studies as Northrop Frye, *Anatomy of Criticism: Four Essays* (Princeton, 1957), esp. pp. 106–7; and Mircea Eliade, *The Myth of the Eternal Return* (Princeton, 1971) as well as the omnibus German study, *Terror und Spiel: Probleme der Mythenrezeption,* ed. Manfred Fuhrmann (Munich, 1971).

7. Samurai leaders did not hesitate to refer to the emperor as a "jewel" (*tama* or *gyoku*) in the political game. See Beasley, *Meiji Restoration,* p. 285; Harry D. Harootunian, *Toward Restoration: The Growth of Political Consciousness in Tokugawa Japan* (Berkeley, 1970), p. 402. Such references abound but do not imply a Machiavellian disrespect; of themselves they are merely a form of code, a shorthand, for the emperor and all that he stood for as an alternative to the existing political system.

8. See Tanaka Akira, *Meiji ishin,* vol. 24 of *Nihon no rekishi* (Tokyo, 1976), pp. 80–81.

9. On the making of rituals suited to an imperial state, see Takashi Fujitani, "Japan's Modern National Ceremonies: A Historical Ethnography, 1868–1912" (Ph.D. dissertation, University of California, Berkeley, 1986).

10. See my article, "Changing Images of the Meiji Restoration in Japanese Historiography," in *Papers of the C.I.C. Far Eastern Language Institute,* ed. Richard B. Mather (Ann Arbor, Mich., 1973), 4:170–81.

11. Jean Piaget's *Structuralism* (New York, 1970) may be the best survey of structuralism as it goes across the hard sciences into literature and philosophy from its origins in linguistics and anthropology. Piaget stresses the features shared by all structuralist arguments: they posit wholeness or *Gestalt,* they are systems of transformation, and they are self-regulating (pp. 3–16). For all he does, Piaget omits mention of the engine of transformation in structuralist approaches to society, which is normally associated with the idea of binary opposition. Structuralism sets forth opposed fea-

tures (traits, aspects, dimensions) of social life that through interaction generate changes (transformations) within the system. For a book that treats five key French thinkers—Claude Lévi-Strauss, Roland Barthes, Michel Foucault, Jacques Lacan, and Jacques Derrida—see John Sturrock, ed., *Structuralism and Since* (Oxford, 1979). For a lucid summary, see Peter Caws, "Structuralism," *Dictionary of the History of Ideas* (New York, 1973), 4:322–30.

12. Collingwood, *Idea of History,* p. 213.

13. Paul Ricoeur, "Explanation and Understanding" (1977), in *The Philosophy of Paul Ricoeur* (Boston, 1978), pp. 149–66.

14. Ricoeur makes this point about action as a "text" in his article "Model of the Text."

15. Michel Foucault, *Language, Counter-memory, Practice* (Ithaca, N.Y., 1977), p. 5.

16. Walter Benjamin, "Theses on the Philosophy of History," in *Illuminations* (New York, 1968), p. 256.

Chapter Two

1. Chester G. Starr, "Historical and Philosophical Time," *History and Theory,* Beiheft 6 (1966): 35, 32.

2. St. Augustine, quoted in *Problems of Space and Time,* ed. J. J. C. Smart (New York, 1964), p. 58. Augustine did not merely muse about time: he was preeminently the theologian who made "progress" a plausible doctrine by systematically setting forth the need for history to proceed along a time line toward *parousia,* the ultimate historical objective of the second coming of Christ. See Frank E. Manuel, *Shapes of Philosophical History* (Stanford, Calif., 1965), pp. 3–4.

3. Immanuel Kant, *Critique of Pure Reason* (New York, 1965), p. 77.

4. Joan Stambaugh, "Time, Finitude, and Finality," *Philosophy East and West* 24 (1974): 129.

5. G. J. Whitrow, *What Is Time?* (London, 1972), pp. 175–77. First president of the International Society for the Study of Time, Whitrow gives a sound interdisciplinary survey of the evolution of time as a concept.

6. On "time's arrow" see A. S. Eddington, *The Nature of the Physical World* (New York, 1929), pp. 68–71. Whole books hold forth on the subject of time and infinite regress. For a philosopher-historian's straightforward view, see R. G. Collingwood, "Some Perplexities about Time, with an Attempted Solution," *Proceedings of the Aristotelian Society,* n.s. 26 (1926): 138–42.

7. G. J. Whitrow, "Reflections on the History of the Concept of Time,"

in *The Study of Time,* ed. J. T. Fraser, F. C. Haber, and G. H. Müller (New York, 1972), p. 6. Whitrow here traces the dominance of linear time in the West back to Galileo, Newton, and Locke, then proclaims it a central but unprovable conviction of Western thinkers since the seventeenth century, hardened into the dogma of progress by the biological evolutionists of the nineteenth century (pp. 8–11).

8. Eliade, *Myth of the Eternal Return,* pp. xiii-xiv, 86–89.

9. Edward W. Said, "On Repetition," in *The Literature of Fact,* ed. Angus Fletcher (New York, 1976), pp. 138–58 passim. Vico's cycles of repetition and "recourse" were combined with the linear pattern of stages—the age of the gods, the age of heroes, the age of man—that he saw in the history of nations; see *The New Science of Giambattista Vico* (Ithaca, N.Y., 1968), pp. xxiv, 336.

10. Joseph Needham, *Time and Eastern Man* (Glasgow, 1965), p. 50.

11. Nathan Sivin, "Chinese Conceptions of Time," *Earlham Review* 1 (1966–67): 82–92; and "On the Limits of Empirical Knowledge in the Traditional Chinese Sciences," in *Time, Science, and Society in China and the West,* ed. J. T. Fraser, N. Lawrence, and F. C. Haber (Amherst, 1986), pp. 151–69.

12. Frederick W. Mote, *Intellectual Foundations of China* (New York, 1971), pp. 17–20.

13. Both chronicles are available in English: Donald L. Philippi, trans., *Kojiki* (Princeton and Tokyo, 1969); and W. G. Aston, trans., *Nihongi: Chronicles of Japan from the Earliest Times to A.D. 697* (London, 1956).

14. See Stambaugh, "Time, Finitude, and Finality," pp. 129, 133–35; and Kenneth K. Inada, "Time and Temporality: A Buddhist Approach," *Philosophy East and West* 24 (1974): 171–79.

15. Mote, *Intellectual Foundations of China,* pp. 22, 27–28.

16. Carl Gustav Jung, *Synchronicity: An Acausal Connecting Principle,* extract from *The Structure and Dynamics of the Psyche,* vol. 8 of *The Collected Works of C. G. Jung* (Princeton, 1973), pp. v-vii, 104–15; and "Letters on Synchronicity," in *The Symbolic Life: Miscellaneous Writings,* vol. 18 of *The Collected Works* (1976), pp. 502–9.

17. *Gukanshō,* vol. 86 of *Nihon koten bungaku taikei* (Tokyo, 1967). For an English translation with elaborate commentary, see *The Future and the Past: A Translation and Study of the "Gukanshō," an Interpretative History of Japan Written in 1219,* ed. and trans. Delmer M. Brown and Ishida Ichirō (Berkeley, 1979).

18. Brown and Ishida argue throughout their extensive commentaries in *The Future and the Past* that politics caused Jien to write the *Gukanshō.*

For a briefer view, see Delmer M. Brown, "Buddhism and Historical Thought in Japan before 1221," *Philosophy East and West* 24 (1974): 215, 223.

19. Ibid., pp. 217, 223–24. A recent gloss of Jien's stage theory of Japanese history emphasizes the role of Buddhist help for the emperor; see Ōyama Kyōhei, *Kamakura bakufu,* vol. 9 of *Nihon no rekishi* (Tokyo, 1974), pp. 322–23. But see Brown and Ishida, *Future and the Past,* chap. 5 passim.

20. This is A. L. Sadler's translation, quoted in *The Taiheiki, a Chronicle of Medieval Japan,* trans. Helen Craig McCullough (New York, 1959), p. xxv. Another genre, the *rekishi monogatari* (historical tale), appeared earlier than the *gunkimono* and similarly appealed to a broader elite than the original court histories. A good example of the *rekishi monogatari* is the *Ōkagami* (Great mirror), composed late in the eleventh century. It too charts a linear course based on the reigns of the emperors, finally coming to focus on the life of the grandest court aristocrat of all—Fujiwara no Michinaga (966–1027; *Ōkagami,* vol. 21 of *Nihon koten bungaku taikei* [Tokyo, 1960]). In English, see *Ōkagami, the Great Mirror,* trans. Helen Craig McCullough (Princeton, 1980).

21. See Basil Hall Chamberlain, trans., *"Ko-ji-ki"; or, "Records of Ancient Matters"* (Tokyo, 1906). A fine example of retreat into Latin occurs during the dance to lure the sun goddess Amaterasu out of a cave (pp. 64–65).

22. Joseph Campbell, *The Masks of God: Oriental Mythology* (New York, 1962), pp. 465–66.

23. Frye, *Anatomy of Criticism,* pp. 99, 365. Frye's "archetype" is a predominant literary symbol or image (p. 365).

24. Philippi, *Kojiki,* p. 15.

25. This rapid survey does scant justice to the mix of later political motives, local lore, and ritual behavior surrounding a host of spirits or deities *(kami).* A compact summary of the creation myth is E. Dale Saunders, "Japanese Mythology," in *Mythologies of the Ancient World,* ed. Samuel Noah Kramer (Garden City, N.Y., 1961), pp. 409–42. For a swiftly paced and authoritative Japanese compendium, see Matsumae Takeshi, *Nihon no kamigami* (Tokyo, 1974).

26. George B. Sansom, *A History of Japan to 1334* (Stanford, Calif., 1958), p. 35. The importance of the concept of *matsurigoto* is underscored by its early appearance in the *Kojiki;* see Philippi, *Kojiki,* p. 140 n. 11.

27. The locus classicus of the idea of "infiguration" is Francis Macdonald Cornford, *Thucydides Mythistoricus* (London, 1907), pp. 130–33. "Infiguration" conveys the point that the demands of an orderly plot oblige

historians to structure a narrative by "the moulding of facts into types of myth contributed by traditional habits of thought" (p. 132). (Cornford argues that this is what Thucydides did in his histories.)

28. For example, Chamberlain wrote that early Japanese Shinto had no organization, dogma, moral code, or canonical texts as did the "civilized religions, such as Buddhism, Christianity, and Islam" (*"Ko-ji-ki"*, p. lxxiv).

29. Mircea Eliade, *No Souvenirs: Journal, 1957–1969* (New York, 1977), pp. 31, 35.

30. John C. Pelzel, "Human Nature in the Japanese Myths," in *Personality in Japanese History,* ed. Albert M. Craig and Donald H. Shively (Berkeley, 1970), p. 45.

31. On the convenient principle of "deterioration . . . followed by improvement," see Brown and Ishida, *Future and the Past,* p. 36. Jien invoked both Buddhist and Shinto law when he said, "We find that all phenomena alternately deteriorate and improve" (ibid.).

32. On the unresolved question of when the *Gukanshō* was actually written, see *Gukanshō,* pp. 8–16; and Brown and Ishida, *Future and the Past,* pp. 347–48, 348 n. 113.

33. *Jinnō shōtōki,* vol. 87 of *Nihon koten bungaku taikei* (Tokyo, 1965), p. 41. For an English translation see *A Chronicle of Gods and Sovereigns,* trans. H. Paul Varley (New York, 1980).

34. George B. Sansom, *A History of Japan 1615–1867* (Stanford, Calif., 1963), p. 94 n. 9. But the same author also praises the *Jinnō shōtōki* as "a remarkable work [and] a fine piece of historical special pleading [for] political reform" (*A History of Japan 1334–1615* [Stanford, Calif., 1961], p. 104).

35. Kurt Singer, *Mirror, Sword, and Jewel: A Study of Japanese Characteristics* (New York, 1973), pp. 145–48.

36. Ibid., pp. 145–47.

37. For the story of the Kenmu Restoration and its place in recent Japanese historiographical debates, see H. Paul Varley, *Imperial Restoration in Medieval Japan* (New York, 1971). For Varley's treatment of Godaigo's intentions and their "reactionary" character, see ibid., p. 95. According to the terms of structural anthropology evoked by Yamaguchi Masao, Godaigo literally and figuratively went too far. A king reaches the apex of his capacity to exercise power at the center of the political arena when he withholds his full potential in order to maintain tension around him: "The history of royalty does not unfold in the shadowy wings of society, but on the contrary occupies the central scene of the area in which a given political community is evolving. This space is loaded with extremely dense tension"

("Kingship as a System of Myth: An Essay in Synthesis," *Diogenes,* no. 77 [1972]: 52, 61). Godaigo expended his authority and spread it on the "margin" of the political arena, losing the "center" (Kyoto) in the process.

38. Erwin Baelz, *Awakening Japan: The Diary of a German Doctor, Erwin Baelz* (Bloomington, 1974), p. 17.

39. The phrase "myth of concern" signifies the ideological basis of a worldview. See Northrop Frye, *The Critical Path: An Essay on the Social Context of Literary Criticism* (Bloomington, 1973), p. 36. For historical writing, William J. Bouwsma compares the operation of a myth to that of a model in the social sciences. Whether true or false, a myth can aid a historian by serving as an axis around which to erect a systematic approach to a topic (Bouwsma, "The Renaissance and the Drama of Western History," *American Historical Review* 84 [1979]: 9).

Chapter Three

1. Fernand Braudel, *The Mediterranean and the Mediterranean World in the Age of Philip II,* 2 vols. (New York, 1972–73).

2. John Whitney Hall, "The New Look of Tokugawa History," in *Studies in the Institutional History of Early Modern Japan,* ed. John Whitney Hall and Marius B. Jansen (Princeton, 1968), p. 55.

3. Many authors have used "centralized feudalism" to characterize Tokugawa Japan; Edwin O. Reischauer described it well in his early work *Japan Past and Present* (New York, 1946), chap. 7; he explicitly speaks of Tokugawa Japan as a "centralized feudal state" in John K. Fairbank, Edwin O. Reischauer, and Albert M. Craig, *East Asia: Tradition and Transformation* (Boston, 1989), chap. 15. The phrase "military-bureaucratic" is that of John Whitney Hall in *Twelve Doors to Japan,* ed. John Whitney Hall and Richard K. Beardsley (New York, 1965), pp. 145–49. The most recent of these labels, "integral bureaucracy," refers to the novel thesis of merchant participation in samurai government asserted by Conrad D. Totman, *Japan before Perry* (Berkeley, 1981), pp. 133–37.

4. Though he treats myths in all his works and devotes whole tomes to exploring the role of mythology, Claude Lévi-Strauss has put his conception of myth and its relation to scholarship into succinct form in *Myth and Meaning* (Toronto, 1978).

5. Hall and Beardsley, *Twelve Doors to Japan,* pp. 159–60.

6. Joseph R. Strayer, *Feudalism* (Princeton, 1965), pp. 11–14. See also the compact article by Strayer, "The Tokugawa Period and Japanese Feudalism," in *Institutional History of Early Modern Japan,* ed. Hall and Jansen, pp. 3–14.

7. The best analysis of the galvanizing effect of *sankin kōtai* on the To-kugawa economy is that of Craig, *Chōshū in the Meiji Restoration,* pp. 27–31.

8. See, e.g., John K. Fairbank, ed., *The Chinese World Order: Traditional China's Foreign Relations* (Cambridge, Mass., 1968); and Donald C. Hellmann, *Japan and East Asia: The New International Order* (New York, 1972), pp. 15–21.

9. George Elison, *Deus Destroyed: The Image of Christianity in Early Modern Japan* (Cambridge, Mass., 1973); Robert N. Bellah, *Tokugawa Religion: The Values of Pre-industrial Japan* (Glencoe, Ill., 1957).

10. An "oblique" study (the author's word) of the push and pull that resulted in "equilibrium between central government and baronial independence [during] the Edo period" is Harold Bolitho, *Treasures among Men: The Fudai Daimyo in Tokugawa Japan* (New Haven, 1974), p. xii.

11. This explanatory pattern was apparent in Thomas C. Smith's classic study *The Agrarian Origins of Modern Japan* (Stanford, Calif., 1959) as well as his *Nakahara: Family Farming and Population in a Japanese Village, 1717–1830* (Stanford, Calif., 1977). It is also present in some of Smith's more recent writings, admirably collected in *Native Sources of Japanese Industrialization, 1750–1920* (Berkeley, 1988).

12. Harry D. Harootunian, "Late Tokugawa Culture and Thought," in *The Nineteenth Century,* ed. Marius B. Jansen (Cambridge, 1989), pp. 168–258.

13. Ibid., pp. 258, 170.

14. See Harootunian, *Toward Restoration;* and Tetsuo Najita, *Visions of Virtue in Tokugawa Japan: The Kaitokudō Merchant Academy of Osaka* (Chicago, 1987).

15. I have studied one such *yōgakusha,* Hashimoto Sanai, who typified the effect of *yōgaku* on events: "The Bakumatsu Intellectual in Action: Hashimoto Sanai in the Political Crisis of 1858," in *Personality in Japanese History,* ed. Craig and Shively, pp. 234–63.

16. Harry D. Harootunian, "The Functions of China in Tokugawa Thought," in *The Chinese and the Japanese: Essays in Political and Cultural Interactions,* ed. Akira Iriye (Princeton, 1980), pp. 9–10, 25–26.

17. Championing the nativist role in bringing about change are Peter Nosco, *Remembering Paradise: Nativism and Nostalgia in Eighteenth-Century Japan* (Cambridge, Mass., 1990); and Harry D. Harootunian, *Things Seen and Unseen: Discourse and Ideology in Tokugawa Nativism* (Chicago, 1988). An earlier and rather different formulation is Harootunian, "The Consciousness of Archaic Form in the New Realism of Koku-

gaku," in *Japanese Thought in the Tokugawa Period, 1600–1868: Methods and Metaphors*, ed. Tetsuo Najita and Irwin Scheiner (Chicago, 1978), pp. 63–104.

18. For the classic thesis about the role of Ogyū Sorai's *kogaku* as the pivotal agent that drove change in Tokugawa Japan, see Maruyama Masao, *Nihon seiji shisōshi kenkyū* (Tokyo, 1952).

19. In the history of Bali (and by inference other parts of Indic Southeast Asia) there is an institution called the *negara*, which can be rendered "state" but has none of the frankly power-related constraints of the European word; indeed, the *negara* appears to cover most of the cultural dimensions that I have associated with *tenka* in Japanese, except that the *negara* might be broader still. See Clifford Geertz, *Negara: The Theatre State in Nineteenth-Century Bali* (Princeton, 1980), pp. 3–10, 121–23. Geertz writes that the *negara* was "a structure of thought [and] a constellation of enshrined ideas" (p. 135). So was the *tenka* or realm—just as much as it was a political institution.

20. Elison, *Deus Destroyed*, p. 246.

21. See the informed discussion of the emergence of *tenka* as an idea in Hayashiya Tatsusaburō, *Tenka ittō*, vol. 12 of *Nihon no rekishi* (Tokyo, 1966), pp. 2–15. See also Hayashiya Tatsusaburō, "Bakumatsu ki no bunkateki shihyō: Bakumatsu bunka kenkyū josetsu," in *Bakumatsu bunka no kenkyū*, ed. Hayashiya Tatsusaburō (Tokyo, 1978), pp. 3–39.

Chapter Four

1. George B. Sansom, *The Western World and Japan* (New York, 1950), p. 281.

2. Claude Lévi-Strauss, *The Savage Mind* (Chicago, 1966), p. 259.

3. Victor W. Turner, "Myth and Symbol," *International Encyclopedia of the Social Sciences* (New York, 1968), 10:576.

4. For paradigmatic examples in English of these opposing appraisals of the Meiji Restoration, see Barrington Moore, *Social Origins of Dictatorship and Democracy: Lord and Peasant in the Making of the Modern World* (Boston, 1966), chap. 5; and John Whitney Hall, *Japan: From Prehistory to Modern Times* (New York, 1970), chaps. 11–14.

5. Collingwood, *Idea of History*, p. 213.

6. Kenneth Burke, *A Grammar of Motives* (Berkeley, 1969), pp. xv–xvi.

7. H. W. Fowler, *A Dictionary of Modern English Usage* (New York, 1944), pp. 470–71.

8. Joan Didion, *The White Album* (New York, 1979), p. 11.

9. Lévi-Strauss, *Savage Mind,* p. 258.

10. Ibid., pp. 258–59.

11. Conrad Totman is an exception to the usual tendency to dwell on the history of the restoration's winners. In his *Collapse of the Tokugawa Bakufu,* he chronicles the dismal if edifying human tragedy that befell the managers of the Tokugawa system notwithstanding their best efforts.

12. Turner, "Myth and Symbol," pp. 576–77.

13. This scheme derives from Hayden White's article "Interpretation in History" (1973), in *Tropics of Discourse: Essays in Cultural Criticism* (Baltimore, 1978), pp. 51–80.

14. Clifford Geertz, *The Interpretation of Cultures* (New York, 1973), pp. 6–10.

15. Frye, *Anatomy of Criticism,* pp. 158–239; see p. 162 for a succinct summary of the four "narrative categories of literature" as "generic plots" or *mythoi.*

16. Geertz, *Interpretation of Cultures,* pp. 89–90, 126–27. In his formulation of the complementary concepts of *ethos* and *worldview,* Geertz defines ethos as "the tone, character, and quality . . . of life, its moral and aesthetic style and mood"; he defines worldview as a people's "picture of the way things in sheer reality are, their concept of nature, of self, of society" (p. 127).

17. For the source and justification of this typology of explanatory strategies, see Stephen C. Pepper, *World Hypotheses: A Study in Evidence* (Berkeley, 1942), chap. 7. Integrative world hypotheses, says Pepper, are inadequate in scope, whereas dispersive ones are inadequately precise (pp. 142–46).

18. On the Richardson affair and its aftermath, see Beasley, *Meiji Restoration,* pp. 183, 199–200.

19. For the French demarche toward the bakufu, see Meron Medzini, *French Policy in Japan during the Closing Years of the Tokugawa Regime* (Cambridge, Mass., 1971), chaps. 8–15.

20. For Mitford's celebrated account of Taki's *harakiri,* apparently the first to be witnessed and described by an Englishman, see his letter to his father, included in Algernon Bertram Freeman-Mitford Redesdale, *Mitford's Japan,* ed. Hugh Cortazzi (London, 1985), pp. 84–91.

21. Ernest Satow, *A Diplomat in Japan* (Tokyo, 1968), p. 347.

22. Ibid., pp. 351–54. The interpretative open-endedness and historical contingency of the Sakai affair are topics treated by Elizabeth A. Wilson, "Reading [Mori] Ōgai's 'Sakai jiken': An Exercise in Disclosing Meanings" (unpublished paper, University of Michigan, 1989).

23. Satow, *Diplomat in Japan*, pp. 358–59.

24. Algernon Bertram Freeman-Mitford Redesdale, *Memories* (New York, n.d.), 2:449–50, 453.

25. Ibid., p. 428.

26. Satow, *Diplomat in Japan*, p. 347.

27. Redesdale, *Memories*, p. 455.

28. Ibid., p. 416.

29. Ibid., p. 418.

30. On situational congruence and situational transcendence as opposing attitudes toward existing social reality, see Karl Mannheim, *Ideology and Utopia: An Introduction to the Sociology of Knowledge* (New York, n.d.), pp. 192–204.

31. *Tōkyō hyakunen shi* (Tokyo, 1979), 1:1556–57.

32. Quoted in Beasley, *Meiji Restoration*, p. 256.

33. William Irwin Thompson, *The Imagination of an Insurrection: Dublin, Easter 1916: A Study of an Ideological Movement* (New York, 1967), p. 242.

34. Murakami Shigeyoshi, *Kindai minshū shūkyōshi no kenkyū*, 2d ed. rev. (Tokyo, 1963), p. 91.

35. Murakami Shigeyoshi, "Bakumatsu ishin ki no minshū shūkyō ni tsuite," in *Minshū shūkyō no shisō*, ed. Murakami Shigeyoshi and Yasumaru Yoshio, vol. 67 of *Nihon shisō taikei* (Tokyo, 1971), pp. 568–69.

36. Ibid., p. 565.

37. Murakami, *Kindai minshū shūkyōshi no kenkyū*, pp. 124–25.

38. Kishimoto Hideo, ed., *Japanese Religion in the Meiji Era* (Tokyo, 1956), pp. 329, 332.

39. Joseph M. Kitagawa, *Religion in Japanese History* (New York, 1966), p. 221 and n. 85.

40. Itō Tadao, "Ee ja nai ka," in *Yonaoshi*, ed. Sasaki Junnosuke, vol. 5 of *Nihon minshū no rekishi* (Tokyo, 1974), pp. 312–13, 327–28.

41. *Ishin no gekidō*, vol. 7 of *Kyōto no rekishi* (Tokyo, 1974), p. 172.

42. Ibid., p. 186.

43. Ibid., p. 360.

44. Geertz, *Interpretation of Cultures*, pp. 89–90.

45. Itō, "Ee ja nai ka," pp. 324–31.

46. Maruyama, *Nihon seiji shisōshi kenkyū*, part 3, chap. 3; in English, see Maruyama Masao, *Studies in the Intellectual History of Tokugawa Japan* (Princeton and Tokyo, 1974), pp. 350–67, esp. p. 366.

47. See Bob Tadashi Wakabayashi, *Anti-foreignism and Western Learning in Early-Modern Japan: The "New Theses" of 1825* (Cambridge, Mass., 1986).

48. Maruyama, *Studies,* pp. 358–63.

49. *Narrative of the Expedition of an American Squadron to the China Seas and Japan,* ed. Sidney Wallach and comp. Francis L. Hawks (New York, 1952), p. 236.

50. Robert Louis Stevenson, "Yoshida-Torajiro," in *Familiar Studies of Men and Books* (New York, 1902), pp. 174–90. Recent treatments of Yoshida include Harootunian, *Toward Restoration,* chap. 4; and Thomas M. Huber, *The Revolutionary Origins of Modern Japan* (Stanford, Calif., 1981), chaps. 2–4.

51. On the mentality of *sonnō jōi* and a suggestion that there were two types of *shishi,* one the zealots who rejected foreigners, the other the "Herodians" who sought to best their enemy through emulation, see Mikiso Hane, *Japan: A Historical Survey* (New York, 1972), pp. 252–56, esp. p. 253 n. 2.

52. Peirce often mentions abductive reasoning. He regarded it as an alternative to both inductive and deductive reasoning (from the particular to the general, from the general to the particular). He said that we can know only the facts that we can observe (perceive), and if they are insufficient to allow inference we must add "guess-work," which leads to "the first starting of a hypothesis": this step itself is what he called "abduction." Even if we cannot prove X, for example, if Y were provable then X would also be provable; hence, abductive reasoning, which in Peirce's view characterizes most of our inferences anyway. See Charles S. Peirce, *Philosophical Writings of Peirce* (New York, 1955), pp. 150–52.

53. Northrop Frye equates the terms "narrative categories," "generic plots," and "mythoi" (*Anatomy of Criticism,* p. 162). Frye holds that there are no unique story lines beyond the four he discusses (as if each of them were a sort of prime number; pp. 158–239). They are of course the four plots used in this book.

54. Also important but outside of the matrix is Kenneth Burke's argument that there are five key terms in assigning motivation (act, scene, agent, agency, purpose); this and his survey of the "four master tropes" (metaphor, metonymy, synecdoche, irony) helped shape the matrix shown here (*Grammar of Motives,* pp. xv, 503–17).

55. The only full-blown attempt to apply the concept of deep structures of consciousness to a standard field of historical inquiry is Hayden White's *Metahistory: The Historical Imagination in Nineteenth-Century Europe* (Baltimore, 1973), esp. pp. ix-xii, 29–42. Trends growing out of structural

linguistics, transformational (generative) grammar, and structural anthropology have contributed to the arrival of this notion that "deep structures" exist beneath the level of rational consciousness.

56. Frye, *Anatomy of Criticism*, pp. 163, 192.

57. Hayden V. White, *Metahistory*, pp. 34–36; Kenneth Burke, *Grammar of Motives*, pp. 507–8.

58. The use of the label *idiographic* (in place of Stephen Pepper's *formist*) is Hayden White's; see *Tropics of Discourse*, pp. 64–66, 79 n. 29.

59. Mannheim, *Ideology and Utopia*, p. 197.

60. Kenneth Burke, *Grammar of Motives*, pp. 506–9, discusses metonymy as a variant of metaphor and (sometimes) a "special category" of synecdoche. It is typical of the mechanistic approach to social problems to see the world in reductionist (metonymic) terms.

61. For the role of catastrophe *(pathos)* in a tragic plot, see Frye, *Anatomy of Criticism*, p. 192.

Chapter Five

1. Sansom, *Western World and Japan*, p. 281.

2. Yasumaru Yoshio, " 'Okagemairi' to 'ee ja nai ka,' " in *Minshū undō no shisō*, ed. Shōji Kichinosuke, Hayashi Motoi, and Yasumaru Yoshio, vol. 58 of *Nihon shisō taikei* (Tokyo, 1970), p. 494.

3. Ibid., pp. 495–96. For a survey of "thanksgiving" *(okagemairi* or *nukemairi)* pilgrimage phenomena throughout the Tokugawa period, see Fujitani Toshio, *"Okagemairi" to "ee ja nai ka"* (Tokyo, 1968), pp. 35–103.

4. Classic statements on these risings are Hayashi Motoi, *Hyakushō ikki no dentō* (Tokyo, 1955) and *Zoku hyakushō ikki no dentō* (Tokyo, 1971); and Shōji Kichinosuke, *Yonaoshi ikki no kenkyū*, 2d ed. rev. (Tokyo, 1970).

5. Victor W. Turner, "Pilgrimages as Social Processes," in *Dramas, Fields, and Metaphors: Symbolic Action in Human Societies* (Ithaca, N.Y., 1974), pp. 166, 197.

6. For example, Yonina Talmon, "Millenarism," in *International Encyclopedia of the Social Sciences* 10:357; and E. J. Hobsbawm, *Primitive Rebels: Studies in Archaic Forms of Social Movement in the Nineteeth and Twentieth Centuries* (New York, 1963), pp. 57–58.

7. Talmon, "Millenarism," p. 349.

8. Peter Worsley, *The Trumpet Shall Sound: A Study of "Cargo" Cults in Melanesia*, 2d ed. rev. (New York, 1968), pp. 12, 225–26.

9. Talmon, "Millenarism," pp. 351–53, 360.

10. See, for example, John Whitney Hall's argument about the high quality of Meiji leadership in *Japan,* pp. 265–72.

11. Totman, *Collapse of the Tokugawa Bakufu,* pp. xiii-xv, 479–81. His argument would be strengthened by applying the concept of systemic crisis elaborated by Jürgen Habermas, *Legitimation Crisis* (Boston, 1975), parts 1–2.

12. On this question see Thomas C. Smith, "Japan's Aristocratic Revolution," *Yale Review* 50 (1960–61): 370–83.

13. This is the gist of a canny argument put forward by Ueyama Shunpei, "Meiji ishin no kakumeisei: Ishin to sonnō jōi shisō," in *Meiji ishin no bunseki shiten* (Tokyo, 1968), pp. 7–41.

14. Turner, "Pilgrimages as Social Processes," p. 197. See also Turner, "Myth and Symbol," pp. 576–77.

15. Nishigaki Seiji, *Kamigami to minshū undō* (Tokyo, 1977), p. 96.

16. Who was the author of *Ukiyo no arisama?* The answer is unclear and probably unimportant when compared with the range of phenomena that the author so carefully describes. We do know that he was an affluent male physician who practiced in Osaka and originally hailed from Katsuyama han in Mimasaka (Yasumaru, "'Okagemairi' to 'ee ja nai ka,'" pp. 497–98). Covering four decades, the text of that part of *Ukiyo no arisama* that deals with *okagemairi* and *hyakushō ikki* is contained in *Minshū undō no shisō,* ed. Shōji Kichinosuke, Hayashi Motoi, and Yasumaru Yoshio, vol. 58 of *Nihon shisō taikei* (Tokyo, 1970), pp. 307–72.

17. Absolute deprivation may elicit less fervent varieties of millenarianism than "relative deprivation"; see Talmon, "Millenarism," pp. 354–55; and David F. Aberle, "A Note on Relative Deprivation Theory as Applied to Millenarian and Other Cult Movements," in *Millennial Dreams in Action: Essays in Comparative History,* ed. Sylvia L. Thrupp (The Hague, 1962), pp. 209–14. But see Worsley, *Trumpet Shall Sound,* pp. xxxix-xlii, for an appraisal of relative deprivation and a defense of his thesis that "the disinherited" are the typical carriers of millenarianism.

18. On Tokisada and his role in the Shimabara Rebellion, see Elison, *Deus Destroyed,* pp. 217–21. See also Ivan Morris, *The Nobility of Failure: Tragic Heroes in the History of Japan* (New York, 1975), pp. 143–79.

19. Elison, *Deus Destroyed,* p. 221.

20. Motoori offered his observations in an extended exercise in social commentary titled *Tama katsuma,* written during the final decade of his life (in *Motoori Norinaga,* ed. Yoshikawa Kōjirō, Satake Akihiro, and Hino Tatsuo, vol. 40 of *Nihon shisō taikei* [Tokyo, 1978], p. 82). *Okagemairi* and *nukemairi* are virtually synonymous. The distinction between

them involves intrafamily relations; it is discussed in the commentary found ibid.

21. Shibahara Takuji, *Kaikoku*, vol. 23 of *Nihon no rekishi* (Tokyo, 1975), p. 332.

22. On "world renewal" *(yonaoshi)*, see Irwin Scheiner, "The Mindful Peasant: Sketches for a Study of Rebellion," *Journal of Asian Studies* 32 (1972–73): 582, and "Benevolent Lords and Honorable Peasants: Rebellion and Peasant Consciousness in Tokugawa Japan," in *Japanese Thought in the Tokugawa Period*, ed. Najita and Scheiner, pp. 39–62 passim. *Yonaori* and *yonaoshi* are often used synonymously. Usage depends partly on regional variations within Japan. There is a distinction between them in the sense that *yonaori* connotes the normal changes of rural life, not the radical departures brought about by natural disasters such as floods, famines, or earthquakes as well as social upheavals. The revitalization process embedded in the idea of *yonaoshi* is much more active than the cyclical changing of "the times of this world" conveyed by *yonaori*. See, e.g., Miyata Noboru, "Nōson no fukkō undō to minshū shūkyō no tenkai," in *Kinsei 5*, vol. 13 of *Iwanami kōza Nihon rekishi* (Tokyo, 1977), pp. 230–33.

23. Yasumaru, "'Okagemairi' to 'ee ja nai ka,'" p. 496. Inoue Kiyoshi writes that *ee ja nai ka* "completely paralyzed the bakufu's military and police functions"; see his *Nihon no rekishi* (Tokyo, 1963–66), 2:112.

24. On the rise of the new religions in nineteenth-century Japan, see Murakami, *Kindai minshū shūkyōshi no kenkyū;* in English, *Japanese Religion in the Modern Century* (Tokyo, 1980), esp. pp. 4–32, 44–51.

25. Shibahara, *Kaikoku*, pp. 338–42, also chooses Tenrikyō and Konkōkyō to illustrate the startling changes that mark Japanese religious behavior in the mid-nineteenth century.

26. H. Neill McFarland, *The Rush Hour of the Gods: A Study of New Religious Movements in Japan* (New York, 1967), p. 103.

27. See Murakami Shigeyoshi, *Kyōso: Kindai Nihon no shūkyō kaikakusha-tachi* (Tokyo, 1975), pp. 74–82.

28. A lucid summary of Konkōkyō and its founder appears in D. C. Holtom, *The National Faith of Japan: A Study in Modern Shinto* (New York, 1938), pp. 257–66.

29. Talmon, "Millenarism," p. 351.

30. On the *jiba*, see Holtom, *National Faith of Japan*, p. 282.

31. Shibahara, *Kaikoku*, p. 338; Murakami, *Kyōso*, pp. 37–39.

32. Murakami, *Kindai minshū shūkyōshi no kenkyū*, pp. 91–92.

33. Many authors agree that Tenrikyō targeted its appeal to the needs of the poor and downtrodden, and its message of joy appealed to those

whose lives were empty: "The wealthy and the scholars could wait" till later (Kishimoto, *Japanese Religion in the Meiji Era,* p. 327).

34. Tenrikyō's large canonical text is available in English: *Ofudesaki, the Tip of the Writing Brush* (Tenri, 1971).

35. Like the Gnostic gospels, heterodox texts antithetical to traditional Japanese mythology exist, and Tenrikyō produced one of them. "One of the secret works of Tenri-kyō doctrine, the *Doroumi-kōki,* which contains its own version of the cosmogonic myths, different from the 'official' myths accepted by the [prewar] Japanese government, was eliminated from the doctrinal systems of Tenri-kyō in 1938" (Kitagawa, *Religion in Japanese History,* p. 222 n. 86). But see also Holtom, *National Faith of Japan,* p. 273.

36. See Kishimoto, *Japanese Religion in the Meiji Era,* pp. 331–32.

37. Ibid., p. 333. See also Murakami, *Japanese Religion in the Modern Century,* p. 15, on the practical aspects of life for Tenrikyo's community of believers. Originally several of the late-Tokugawa new religions were called *kō* (or *kōsha*), a term indicating an association for mutual financial benefit, a kind of credit union. They rendered a valuable service to the members, considering the ups and downs of the economy.

38. In 1858–59 Japan faced a remarkable opportunity to achieve productive reform. Tired of suffocating bakufu direction from the center, reformers acted to enlarge political participation and to adapt from Western models in order to promote industrialization. It all collapsed when the shogunal succession for Tokugawa Yoshinobu fell through. I am working on a book that engages this fertile moment in Japanese history, focusing on some of the victims of the bakufu's Ansei Purge, conducted by Ii Naosuke: "Trial of a Samurai: Hashimoto Sanai in the Ansei Purge, 1858–1859."

39. See, e.g., Inoue Kiyoshi, *Nihon no rekishi* 2:121–22; or Tōyama Shigeki, *Meiji ishin to gendai* (Tokyo, 1968), pp. 93–108.

40. Harry D. Harootunian, "From Principle to Principal: Restoration and Emperorship in Japan," in *The Uses of History: Essays in Intellectual and Social History,* ed. Hayden V. White (Detroit, 1968), pp. 221–45. See also Harootunian's essay on the theoretical basis of his concern with nativism, "Consciousness of Archaic Form," pp. 63–104.

41. Carol N. Gluck examines the rise of a Japanese school of historiography based on the exploits of the "common people" *(minshū)* (as opposed to the samurai elite) in "The People in History: Recent Trends in Japanese Historiography," *Journal of Asian Studies* 38 (1978–79): 25–50.

42. Harootunian, *Toward Restoration,* pp. 42–43, 251–54, 278–320, 390–91. On Kusaka and Takasugi, see also Huber, *Revolutionary Origins of Modern Japan,* chaps. 5–8.

43. Talmon, "Millenarism," p. 360. She also points out that millenarianism (unlike modern science) can sustain both a linear and a cyclical concept of time; but when the millennium actually dawns, time must stop as myth become reality ("Pursuit of the Millennium: The Relation between Religious and Social Change," *Archives européennes de sociologie* 3 [1962]: 130–31).

Chapter Six

1. The most accessible survey and the only comprehensive study of *ee ja nai ka* as a cultural and political phenomenon is Takagi Shunsuke, *Ee ja nai ka* (Tokyo, 1979).

2. Ibid., p. 13.

3. Sasaki Junnosuke, "Bakumatsu no shakai jōsei to yonaoshi," in *Kinsei 5*, p. 275.

4. Takagi Shunsuke, *Ee ja nai ka,* pp. 13–14; Tanaka Akira, *Mikan no Meiji ishin* (Tokyo, 1968), p. 16.

5. It is a peculiar fact of the history of this peculiar phenomenon that nowhere east of Nagoya was *ee ja nai ka* the actual phrase used to close the reiterative verses. Instead any of several other phrases fulfilled the same function. The most common of these alternative verse endings was *rokkon shōjō,* a pietistic urging for ritual purification often spoken by ascetics as they traveled together. See Takagi Shunsuke, *Ee ja nai ka,* pp. 16–17 et passim.

6. See Tanaka, *Meiji ishin,* p. 28. A graph showing the frequency of *hyakushō ikki* (regional or multivillage peasant uprisings), *toshi sōjō* (urban disturbances), and *murakata sōdō* (intravillage disputes) for the twelve years 1858–69 inclusive appears in Shibahara, *Kaikoku,* p. 333. The year 1866 witnessed by far the largest total number of outbreaks; Shibahara points out that the situation was exacerbated because *ikki* greatly outnumbered *murakata sōdō,* reversing the relationship present in a normal year and doing so just when a great rise in urban disturbances was also taking place.

7. E. Herbert Norman, "Feudal Background of Japanese Politics," in *Origins of the Modern Japanese State: Selected Writings of E. H. Norman,* ed. John W. Dower (New York, 1975), pp. 343–44.

8. My use of *antinomian* refers to the "unlawful" behavior of crowds going against accepted norms and mores. Whether specific legal restraints are violated is not as important as the disrespectful conduct of the crowds in public places, in contrast to their usual orderly public behavior.

9. My use of *disnomic* and *disnomy* follows that of Kenelm O. Burridge,

Mambu: A Melanesian Millennium (London, 1960), pp. xxi, 274–75, 281–82: "This characteristic is probably best described as 'incertaintie.'
. . . Disnomic describes an acceleration in the number of particulars in an environment without a corresponding series of categories within terms of which they might be comprehended and mastered." Again, "Not so much the protest of the oppressed against an oppressor . . . a Cargo movement is a protest against the disnomy. Participants look back—and forward—to times of certainty. They are searching for criteria of definitive consent" (pp. 274, 281). Antinomian and disnomic are related: antinomian stresses the violation of mores; disnomic, the uncertainty of the situation (which often leads to antinomian behavior).

10. The sense of relief at the bumper crops of 1867 is noted by Totman, *Collapse of the Tokugawa Bakufu,* pp. 377–79.

11. Sasaki, "Bakumatsu no shakai jōsei to yonaoshi," pp. 273–74, says that his associate Itō Tadao has fixed the time of the first *ofudafuri* episode as one that occurred in Mikawa during the seventh month of 1867, rather than the eighth month, as had been thought. Itō's published view is that *ee ja nai ka* began early in the eighth month in Mikawa (Itō, "Ee ja nai ka," p. 303).

12. Ochiai Nobutaka, "Yonaoshi," in *Ikki no rekishi,* vol. 2 of *Ikki* (Tokyo, 1981), pp. 300–301. One might use speech-act theory to propose a way to read the "intentions" of the dancers. Thus it could be argued that *ee ja nai ka* was neither a simple locutionary act nor an utterance act; instead, in behavioral terms it constituted a perlocutionary act. John Austin, *How to Do Things with Words,* 2d ed. (Cambridge, Mass., 1975), pp. 118–19, explicitly allows for a perlocutionary act to happen as a "sequel" to a locutionary act, or even to a nonverbal action of some sort. The modifications in theory introduced by John R. Searle, *Speech Acts* (London, 1969), pp. 24–25, 29, 71, still allow for perlocutionary acts to result if illocutionary acts give rise to them. Certainly some of the behavior in the *ee ja nai ka* demonstrations (trashings, arson, petty thievery) carried illocutionary force and had perlocutionary effects; and some of the *ee ja nai ka* verses made assertions that were illocutionary acts—assertions that had results that made them perlocutionary acts as well.

13. Yasumaru, "'Okagemairi' to 'ee ja nai ka,'" p. 496; Inoue Kiyoshi, *Nihon gendaishi 1: Meiji ishin* (Tokyo, 1951), pp. 283–84.

14. Yasumaru Yoshio, "Minshū undō no shisō," in *Minshū undō no shisō,* ed. Shōji, Hayashi, and Yasumaru, p. 412. Takagi Shunsuke, *Ee ja nai ka,* pp. 97–116, presents the situation in Shinano Province, east of the Kansai, where the heroism of Chōshū, Satsuma, and Tosa was celebrated in the *ee ja nai ka* festivities. Shimazaki Tōson (1872–1943) situated his

vast historical novel *Yoakemae* in the Kiso valley in Shinano, along the Nakasendō highway. Other areas in the *ee ja nai ka* belt of east-central Japan are also famous for displaying strong anti-bakufu sentiment on the eve of the restoration.

15. Nishigaki Seiji, *Ee ja nai ka: Minshū undō no keifu* (Tokyo, 1973), p. 277.

16. Fukuchi Gen'ichirō, *Kaiō jidan / Bakumatsu seijika* (Tokyo, 1979), p. 166.

17. Tanaka, *Meiji ishin*, pp. 31–32, goes out of his way to rebut the "thesis" *(setsu)* that *ee ja nai ka* was all a plot on the part of the bakufu's opponents. Even Tōyama Shigeki, who belittles *ee ja nai ka* as an illusory approach to the hoped-for *yonaoshi*, admits that it was far too widespread to be the result of a conspiracy; see his *Meiji ishin to gendai*, pp. 102–3. Takagi Shunsuke, *Ee ja nai ka*, pp. 211–12, goes further to close off this kind of explanation: the *shishi*, he argues, could make use of *ee ja nai ka* demonstrations for their own purposes, but they never could have contrived to produce disturbances on so wide a scale over so many months.

18. Sasaki, "Bakumatsu no shakai jōsei to yonaoshi," p. 273.

19. *Chūgai shinbun*, 3/2/1868, reprinted in *Shinbun hen*, vol. 4 of *Meiji bunka zenshū* (Tokyo, 1928), p. 222.

20. Ochiai, "Yonaoshi," p. 299. The figure should be ninety-six houses, according to a document cited by Miura Toshiaki, "Tōkaidō no 'ee ja nai ka,'" in *Bakuhansei kokka no hōkai*, ed. Satō Shigerō and Kawachi Hachirō, vol. 8 of *Kōza Nihon kinseishi* (Tokyo, 1981), p. 193.

21. Itō, "Ee ja nai ka," p. 329.

22. Nishigaki, *Kamigami to minshū undō*, p. 113. On the antiforeign episode at Fujisawa Station, see chapter 7.

23. Ochiai, "Yonaoshi," p. 303.

24. Shibahara, *Kaikoku*, p. 381; Takagi Shunsuke, *Ee ja nai ka*, p. 205; Sasaki Junnosuke, *Yonaoshi* (Tokyo, 1979), p. 103; Itō, "Ee ja nai ka," p. 312.

25. Georges Lefebvre, *The Great Fear of 1789: Rural Panic in Revolutionary France* (New York, 1973), p. 1.

26. Redesdale, *Memories*, p. 414.

27. Satow, *Diplomat in Japan*, pp. 289, 286.

28. Ibid., p. 289; emphasis mine. The absence of solid doors in Japanese domestic architecture made the *ee ja nai ka* demonstrations all the more invasive of everyday private life.

29. Ibid., p. 286.

30. The situation in Kyoto is treated by the municipal history, *Ishin no gekidō,* pp. 185–86, 357–61, 383–87; by Fukawa Kiyoshi, "Bakumatsu ki chōnin no seiji ishiki: Kyōto chōnin no yonaoshi ishiki o chūshin ni," in Hayashiya, *Bakumatsu bunka no kenkyū,* pp. 271–304; and by Abe Masakoto, " 'Ee ja nai ka' no minshū undō," in *Kinsei shakai no seiritsu to hōkai* (Tokyo, 1976), pp. 195–200.

31. *Ishin no gekidō,* p. 172, contains a table listing the prices for major commodities in Kyoto for the three years 1865–67 inclusive.

32. Takagi Zaichū, *Bakumatsu ishin Kyōto chōnin nikki: Takagi Zaichū nikki* (Osaka, 1989), pp. 275–76.

33. Iwakura Tomomi, *Iwakura Kō jikki* (Tokyo, 1926), 2:102–3. Norman quotes Iwakura in "Feudal Background of Japanese Politics," p. 348.

34. Takagi Shunsuke, *Ee ja nai ka,* pp. 132–33.

35. Takagi Zaichū, *Chōnin nikki,* p. 276.

36. The text of the 11/25 decree appears in *Shiryō Kyōto no rekishi* (Tokyo, 1979), 3:626.

37. Takagi Zaichū, *Chōnin nikki,* p. 278; Iwakura, *Iwakura Kō jikki* 2:103.

38. The map and the source that contains it are described and depicted in *Ishin no gekidō,* pp. 359–61.

39. Ibid, p. 186.

40. The evidence is presented by Kinugasa Yasuki, "Bakumatsu no minshū undō," *Nihonshi kenkyū,* no. 128 (September 1972): 77–78.

41. The oilman's diary notes that in Funamachi village *ee ja nai ka* began on 12/15/1867 and never really ceased until 1/4/1868 (cited ibid., pp. 78–79).

42. Ibid., p. 80.

43. Few Japanese authors explore millenarianism or seek a comparative cultural explanation (e.g., utopia) for the convenient but elusive concept of *yonaoshi.* Some useful distinctions between *yonaoshi* and European and Chinese chiliastic movements are drawn by Yasumaru, "Minshū undō no shisō," pp. 413–20.

44. Takagi Shunsuke, *Ee ja nai ka,* p. 233; Sasaki, *Yonaoshi,* pp. 98, 102.

45. Miura, "Tōkaidō no 'ee ja nai ka,' " pp. 180, 203–5; Takagi Shunsuke, *Ee ja nai ka,* p. 233; Sasaki, *Yonaoshi,* p. 98. (For Fujisawa Station, see chapter 7.)

46. Tsuchiya Takao, "Ishinshijō no nansensu," *Chūō kōron* 46, no. 12 (December 1931): 282–90.

47. Hani Gorō, "Bakumatsu ni okeru seiji dōkō," in *Meiji ishinshi kenkyū* (Tokyo, 1956), p. 231.

48. Inoue, *Nihon gendaishi 1*, pp. 282–83; Tōyama Shigeki, *Meiji ishin* (Tokyo, 1951), pp. 187–89, and *Meiji ishin to gendai*, pp. 102ff. For a consideration of Hani's "negative critique" of *ee ja nai ka* and Inoue's "extremely subjective" interpretation that accords it a highly revolutionary evaluation, see Ishii Takashi, *Gakusetsu hihan Meiji ishin* (Tokyo, 1961), pp. 242–52.

49. Sasaki, *Yonaoshi*, pp. 101–3.

50. Totman, *Collapse of the Tokugawa Bakufu*, pp. 377–79, 531–32 n. 9; Beasley, *Meiji Restoration*, pp. 292–93.

51. Norman, "Feudal Background of Japanese Politics," pp. 344, 354. This appraisal is also included in an unpublished essay by E. H. Norman, "Okage-mairi: Observations on the Dancing Mania in Tokugawa Japan and in Europe," mimeo (New York, n.d.). I am grateful to Roger W. Bowen for letting me have a copy of this essay.

52. On the practice and justification of *shoshi ōgi*, see Haga Noboru, *Bakumatsu shishi no seikatsu* (Tokyo, 1982), pp. 11–22.

53. Shibahara, *Kaikoku*, pp. 336–38. At root there seems to be a resonance between Shibahara's use of revolutionary situation and what Sasaki refers to as *yonaoshi no jōkyō* (utopian condition).

54. The manifesto is titled "Tora hachigatsu Koishikawa" and appears in *Bakumatsu hishi shinbun waisō*, ed. Meiji Bunka Kenkyūkai (Tokyo, 1968), pp. 269–71. For some of Tanaka's numerous comments on this document, see his *Meiji kokka*, vol. 5 of *Taikei / Nihon rekishi* (Tokyo, 1967), pp. 78–79; *Mikan no Meiji ishin*, pp. 14–15; *Meiji ishin*, pp. 26–29; and "Bakufu no tōkai," in *Kinsei 5*, p. 344.

55. "Tora hachigatsu Koishikawa," p. 269.

56. Ibid., p. 270.

57. Ryusaku Tsunoda, William Theodore de Bary, and Donald Keene, comps., *Sources of the Japanese Tradition* (New York, 1958), p. 644.

58. On popular consciousness and rebellion at Fukushima, Kabasan, and Chichibu during the 1880s, see Roger W. Bowen, *Rebellion and Democracy in Meiji Japan* (Berkeley, 1980).

59. Imamura Shōhei, director, *Ee ja nai ka* (1981; English-subtitle videotape, New York, 1990).

60. Minami Kazuo, *Ishin zen'ya no Edo shomin* (Tokyo, 1980), pp. 172–81, traces the fall of *ofuda* in Edo and goes on to consider *ee ja nai ka* in Osaka and Kyoto against the surprising backdrop of the "undancing Edoites" (p. 178). See also Takagi Shunsuke, *Ee ja nai ka*, pp. 68–72.

61. Minami Kazuo, *Bakumatsu Edo shakai no kenkyū* (Tokyo, 1978), p. 313.

62. For an argument that "fear and ambition" caused the Meiji Restoration, see Harold Bolitho, "Idealization and Restoration," *Harvard Journal of Asiatic Studies* 45 (1985): 667–84.

63. Johan Huizinga, *Homo Ludens: A Study of the Play-Element in Culture* (London, 1949), p. 5.

64. Thomas C. Smith, "Ōkura Nagatsune and the Technologists," in *Personality in Japanese History,* ed. Craig and Shively, p. 154.

Chapter Seven

1. Mikhail M. Bakhtin, *Rabelais and His World* (Cambridge, Mass., 1968).

2. Shimazaki Tōson, *Before the Dawn,* trans. William E. Naff (Honolulu, 1987), pp. 375–76.

3. Aoki Michio and Miura Toshiaki, "Minami Kantō ni okeru 'ee ja nai ka,'" *Rekishigaku kenkyū,* no. 385 (June 1972): 56.

4. Miura Toshiaki, *Tōkaidō Fujisawajuku* (Tokyo, 1980), p. 150.

5. Aoki and Miura, "Minami Kantō ni okeru 'ee ja nai ka,'" pp. 55–57; Nishigaki, *Kamigami to minshū undō,* pp. 100–114.

6. Horiguchi Yoshibee, "Keiō Ise okage kenbun shokoku fushigi no hikae," in *Minshū undō no shisō,* ed. Shōji, Hayashi, and Yasumaru, pp. 374–81.

7. Aoki and Miura, "Minami Kantō ni okeru 'ee ja nai ka,'" p. 56.

8. Mona Ozouf, *Festivals and the French Revolution* (Cambridge, Mass., 1988), p. 90. A large literature has recently appeared on carnival. Apart from Bakhtin's *Rabelais and His World,* systematic inquiry began when the Arbeitskreis für Fasnachtsforschung at Tübingen launched a multivolume project on forms of Lenten and carnivalesque rituals and the behavior of celebrants in specific localities. In English, Robert W. Scribner works on play in political culture during the German Reformation; e.g., "Reformation, Carnival, and the World Turned Upside-down," *Social History* 3 (1978): 303–29. Helpful approaches to carnival can be found in Natalie Zemon Davis, *Society and Culture in Early Modern France* (Stanford, Calif., 1975), chaps. 4–5; and Peter Burke, *Popular Culture in Early Modern Europe* (London, 1978), chap. 7.

9. Miura, "Tōkaidō no 'ee ja nai ka,'" pp. 200–201.

10. Aoki and Miura, "Minami Kantō ni okeru 'ee ja nai ka,'" p. 56.

11. Yano Yoshiko, "'Okagemairi' to 'ee ja nai ka,'" in *Seikatsu / bunka / shisō,* vol. 4 of *Ikki,* p. 353.

12. Satow, *Diplomat in Japan*, p. 286.

13. Nishigaki, *Kamigami to minshū undō*, pp. 96–97.

14. Charles Tilly, *The Contentious French* (Cambridge, Mass., 1986), p. 404.

15. The social imaginary is a construct associated with Cornelius Castoriadis, *The Imaginary Institution of Society* (Cambridge, Mass., 1987). For capsule analyses of the social imaginary, see Brian C. J. Singer, *Society, Theory, and the French Revolution: Studies in the Revolutionary Imaginary* (New York, 1986), p. 205 n. 1; and Harootunian, "Late Tokugawa Culture and Thought," p. 170 n. 4.

16. A "circumstantial picture" of political organization is what Clifford Geertz seeks to provide in his reconstruction of Balinese history, *Negara: The Theatre State in Nineteenth-Century Bali* (see p. 7). By extension I would argue that no version of the past is ever more than a circumstantial picture, arrived at by a combination of Peirce's "abductive" reasoning and the inductive and deductive means that Geertz mentions (pp. 5–7); this combination differs with the data available, the degree of generalization, and the historian's intent.

Glossary

Abe Masahiro 阿部正弘

Amakusa Shirō Tokisada 天草四郎時貞

Amaterasu 天照

Andō Hiroshige 安藤広重

Ansei 安政

Awa 阿波

Awaji 淡路

bakufu 幕府

bakuhan taisei 幕藩体制

bakumatsu 幕末

Bizen 備前

bushi 武士

Chiba 千葉

Chichibu 秩父

chōchō 蝶々

Chōshū　　長州

Daikokuten　　大黒天

daimyō　　大名

dōri　　道理

Ebisu　　恵比須

Edo　　江戸

ee ja nai ka　　ええじゃないか

emaki　　絵巻

emakimono　　絵巻物

Fujisawa　　藤沢

Fujiwara　　藤原

fukoku kyōhei　　富国強兵

Fukuchi Gen'ichirō　　福地源一郎

Fukui　　福井

Fukushima　　福島

Funamachimura　　舟町村

genrō　　元老

Gion　　祇園

Godaigo　　後醍醐

goisshin　　御一新

Gojō　　五条

Gotō Shōjirō　　後藤象二郎

gunki monogatari　　軍記物語

gunkimono　　軍記物

gyoku　　玉

han　　藩

Hani Gorō　　羽仁五郎

harakiri　　腹切

Harima　　播磨

Hashimoto Sanai　　橋本左内

hayabikyaku　　早飛脚

Higashi Honganji　　東本願寺

Hikone　　彦根

Hiroshima　　広島

Hitotsubashi　　一橋

Honshū　　本州

Horikawa　　堀川

Horiuchi Ikunosuke　　堀内郁之助

Horiuchi Tōhisa　　堀内悠久

Hotta Masayoshi　　堀田正睦

hyakushō ikki   百姓一揆

Hyōgo   兵庫

Ii Naosuke   井伊直弼

ijin taiji   異人退治

Ikigami Konkō Daijin   生神金光大神

ikki   一揆

Imamura Shōhei   今村昌平

Inoue Kiyoshi   井上清

Ise   伊勢

ishiki   意識

ishin   維新

isshin   一新

Itō Tadao   伊藤忠士

Iwakura Tomomi   岩倉具視

jiba   地場

Jien   慈円

Jinmu Tennō   神武天皇

jitsugaku   実学

jitsuzai   実在

jiyū minken   自由民権

Jōdo Shin   浄土真

jōi   攘夷

Jōkyū no ran   承久の乱

Kabasan   加波山

Kagoshima   鹿児島

kaikoku   開国

Kakogawa   加古川

kakubutsu kyūri   格物窮理

kakumeiteki jōsei   革命的情勢

Kamakura   鎌倉

kami   神

kamigakari   神掛り

Kanagawa   神奈川

Kansai   関西

Katsuyama   勝山

Kawaramachi   河原町

Kawate Bunjirō   川手文治郎

Keiō   慶応

Kenmu   建武

Kinugasa Yasuki   衣笠安喜

Kiso　　木曽

Kita　　喜多

Kitabatake Chikafusa　　北畠親房

kō　　講

Kōbe　　神戸

kōbu gattai　　公武合体

kogaku　　古学

kogakuha　　古学派

Koishikawa　　小石川

kōken　　後見

kokon tairan　　古今大乱

kokugaku　　国学

kokutai　　国体

Konjin　　金神

Konkōkyō　　金光教

kōsha　　講社

kotobagaki　　詞書

Kōza　　講座

Kusaka Genzui　　久坂玄瑞

Kyōto　　京都

Kyūshū　　九州

Maki Izumi　　真木和泉

mappō　　末法

Matsudaira Shungaku　　松平春嶽

matsurigoto　　政

Meiji ishin　　明治維新

mikado　　御門

Mikawa　　三河

Mimasaka　　美作

Minami Kazuo　　南和男

Minamoto　　源

minshū　　民衆

miso　　味噌

Mito　　水戸

Motoori Norinaga　　本居宣長

Murakami Shigeyoshi　　村上重良

murakata sōdō　　村方騒動

Mutsuhito　　睦仁

Nagasaki　　長崎

Nagoya　　名古屋

Nakaoka Shintarō 中岡慎太郎

Nakasendō 中仙道

Nakayama Miki 中山みき

nanushi 名主

Narita 成田

Nihonbashi 日本橋

Nijō 二条

Ninigi 瓊瓊杵

Nikkōsan Tōshōgū 日光山東照宮

Nipponkoku 日本国

Nishi Honganji 西本願寺

nukemairi 抜け参り

Numazu 沼津

ofuda 御札

ofudafuri 御札降り

Ogyū Sorai 荻生徂徠

okagemairi 御蔭参り

okageodori 御蔭踊り

Ōkawabe Chikara 大河辺主税

Okayama 岡山

Ōkubochō   大久保町

Ōsaka   大阪

ōsei fukko   王政復古

oyasama   親様

Pontochō   先斗町

rangakusha   蘭学者

rekishi monogatari   歴史物語

rōjū   老中

rokkon shōjō   六根清浄

rōnin   浪人

Rōnō   労農

Ryōgoku   両国

Sagami   相模

Saigō Takamori   西郷隆盛

saitoku sugureru mono   才徳勝れる者

Sakai   堺

Sakamoto Ryōma   坂本竜馬

sakoku   鎖国

Sanjō Ōhashi   三条大橋

sankin kōtai   参勤交代

Sasaki Junnosuke　佐々木潤之介

satori　悟り

Satsuma　薩摩

seii tai shōgun　征夷大将軍

seiji sōsai　政事総裁

sekai daiichi no zenkoku　世界第一の善国

sengoku　戦国

setsu　説

Shibahara Takuji　芝原拓自

Shibata Takenaka　柴田剛中

Shijō Ōmiya　四条大宮

Shikoku　四国

Shimabara　島原

Shimazaki Tōson　島崎藤村

Shimoda　下田

Shimonoseki　下の関

Shinano　信濃

Shintō　神道

shishi　志士

Shizuoka　静岡

Shōchiku 松竹

shōgun 将軍

shoshi ōgi 諸士横義

shukuba 宿場

shukubamachi 宿場町

shūmatsuron 終末論

sōbyō no kami 宗廟の神

sonnō jōi 尊王攘夷

Susanoo 須佐之男

tairō 大老

taisei hōkan 大政奉還

Takagi Zaichū 高木在中

Takasugi Shinsaku 高杉晋作

Takeda Shūunsai 竹田秋雲斎

Taki Zensaburō 滝善三郎

tama 玉

Tanaka Akira 田中彰

Tango 丹後

Tenchi Kanenokami 天地金乃神

Tendai 天台

tenjo 天助

tenka 天下

tennō 天皇

Tenri Ōnomikoto 天理王命

Tenrikyō 天理教

Teramachi 寺町

Tōkaidō 東海道

Tokugawa Ieyasu 徳川家康

Tokugawa Nariaki 徳川斉昭

Tokugawa Yoshinobu 徳川慶喜

Tokushima 徳島

Tosa 土佐

toshi sōjō 都市騒擾

Tōyama Shigeki 遠山茂樹

Tsuchiya Takao 土屋喬雄

uchikowashi 打ち毀し

yakiharai 焼き払い

Yamato 大和

Yamatodamashii 大和魂

Yano Yoshiko 矢野芳子

Yasumaru Yoshio　安丸良夫

yōgaku　洋学

yōkisuru　揚棄する

Yokohama　横浜

yonaori　世直り

yonaoshi　世直し

yonaoshi ikki　世直し一揆

yonaoshi no jōkyō　世直しの情況

Yoshida Shōin　吉田松陰

Yoshii Tomozane　吉井友実

Zen　禅

zentaiseiteki na shakai no henkaku　全体制的な社会の変革

Bibliography

Most of the items included below are cited in the chapter notes. Also included are items that proved to be useful but do not appear in the notes. Both types of items appear here so that readers may know something of the overall base of "authority" that grounds this study.

Names follow customary usage: surname first, followed by the given name, for Japanese authors; for others, surname, followed by a comma, then the given name. The names of second authors or editors appear in the order of spoken usage.

All of these items are published materials except for two papers, a Ph.D. thesis, and a picture scroll in the Fujisawa Archives. Of the rest, all are books or articles, except for Imamura Shōhei's motion picture *Ee ja nai ka.*

Materials in Japanese and English are intermixed, as are primary and secondary sources. Specialists know what is involved, while generalists do not suffer over such matters.

Abe Masakoto. "'Ee ja nai ka' no minshū undō." In *Kinsei shakai no seiritsu to hōkai,* edited by Ōsaka Rekishi Gakkai, pp. 169–229. Tokyo: Yoshikawa Kōbunkan, 1976.

Aberle, David F. "A Note on Relative Deprivation Theory as Applied to Millenarian and Other Cult Movements." In *Millennial Dreams in Action: Essays in Comparative History,* edited by Sylvia Thrupp, pp. 209–14. The Hague: Mouton, 1962.

Akamatsu, Paul. *Meiji 1868: Revolution and Counter-revolution in Japan.* Translated by Miriam Kochan. New York: Harper and Row, 1972.

Alcock, Rutherford. *The Capital of the Tycoon: A Narrative of Three Years' Residence in Japan.* 2 vols. 1863. Reprint. New York: Greenwood Press, 1969.

Anderson, Benedict. *Imagined Communities: Reflections on the Origin and Spread of Nationalism.* New York: Schocken Books, 1983.

Anscombe, G. E. M. *Intention.* 2d ed. Ithaca, N.Y.: Cornell University Press, 1963.

Aoki Michio. "Bakumatsu / ishin ki no yonaoshi sōdō: Minami Kantō chihō o chūshin ni." In *Bakuhansei kokka no hōkai,* edited by Satō Shigerō and Kawachi Hachirō, pp. 133–72. Vol. 8 of *Kōza Nihon kinseishi.* Tokyo: Yūhikaku, 1981.

Aoki Michio and Kawachi Hachirō, eds. *Kaikoku.* Vol. 7 of *Kōza Nihon kinseishi.* Tokyo: Yūhikaku, 1985.

Aoki Michio and Miura Toshiaki. "Minami Kantō ni okeru 'ee ja nai ka.'" *Rekishigaku kenkyū,* no. 385 (June 1972): 55–57.

Aoki Michio and Yamada Tadao, eds., *Tenpō ki no seiji to shakai.* Vol. 6 of *Kōza Nihon kinseishi.* Tokyo: Yūhikaku, 1981.

Arbeitskreis für Fasnachtsforschung. *Dörfliche Fasnacht zwischen Neckar und Bodensee.* Tübingen: Tübinger Vereinigung für Volkskunde, 1966.

Aston, W. G., trans. *Nihongi: Chronicles of Japan from the Earliest Times to A.D. 697.* 1896. Reprint. London: George Allen and Unwin, 1956.

Austin, John. *How to Do Things with Words.* 2d ed. Cambridge, Mass.: Harvard University Press, 1975.

Baelz, Erwin. *Awakening Japan: The Diary of a German Doctor, Erwin Baelz.* Introduced by George M. Wilson. Bloomington: Indiana University Press, 1974.

Bakhtin, Mikhail M. *The Dialogic Imagination.* Edited by Michael Holquist; translated by Caryl Emerson and Michael Holquist. Austin: University of Texas Press, 1981.

———. *Rabelais and His World.* Translated by Helene Iswolsky. Cambridge, Mass.: MIT Press, 1968.

Bakufu sei-Chō kiroku. 1919. Nihon Shiseki Kyōkai reprint. Tokyo: Tōkyō Daigaku Shuppankai, 1973.

Bakumatsu hishi shinbun waisō. Edited by Meiji Bunka Kenkyūkai. 1934. Reprint. Tokyo: Meicho Kankōkai, 1968.

Bakumatsu ishin shi jiten. Edited by Kamiya Jirō and Yasuoka Akio; supervised by Konishi Shirō. Tokyo: Shinjinbutsu Ōraisha, 1983.

Barthes, Roland. *Empire of Signs.* Translated by Richard Howard. New York: Hill and Wang, 1982.

Beasley, William G. *The Meiji Restoration.* Stanford, Calif.: Stanford University Press, 1972.

Becker, Carl L. *The Heavenly City of the Eighteenth-Century Philosophers.* New Haven: Yale University Press, 1932.

Bellah, Robert N. *Tokugawa Religion: The Values of Pre-industrial Japan.* Glencoe, Ill.: Free Press, 1957.

Belsey, Catherine. *Critical Practice*. London: Methuen, 1980.

——. *The Subject of Tragedy: Identity and Difference in Renaissance Drama*. London: Methuen, 1985.

Benjamin, Walter. *Illuminations*. Translated by Harry Zohn. New York: Harcourt, Brace and World, 1968.

Berger, Peter L., and Thomas Luckmann. *The Social Construction of Reality: A Treatise in the Sociology of Knowledge*. Garden City, N.Y.: Doubleday, 1967.

Bitō Masahide. "*Bushi* and the Meiji Restoration." *Acta Asiatica*, no. 49 (August 1985): 78–96.

——. "Meiji ishin to bushi: 'Kōron' no rinen ni yoru ishin zō saikōsei no kokoromi." *Shisō*, no. 735 (September 1985): 1–16.

Bix, Herbert P. *Peasant Protest in Japan, 1590–1884*. New Haven: Yale University Press, 1986.

Bloom, Harold. *The Anxiety of Influence: A Theory of Poetry*. New York: Oxford University Press, 1973.

——. *Kabbalah and Criticism*. New York: Seabury, 1975.

——. *A Map of Misreading*. New York: Oxford University Press, 1975.

Bolitho, Harold. "Idealization and Restoration." *Harvard Journal of Asiatic Studies* 45 (1985): 667–84.

——. *Treasures among Men: The Fudai Daimyo in Tokugawa Japan*. New Haven: Yale University Press, 1974.

Bouwsma, William J. "The Renaissance and the Drama of Western History." *American Historical Review* 84 (1979): 1–15.

Bowen, Roger W. *Rebellion and Democracy in Meiji Japan*. Berkeley and Los Angeles: University of California Press, 1980.

Bradley, F. H. *The Presuppositions of Critical History*. Edited and introduced by Lionel Rubinoff. 1874. Reprint. Chicago: Quadrangle Books, 1968.

Braudel, Fernand. *The Mediterranean and the Mediterranean World in the Age of Philip II*. Translated by Siân Reynolds. 2 vols. New York: Harper and Row, 1972–73.

Brown, Delmer M. "Buddhism and Historical Thought in Japan before 1221." *Philosophy East and West* 24 (1974): 215–25.

Brown, Delmer M., and Ishida Ichirō, eds. and trans. *The Future and the Past: A Translation and Study of the "Gukanshō," an Interpretative History of Japan Written in 1219*. Berkeley and Los Angeles: University of California Press, 1979.

Brownlee, John S., ed. *History in the Service of the Japanese Nation*. Toronto: University of Toronto-York University Joint Centre on Modern East Asia, 1983.

Burckhardt, Jacob. *The Civilization of the Renaissance in Italy: An Essay.* Translated by S. G. C. Middlemore. 1878. Reprint. New York: Random House, 1954.

Burke, Kenneth. *A Grammar of Motives.* Berkeley and Los Angeles: University of California Press, 1969.

Burke, Peter. *Popular Culture in Early Modern Europe.* London: Maurice Temple Smith, 1978.

Burridge, Kenelm O. *Mambu: A Melanesian Millennium.* London: Methuen, 1960.

Callinicos, Alex. *Making History: Agency, Structure, and Change in Social Theory.* Ithaca, N.Y.: Cornell University Press, 1988.

Campbell, Joseph. *The Masks of God: Oriental Mythology.* New York: Viking Press, 1962.

Canary, Robert H., and Henry Kozicki, eds. *The Writing of History: Literary Form and Historical Understanding.* Madison: University of Wisconsin Press, 1978.

Castoriadis, Cornelius. *The Imaginary Institution of Society.* Translated by Kathleen Blamey. Cambridge, Mass.: MIT Press, 1987.

Caws, Peter. "Structuralism." *Dictionary of the History of Ideas* 4:322–30. New York: Charles Scribner's Sons, 1973.

Chamberlain, Basil Hall, trans. *"Ko-ji-ki"; or, "Records of Ancient Matters".* 1882. Reprint. Tokyo: Asiatic Society of Japan, 1906.

Clifford, James, and George E. Marcus, eds. *Writing Culture: The Poetics and Politics of Ethnography.* Berkeley and Los Angeles: University of California Press, 1986.

Cohen, Sande. *Historical Culture: On the Recoding of an Academic Discipline.* Berkeley and Los Angeles: University of California Press, 1986.

Cohn, Norman. *The Pursuit of the Millennium: Revolutionary Millenarians and Mystical Anarchists of the Middle Ages.* 3d ed. New York: Oxford University Press, 1970.

Collingwood, R. G. *The Idea of History.* Oxford: Clarendon Press, 1946.

———. "Some Perplexities about Time, with an Attempted Solution." *Proceedings of the Aristotelian Society,* n.s. 26 (1926): 138–42.

Cornford, Francis Macdonald. *Thucydides Mythistoricus.* London: Edward Arnold, 1907.

Craig, Albert M. *Chōshū in the Meiji Restoration.* Harvard Historical Monographs, 47. Cambridge, Mass.: Harvard University Press, 1961.

Craig, Albert M., and Donald H. Shively, eds. *Personality in Japanese History.* Berkeley and Los Angeles: University of California Press, 1970.

Crapanzano, Vincent. "Hermes' Dilemma: The Masking of Subversion in Ethnographic Description." In *Writing Culture,* edited by James Clifford and George E. Marcus, pp. 51–76. Berkeley and Los Angeles: University of California Press, 1986.

Crowley, James B., ed. *Modern East Asia: Essays in Interpretation.* New York: Harcourt, Brace and World, 1970.

Darnton, Robert. *The Literary Underground of the Old Regime.* Cambridge, Mass.: Harvard University Press, 1982.

Davis, Natalie Zemon. *Society and Culture in Early Modern France.* Stanford, Calif.: Stanford University Press, 1975.

Didion, Joan. *The White Album.* New York: Simon and Schuster, 1979.

Dray, William H. "Narrative versus Analysis in History." *Philosophy of the Social Sciences* 15 (1985): 125–45.

Earl, David Magarey. *Emperor and Nation in Japan: Political Thinkers of the Tokugawa Period.* Seattle: University of Washington Press, 1964.

Ebersole, Gary L. *Ritual Poetry and the Politics of Death in Early Japan.* Princeton: Princeton University Press, 1989.

Eddington, A. S. *The Nature of the Physical World.* New York: Macmillan, 1929.

Eliade, Mircea. *The Myth of the Eternal Return.* Translated by Willard R. Trask. Bollingen Series, 46. Princeton: Princeton University Press, 1971.

———. *No Souvenirs: Journal, 1957–1969.* Translated by Fred H. Johnson, Jr., New York: Harper and Row, 1977.

Elison, George. *Deus Destroyed: The Image of Christianity in Early Modern Japan.* Harvard East Asian Series, 72. Cambridge, Mass.: Harvard University Press, 1973.

Fairbank, John K., ed. *The Chinese World Order: Traditional China's Foreign Relations.* Harvard East Asian Series, 32. Cambridge, Mass.: Harvard University Press, 1968.

Fairbank, John K., Edwin O. Reischauer, and Albert M. Craig. *East Asia: Tradition and Transformation.* Rev. ed. Boston: Houghton Mifflin, 1989.

Fletcher, Angus, ed. *The Literature of Fact.* New York: Columbia University Press, 1976.

Foucault, Michel. *Language, Counter-memory, Practice.* Translated by Donald F. Bouchard and Sherry Simon. Ithaca, N.Y.: Cornell University Press, 1977.

Fowler, H. W. *A Dictionary of Modern English Usage*. New York: Oxford University Press, 1944.

Fraser, J. T., F. C. Haber, and G. H. Müller, eds. *The Study of Time*. New York: Springer-Verlag, 1972.

Fraser, J. T., N. Lawrence, and F. C. Haber, eds. *Time, Science, and Society in China and the West*. Amherst: University of Massachusetts Press, 1986.

Friedman, Barton R. *Fabricating History: English Writers on the French Revolution*. Princeton: Princeton University Press, 1988.

Frye, Northrop. *Anatomy of Criticism: Four Essays*. Princeton: Princeton University Press, 1957.

———. *The Critical Path: An Essay on the Social Context of Literary Criticism*. Bloomington: Indiana University Press, 1973.

Fujitani, Takashi. "Japan's Modern National Ceremonies: A Historical Ethnography, 1868–1912." Ph.D. dissertation, Department of History, University of California, Berkeley, 1986.

Fujitani Toshio. *"Okagemairi" to "ee ja nai ka"*. Tokyo: Iwanami Shoten, 1968.

Fukawa Kiyoshi. "Bakumatsu ki chōnin no seiji ishiki: Kyōto chōnin no yonaoshi ishiki o chūshin ni." In *Bakumatsu bunka no kenkyū*, edited by Hayashiya Tatsusaburō, pp. 271–304. Tokyo: Iwanami Shoten, 1978.

———. *Kinsei minshū no rinriteki enerugii*. Nagoya: Fūbaisha, 1976.

Fukuchi Gen'ichirō. *Bakufu suibō ron*. 1892. Nihon Shiseki Kyōkai reprint. Tokyo: Tōkyō Daigaku Shuppankai, 1967.

———. *Kaiō jidan / bakumatsu seijika*. 1900. Nihon Shiseki Kyōkai reprint. Tokyo: Tōkyō Daigaku Shuppankai, 1979.

Fukuzawa Yukichi. *The Autobiography of Yukichi Fukuzawa*. Translated by Eiichi Kiyooka. New York: Columbia University Press, 1966.

Geertz, Clifford. *The Interpretation of Cultures*. New York: Basic Books, 1973.

———. *Negara: The Theatre State in Nineteenth-Century Bali*. Princeton: Princeton University Press, 1980.

———. *Works and Lives: The Anthropologist as Author*. Stanford, Calif.: Stanford University Press, 1988.

Gibbon, Edward. *The History of the Decline and Fall of the Roman Empire*. 8 vols. Philadelphia: Birch and Small, 1804–5.

Gluck, Carol N. *Japan's Modern Myths: Ideology in the Late Meiji Period*. Princeton: Princeton University Press, 1985.

———. "The People in History: Recent Trends in Japanese Historiography." *Journal of Asian Studies* 38 (1978–79): 25–50.

"Gods of the Old Japanese Mythology." *Illustrated London News* 37 (1860): 570.

Goodman, Nelson. "Time and Language, and the Passage of Time." In *Problems of Space and Time,* edited by J. J. C. Smart, pp. 356–69. New York: Macmillan, 1964.

Green, Martin. *Dreams of Adventure, Deeds of Empire.* New York: Basic Books, 1979.

Griffis, William Elliot. *The Mikado's Empire.* 8th ed. rev. 1895. Reprint. Wilmington, Del.: Scholarly Resources, 1973.

Gukanshō. Vol. 86 of *Nihon koten bungaku taikei.* Tokyo: Iwanami Shoten, 1967.

Gurvitch, Georges. *The Spectrum of Social Time.* Translated by Myrtle Korenbaum. Dordrecht, Netherlands: D. Reidel, 1974.

Habermas, Jürgen. *Legitimation Crisis.* Translated by Thomas McCarthy. Boston: Beacon Press, 1975.

———. *The Philosophical Discourse of Modernity: Twelve Lectures.* Translated by Frederick G. Lawrence. Cambridge, Mass.: MIT Press, 1987.

Haga Noboru. *Bakumatsu shishi no seikatsu.* Seikatsushi sōsho, 8. Tokyo: Yūzankaku, 1982.

———. *Ishin o motomete.* Edo Series, 2. Tokyo: Mainichi Shinbunsha, 1976.

———. *Meiji kokka to minshū.* Tokyo: Yūzankaku, 1974.

———. *Yonaoshi no shisō.* Tokyo: Yūzankaku, 1973.

Haga Noboru and Matsumoto Sannosuke, eds., *Kokugaku undō no shisō.* Vol. 51 of *Nihon shisō taikei.* Tokyo: Iwanami Shoten, 1971.

Hall, John Whitney. *Japan: From Prehistory to Modern Times.* New York: Delacorte Press, 1970.

———. "Japanese History in World Perspective." In *The Future of History,* edited by Charles F. Delzell, pp. 173–88. Nashville: Vanderbilt University Press, 1977.

———. "The New Look of Tokugawa History." in *Studies in the Institutional History of Early Modern Japan,* edited by John Whitney Hall and Marius B. Jansen, pp. 55–64. Princeton: Princeton University Press, 1968.

———. "Tokugawa Japan: 1600–1853." In *Modern East Asia: Essays in Interpretation,* edited by James B. Crowley, pp. 62–94. New York: Harcourt, Brace and World, 1970.

Hall, John Whitney, and Richard K. Beardsley, eds. *Twelve Doors to Japan.* New York: McGraw-Hill, 1965.

Hall, John Whitney, and Marius B. Jansen, eds. *Studies in the Institutional History of Early Modern Japan.* Princeton: Princeton University Press, 1968.

Hane, Mikiso. *Japan: A Historical Survey.* New York: Charles Scribner's Sons, 1972.

Hani Gorō. *Meiji ishinshi kenkyū.* Tokyo: Iwanami Shoten, 1956.

Hanley, Susan B., and Kozo Yamamura. *Economic and Demographic Change in Preindustrial Japan, 1600–1868.* Princeton: Princeton University Press, 1977.

Harootunian, Harry D. "Between Principle and Personality." *Journal of Asian Studies* 24 (1964–65): 115–21.

―――. "The Consciousness of Archaic Form in the New Realism of Kokugaku." In *Japanese Thought in the Tokugawa Period, 1600–1868: Methods and Metaphors,* edited by Tetsuo Najita and Irwin Scheiner, pp. 63–104. Chicago: University of Chicago Press, 1978.

―――. "From Principle to Principal: Restoration and Emperorship in Japan." In *The Uses of History: Essays in Intellectual and Social History,* edited by Hayden V. White, pp. 221–45. Detroit: Wayne State University Press, 1968.

―――. "The Functions of China in Tokugawa Thought." In *The Chinese and the Japanese: Essays in Political and Cultural Interactions,* edited by Akira Iriye, pp. 9–36. Princeton: Princeton University Press, 1980.

―――. "Ideology as Conflict." In *Conflict in Modern Japanese History,* edited by Tetsuo Najita and J. Victor Koschmann, pp. 25–61. Princeton: Princeton University Press, 1982.

―――. "Late Tokugawa Culture and Thought." In *The Nineteenth Century,* edited by Marius B. Jansen, pp. 168–258. Vol. 5 of *The Cambridge History of Japan.* Cambridge: Cambridge University Press, 1989.

―――. *Things Seen and Unseen: Discourse and Ideology in Tokugawa Nativism.* Chicago: University of Chicago Press, 1988.

―――. *Toward Restoration: The Growth of Political Consciousness in Tokugawa Japan.* Berkeley and Los Angeles: University of California Press, 1970.

Hayashi Motoi. *Hyakushō ikki no dentō.* Tokyo: Shinhyōron, 1955.

―――. *Zoku hyakushō ikki no dentō.* Tokyo: Shinhyōron, 1971.

Hayashiya Tatsusaburō. "Bakumatsu ki no bunkateki shihyō: Bakumatsu bunka kenkyū josetsu." In *Bakumatsu bunka no kenkyū,* edited by Hayashiya Tatsusaburō, pp. 3–39. Tokyo: Iwanami Shoten, 1978.

———. *Tenka ittō.* Vol. 12 of *Nihon no rekishi.* Tokyo: Chūō Kōronsha, 1966.

———, ed. *Bakumatsu bunka no kenkyū.* Tokyo: Iwanami Shoten, 1978.

Hellmann, Donald C. *Japan and East Asia: The New International Order.* New York: Frederick A. Praeger, 1972.

Hexter, Jack H. *Doing History.* Bloomington: Indiana University Press, 1971.

———. *The History Primer.* New York: Basic Books, 1971.

Hill, Christopher. *The World Turned Upside Down: Radical Ideas during the English Revolution.* New York: Viking Press, 1972.

Hirsch, E. D. *The Aims of Interpretation.* Chicago: University of Chicago Press, 1976.

Hobsbawm, E. J. *Primitive Rebels: Studies in Archaic Forms of Social Movement in the Nineteenth and Twentieth Centuries.* New York: Frederick A. Praeger, 1963.

Holtom, D. C. *The National Faith of Japan: A Study in Modern Shinto.* New York: E. P. Dutton, 1938.

Hookway, Christopher, and Philip Pettit, eds. *Action and Interpretation: Studies in the Philosophy of the Social Sciences.* Cambridge: Cambridge University Press, 1978.

Horiguchi Yoshibee. "Keiō Ise okage kenbun shokoku fushigi no hikae." In *Minshū undō no shisō,* edited by Shōji Kichinosuke, Hayashi Motoi, and Yasumaru Yoshio, pp. 373–81. Vol. 58 of *Nihon shisō taikei.* Tokyo: Iwanami Shoten, 1970.

Horiuchi Tōhisa and Horiuchi Ikunosuke. "Shinbutsu miei kōrin no keikyō." Picture scroll with text, ca. 1867. Fujisawa Monjokan, Fujisawa.

Hoston, Germaine A. *Marxism and the Crisis of Development in Prewar Japan.* Princeton: Princeton University Press, 1986.

Howard, Roy J. *Three Faces of Hermeneutics: An Introduction to Current Theories of Understanding.* Berkeley and Los Angeles: University of California Press, 1982.

Huber, Thomas M. *The Revolutionary Origins of Modern Japan.* Stanford, Calif.: Stanford University Press, 1981.

Huizinga, Johan. *Homo Ludens: A Study of the Play-Element in Culture.* Translated by R. F. C. Hull. London: Routledge and Kegan Paul, 1949.

Hunt, Lynn A. *Politics, Culture, and Class in the French Revolution.* Berkeley and Los Angeles: University of California Press, 1984.

——, ed. *The New Cultural History.* Berkeley and Los Angeles: University of California Press, 1989.

Ichii Saburō. *"Meiji ishin" no tetsugaku.* Tokyo: Kōdansha, 1967.

Ikki. Vol. 2, *Ikki no rekishi.* Vol. 4, *Seikatsu / bunka / shisō.* Tokyo: Tōkyō Daigaku Shuppankai, 1981.

Imamura Shōhei, director. *Ee ja nai ka.* Tokyo: Shōchiku Studios, 1981. Motion picture. English-subtitle videotape, *Eijanaika.* New York: Kino International, 1990.

Imanaka Kanji, ed. *Nihon no kindaika to ishin.* Tokyo: Perikansha, 1982.

Inada, Kenneth K. "Time and Temporality: A Buddhist Approach." *Philosophy East and West* 24 (1974): 171–79.

Inoue Kiyoshi. *Nihon gendaishi 1: Meiji ishin.* Tokyo: Tōkyō Daigaku Shuppankai, 1951.

——. *Nihon no rekishi.* 3 vols. Tokyo: Iwanami Shoten, 1963–66.

Iriye, Akira, ed. *The Chinese and the Japanese: Essays in Political and Cultural Interactions.* Princeton: Princeton University Press, 1980.

Ishii Kanji. *Kaikoku to ishin.* Vol. 12 of *Taikei Nihon no rekishi.* Tokyo: Shōgakkan, 1989.

Ishii Takashi. *Gakusetsu hihan Meiji ishin.* Tokyo: Yoshikawa Kōbunkan, 1961.

Ishin no gekidō. Vol. 7 of *Kyōto no rekishi.* Tokyo: Gakugei Shorin, 1974.

Itō Tadao. "Ee ja nai ka." In *Yonaoshi,* edited by Sasaki Junnosuke, pp. 300–331. Vol. 5 of *Nihon minshū no rekishi.* Tokyo: Sanseidō, 1974.

Iwakura Tomomi. *Iwakura Kō jikki.* 2 vols. 1906. Reprint. Tokyo: Iwakura Kō Kyūseki Hozonkai, 1926.

Iwanami kōza Nihon rekishi. Vol. 13, *Kinsei 5.* Tokyo: Iwanami Shoten, 1977.

Jansen, Marius B. "The Meiji State: 1868–1912." In *Modern East Asia: Essays in Interpretation,* edited by James B. Crowley, pp. 95–121. New York: Harcourt, Brace and World, 1970.

——, ed. *Changing Japanese Attitudes toward Modernization.* Princeton: Princeton University Press, 1965.

——. *The Nineteenth Century.* Vol. 5 of *The Cambridge History of Japan.* Cambridge: Cambridge University Press, 1989.

"Japanese Mythology and Religion." *Illustrated London News* 37 (1860): 568.

Jauss, Hans Robert, ed. *Die nicht mehr schönen Künste: Grenzphänomene des ästhetischen.* Munich: Wilhelm Fink Verlag, 1968.

Jinnō shōtōki. Vol. 87 of *Nihon koten bungaku taikei.* Tokyo: Iwanami Shoten, 1965.

Jung, Carl Gustav. *The Structure and Dynamics of the Psyche.* Translated by R. F. C. Hull. Vol. 8 of *The Collected Works of C. G. Jung.* Bollingen Series, 20. Princeton: Princeton University Press, 1969.

Kanai Madoka, ed. and trans. *Egakareta bakumatsu Meiji.* Tokyo: Yūshōdō Shoten, 1973.

Kant, Immanuel. *Critique of Pure Reason.* Translated by Norman Kemp Smith. 1929. Reprint. New York: St. Martin's, 1965.

Kawakita Nobuo. *Bakumatsu no seisō.* Tokyo: Kōdansha, 1968.

Kelly, William W. *Deference and Defiance in Nineteenth-Century Japan.* Princeton: Princeton University Press, 1985.

Kida Jun'ichirō. *Kaikoku no seishin: Ishin Nippon no yūtopia.* Tokyo: San'ichi Shobō, 1969.

Kinbara Samon. *"Nihon kindaika" no rekishizō.* Tokyo: Chūō Daigaku Shuppanbu, 1968.

Kinugasa Yasuki. "Bakumatsu no minshū undō." *Nihonshi kenkyū,* no. 128 (September 1972): 77–80.

Kishimoto Hideo, ed. *Japanese Religion in the Meiji Era.* Translated by John F. Howes. Tokyo: Ōbunsha, 1956.

Kitagawa, Joseph M. *Religion in Japanese History.* New York: Columbia University Press, 1966.

Kōno Kenji. *Furansu kakumei to Meiji ishin.* Tokyo: Nihon Hōsō Shuppan Kyōkai, 1966.

Koschmann, J. Victor. *The Mito Ideology: Discourse, Reform, and Insurrection in Late Tokugawa Japan, 1790–1864.* Berkeley and Los Angeles: University of California Press, 1987.

Kracauer, Siegfried. "General History and the Aesthetic Approach." In *Die nicht mehr schönen Künste: Grenzphänomene des ästhetischen,* edited by Hans Robert Jauss, pp. 111–27. Munich: Wilhelm Fink Verlag, 1968.

Kramer, Samuel Noah, ed. *Mythologies of the Ancient World.* Garden City, N.Y.: Doubleday, 1961.

Krauss, Ellis S., Thomas P. Rohlen, and Patricia G. Steinhoff, eds. *Conflict in Japan.* Honolulu: University of Hawaii Press, 1984.

Kuwabara Takeo. *Japan and Western Civilization: Essays on Comparative Culture.* Edited by Katō Hidetoshi; translated by Kano Tsutomu and Patricia Murray. Tokyo: University of Tokyo Press, 1983.

————, ed. *Burujowa kakumei no hikaku kenkyū*. Tokyo: Chikuma Shobō, 1964.

Kuzminski, Adrian. "The Paradox of Historical Knowledge." *History and Theory* 12 (1973): 269–89.

LaCapra, Dominick. *History and Criticism*. Ithaca, N.Y.: Cornell University Press, 1985.

————. "Rethinking Intellectual History and Reading Texts." In *Rethinking Intellectual History: Texts, Contexts, Language*, pp. 23–71. Ithaca, N.Y.: Cornell University Press, 1983.

————. *Soundings in Critical Theory*. Ithaca, N.Y.: Cornell University Press, 1989.

LaCapra, Dominick, and Steven L. Kaplan, eds. *Modern European Intellectual History: Reappraisals and New Perspectives*. Ithaca, N.Y.: Cornell University Press, 1982.

Ladurie, Emmanuel Le Roy. *The Mind and Method of the Historian*. Translated by Siân Reynolds and Ben Reynolds. Chicago: University of Chicago Press, 1981.

Lefebvre, Georges. *The Great Fear of 1789: Rural Panic in Revolutionary France*. Introduced by George Rudé; translated by Joan White. New York: Pantheon Books, 1973.

Lefort, Claude. *The Political Forms of Modern Society*. Edited and introduced by John B. Thompson. Cambridge, Mass.: MIT Press, 1986.

Lévi-Strauss, Claude. *Myth and Meaning*. Toronto: University of Toronto Press, 1978.

————. *The Savage Mind*. Chicago: University of Chicago Press, 1966.

Lowenthal, David. *The Past Is a Foreign Country*. Cambridge: Cambridge University Press, 1985.

McCullough, Helen Craig, trans. *Ōkagami, the Great Mirror*. Princeton: Princeton University Press, 1980.

————. *The Taiheiki, a Chronicle of Medieval Japan*. New York: Columbia University Press, 1959.

McFarland, H. Neill. *The Rush Hour of the Gods: A Study of New Religious Movements in Japan*. New York: Macmillan, 1967.

Macherey, Pierre. *A Theory of Literary Production*. Translated by Geoffrey Wall. London: Routledge and Kegan Paul, 1978.

Mannheim, Karl. *Ideology and Utopia: An Introduction to the Sociology of Knowledge*. 1936. Reprint. New York: Harcourt Brace Jovanovich, n.d.

Manuel, Frank E. *Shapes of Philosophical History.* Stanford, Calif.: Stanford University Press, 1965.

Maruya Sai'ichi. *Chūshingura to wa nani ka?* Tokyo: Kōdansha, 1984.

Maruyama Masao. *Nihon seiji shisōshi kenkyū.* Tokyo: Tōkyō Daigaku Shuppankai, 1952.

———. *Studies in the Intellectual History of Tokugawa Japan.* Translated by Mikiso Hane. Princeton: Princeton University Press; Tokyo: University of Tokyo Press, 1974.

Mass, Jeffrey P., and William B. Hauser, eds. *The Bakufu in Japanese History.* Stanford, Calif.: Stanford University Press, 1985.

Matsumae Takeshi. *Nihon no kamigami.* Tokyo: Chūō Kōronsha, 1974.

Matsuura Rei. *Ansatsu: Meiji ishin no shisō to kōdō.* Tokyo: Keisō Shobō, 1979.

Medzini, Meron. *French Policy in Japan during the Closing Years of the Tokugawa Regime.* Harvard East Asian Monographs, 41. Cambridge, Mass.: Harvard University Press, 1971.

Meiji bunka zenshū. Vol. 4, *Shinbun hen.* Tokyo: Nihon Hyōron Shinsha, 1928.

Minami Kazuo. *Bakumatsu Edo shakai no kenkyū.* Tokyo: Yoshikawa Kōbunkan, 1978.

———. *Ishin zen'ya no Edo shomin.* Tokyo: Kyōikusha, 1980.

Minshūshi o kangaeru. Edited by Minshūshi Kenkyūkai. Tokyo: Azekura Shobō, 1988.

Miura Toshiaki. *Tōkaidō Fujisawajuku.* Tokyo: Meicho Shuppan, 1980.

———. "Tōkaidō no 'ee ja nai ka.'" In *Bakuhansei kokka no hōkai,* edited by Satō Shigerō and Kawachi Hachirō, pp. 173–210. Vol. 8 of *Kōza Nihon kinseishi.* Tokyo: Yūhikaku, 1981.

Miyata Noboru. "Nōson no fukkō undō to minshū shūkyō no tenkai." In *Kinsei 5,* pp. 209–45. Vol. 13 of *Iwanami kōza Nihon rekishi.* Tokyo: Iwanami Shoten, 1977.

Moore, Barrington. *Social Origins of Dictatorship and Democracy: Lord and Peasant in the Making of the Modern World.* Boston: Beacon Press, 1966.

Morikawa Tetsurō. *Bakumatsu ansatsu shi: Terorizumu to Meiji ishin.* Tokyo: San'ichi Shobō, 1967.

Moriya Takeshi. *Kyō no chōnin: Kinsei toshi seikatsu shi.* Tokyo: Kyōikusha, 1980.

———. "Shisei no jōhō: 'Ukiyo no arisama' o meguru nōto." In *Baku-*

matsu bunka no kenkyū, edited by Hayashiya Tatsusaburō, pp. 239–69. Tokyo: Iwanami Shoten, 1978.

Morris, Ivan. *The Nobility of Failure: Tragic Heroes in the History of Japan.* New York: Holt, Rinehart and Winston, 1975.

Mote, Frederick W. *Intellectual Foundations of China.* New York: Alfred A. Knopf, 1971.

Motoyama Yukihiko. "Bakumatsu ki ni okeru minshū no ishiki to kōdō." *Kyōto Daigaku Kyōiku Gakubu kiyō,* no. 30 (1984): 51–79.

Motoyama Yukihiko Kyōju Taikan Kinen Ronbunshū Henshū Iinkai, ed. *Nihon kyōiku shi ronsō: Motoyama Yukihiko Kyōju taikan kinen ronbunshū.* Kyoto: Shibunkaku Shuppan, 1988.

Munz, Peter. *The Shapes of Time: A New Look at the Philosophy of History.* Middletown, Conn.: Wesleyan University Press, 1977.

Murakami Shigeyoshi. *Japanese Religion in the Modern Century.* Translated by H. Byron Earhart. Tokyo: University of Tokyo Press, 1980.

———. *Kindai minshū shūkyōshi no kenkyū.* 2d ed. rev. Tokyo: Hōzōkan, 1963.

———. *Kyōso: Kindai Nihon no shūkyō kaikakusha-tachi.* Tokyo: Yomiuri Shinbunsha, 1975.

———, ed. *Konkō Daijin oboe.* Tōyō bunko, 304. Tokyo: Heibonsha, 1977.

Murakami Shigeyoshi and Yasumaru Yoshio, eds. *Minshū shūkyō no shisō.* Vol. 67 of *Nihon shisō taikei.* Tokyo: Iwanami Shoten, 1971.

Mythology. Compiled by Yves Bonnefoy; translated under the direction of Wendy Doniger O'Flaherty. 2 vols. Chicago: University of Chicago Press, 1991.

Nagafuji Yasushi. *Jikan no shisō: Kodaijin no seikatsu kanjō.* Tokyo: Kyōikusha, 1979.

Nagai Michio and Miguel Urrutia, eds. *Meiji Ishin: Restoration and Revolution.* UNU Series on Social Transformation, 1. Tokyo: United Nations University, 1985.

Nagel, Ernest, and James R. Newman. *Gödel's Proof.* New York: New York University Press, 1958.

Najita, Tetsuo. *Japan: The Intellectual Foundations of Modern Japanese Politics.* Chicago: University of Chicago Press, 1980.

———. *Visions of Virtue in Tokugawa Japan: The Kaitokudō Merchant Academy of Osaka.* Chicago: University of Chicago Press, 1987.

Najita, Tetsuo, and J. Victor Koschmann, eds. *Conflict in Modern Japanese History.* Princeton: Princeton University Press, 1982.

Najita, Tetsuo, and Irwin Scheiner, eds. *Japanese Thought in the Tokugawa Period, 1600–1868: Methods and Metaphors*. Chicago: University of Chicago Press, 1978.

Naramoto Tatsuya. *Meiji ishin ron*. Tokyo: Tokuma Shoten, 1968.

Naramoto Tatsuya and Nakai Nobuhiko, eds. *Ninomiya Sontoku / Ōhara Yūgaku*. Vol. 52 of *Nihon shisō taikei*. Tokyo: Iwanami Shoten, 1973.

Narrative of the Expedition of an American Squadron to the China Seas and Japan. Edited by Sidney Wallach; compiled by Francis L. Hawks. New York: Coward-McCann, 1952.

Needham, Joseph. *Time and Eastern Man*. Royal Anthropological Institute Occasional Paper, 21. Glasgow: Royal Anthropological Institute of Great Britain and Ireland, 1965.

Nietzsche, Friedrich. *On the Advantage and Disadvantage of History for Life*. Translated by Peter Preuss. Indianapolis: Hackett, 1980.

Nishigaki Seiji. *Ee ja nai ka: Minshū undō no keifu*. Tokyo: Shinjinbutsu Ōraisha, 1973.

———. *Kamigami to minshū undō*. Edo Series, 9. Tokyo: Mainichi Shinbunsha, 1977.

Norman, E. Herbert. "Feudal Background of Japanese Politics." In *Origins of the Modern Japanese State: Selected Writings of E. H. Norman*, edited by John W. Dower, pp. 319–464. New York: Pantheon Books, 1975.

———. "Mass Hysteria in Japan." *Far Eastern Survey* 14 (1945): 65–70.

———. "Okage-mairi: Observations on the Dancing Mania in Tokugawa Japan and in Europe." New York: Institute of Pacific Relations, n.d. Mimeo.

Nosco, Peter. *Remembering Paradise: Nativism and Nostalgia in Eighteenth-Century Japan*. Harvard-Yenching Institute Monographs, 31. Cambridge, Mass.: Harvard University, Council on East Asian Studies, 1990.

Ochiai Nobutaka. "Yonaoshi." In *Ikki no rekishi*, pp. 283–325. Vol. 2 of *Ikki*. Tokyo: Tōkyō Daigaku Shuppankai, 1981.

Odera Gyokuchō, comp. *Teibō zasshūroku*. 2 vols. 1922. Nihon Shiseki Kyōkai reprint. Tokyo: Tōkyō Daigaku Shuppankai, 1972–73.

O'Flaherty, Wendy Doniger. *Other Peoples' Myths: The Cave of Echoes*. New York: Macmillan, 1988.

Ofudesaki, the Tip of the Writing Brush. Tenri: Tenrikyō Church Headquarters, 1971.

Ohara Shin. *Nihonjin no jikan*. Tokyo: Gendai Kenkyūkai, 1980.

Ōkagami. Vol. 21 of *Nihon koten bungaku taikei*. Tokyo: Iwanami Shoten, 1960.

Ooms, Herman. *Tokugawa Ideology: Early Constructs, 1570–1680*. Princeton: Princeton University Press, 1985.

Ōsaka Rekishi Gakkai, ed. *Kinsei shakai no seiritsu to hōkai*. Tokyo: Yoshikawa Kōbunkan, 1976.

Ōyama Kyōhei. *Kamakura bakufu*. Vol. 9 of *Nihon no rekishi*. Tokyo: Shōgakkan, 1974.

Ozouf, Mona. *Festivals and the French Revolution*. Translated by Alan Sheridan. Cambridge, Mass.: Harvard University Press, 1988.

Peirce, Charles S. *Philosophical Writings of Peirce*. Edited by Justus Buchler. New York: Dover Books, 1955.

Pelzel, John C. "Human Nature in the Japanese Myths." In *Personality in Japanese History*, edited by Albert M. Craig and Donald H. Shively, pp. 29–56. Berkeley and Los Angeles: University of California Press, 1970.

Pepper, Stephen C. *World Hypotheses: A Study in Evidence*. Berkeley and Los Angeles: University of California Press, 1942.

Philippi, Donald L., trans. *Kojiki*. Princeton: Princeton University Press; Tokyo: University of Tokyo Press, 1969.

Piaget, Jean. *Structuralism*. Translated and edited by Chaninah Maschler. New York: Harper and Row, 1970.

Rabinow, Paul. "Representations Are Social Facts: Modernity and Postmodernity in Anthropology." In *Writing Culture: The Poetics and Politics of Ethnography*, edited by James Clifford and George E. Marcus, pp. 234–61. Berkeley and Los Angeles: University of California Press, 1986.

Ranke, Leopold von. *The Secret of World History: Selected Writings on the Art and Science of History*. Edited and translated by Roger Wines. New York: Fordham University Press, 1981.

Redesdale, Algernon Bertram Freeman-Mitford, Baron. *Memories*. 2 vols. New York: E. P. Dutton, n.d.

———. *Mitford's Japan*. Edited by Hugh Cortazzi. London: Athlone, 1985.

Reischauer, Edwin O. *Japan Past and Present*. New York: Alfred A. Knopf, 1946.

Rekishigaku Kenkyūkai and Nihonshi Kenkyūkai, eds. *Kindai 1*. Vol. 7 of *Kōza Nihon rekishi*. Tokyo: Tōkyō Daigaku Shuppankai, 1985.

———. *Meiji ishin*. Vol. 5 of *Kōza Nihonshi*. Tokyo: Tōkyō Daigaku Shuppankai, 1970.

Ricoeur, Paul. *Hermeneutics and the Human Sciences: Essays on Language, Action, and Interpretation*. Edited and translated by John B. Thompson. Cambridge: Cambridge University Press; Paris: Editions de la Maison des Sciences de l'Homme, 1981.

————. "The Model of the Text: Meaningful Action Considered as a Text." *New Literary History 5* (1973–74): 91–117.

————. *The Philosophy of Paul Ricoeur*. Edited by Charles E. Reagan and David Stewart. Boston: Beacon Press, 1978.

————. *Time and Narrative*. Vol. 1. Translated by Kathleen McLaughlin and David Pellauer. Chicago: University of Chicago Press, 1984.

Rudé, George. *The Crowd in the French Revolution*. London: Oxford University Press, 1959.

Sagara Tōru, Bitō Masahide, and Akiyama Ken. *Jikan*. Vol. 4 of *Kōza Nihon shisō*. Tokyo: Tōkyō Daigaku Shuppankai, 1984.

Said, Edward W. "On Repetition." In *The Literature of Fact*, edited by Angus Fletcher, pp. 135–58. New York: Columbia University Press, 1976.

————. *Orientalism*. New York: Pantheon Books, 1978.

Sakata Yoshio. *Meiji ishin shi*. Tokyo: Miraisha, 1960.

————, ed. *Meiji ishin shi no mondaiten*. Tokyo: Miraisha, 1962.

Sakata Yoshio and John Whitney Hall. "The Motivation of Political Leadership in the Meiji Restoration." *Journal of Asian Studies* 16 (1956–57): 31–50.

Sansom, George B. *A History of Japan to 1334*. Stanford, Calif.: Stanford University Press, 1958.

————. *A History of Japan 1334–1615*. Stanford, Calif: Stanford University Press, 1961.

————. *A History of Japan 1615–1867*. Stanford, Calif.: Stanford University Press, 1963.

————. *The Western World and Japan*. New York: Alfred A. Knopf, 1950.

Sasaki Junnosuke. "Bakumatsu no shakai jōsei to yonaoshi." In *Kinsei 5*, pp. 247–308. Vol. 13 of *Iwanami kōza Nihon rekishi*. Tokyo: Iwanami Shoten, 1977.

————. *Bakumatsu shakai ron*. Tokyo: Hanawa Shobō, 1969.

————. *Kinsei minshūshi no saikōsei*. Tokyo: Azekura Shobō, 1984.

————. *Yonaoshi*. Tokyo: Iwanami Shoten, 1979.

————. "Yonaoshi no jōkyō." In *Meiji ishin*, pp. 87–112. vol. 5 of *Kōza Nihonshi*. Tokyo: Tōkyō Daigaku Shuppankai, 1970.

Satō Shigerō and Kawachi Hachirō, eds. *Bakuhansei kokka no hōkai*. Vol. 8 of *Kōza Nihon kinseishi*. Tokyo: Yūhikaku, 1981.

Satow, Ernest. *A Diplomat in Japan*. Introduced by Gordon Daniels. Tokyo: Oxford University Press, 1968.

Saunders, E. Dale. "Japanese Mythology." In *Mythologies of the Ancient World*, edited by Samuel Noah Kramer, pp. 409–42. Garden City, N.Y.: Doubleday, 1961.

Sawada Akira. *Sokumenkan bakumatsushi*. 2 vols. 1905. Nihon Shiseki Kyōkai reprint. Tokyo: Tōkyō Daigaku Shuppankai, 1982.

Scheiner, Irwin. "Benevolent Lords and Honorable Peasants: Rebellion and Peasant Consciousness in Tokugawa Japan." In *Japanese Thought in the Tokugawa Period, 1600–1868: Methods and Metaphors,* edited by Tetsuo Najita and Irwin Scheiner, pp. 39–62. Chicago: University of Chicago Press, 1978.

―――. "The Mindful Peasant: Sketches for a Study of Rebellion." *Journal of Asian Studies* 32 (1972–73): 579–91.

Scott, James C. *Weapons of the Weak: Everyday Forms of Peasant Resistance*. New Haven: Yale University Press, 1985.

Scribner, Robert W. *Popular Culture and Popular Movements in Reformation Germany*. London: Hambledon Press, 1987.

―――. "Reformation, Carnival, and the World Turned Upside-down." *Social History* 3 (1978): 303–29.

Searle, John R. *Intentionality: An Essay in the Philosophy of Mind*. Cambridge: Cambridge University Press, 1983.

―――. *Speech Acts*. London: Cambridge University Press, 1969.

Shibahara Takuji. *Kaikoku*. Vol. 23 of *Nihon no rekishi*. Tokyo: Shōgakkan, 1975.

―――. *Sekaishi no naka no Meiji ishin*. Tokyo: Iwanami Shoten, 1977.

Shimazaki Tōson. *Before the Dawn*. Translated by William E. Naff. Honolulu: University of Hawaii Press, 1987.

Shiryō Kyōto no rekishi. Vol. 3, *Seiji / gyōsei*. Tokyo: Heibonsha, 1979.

Shōji Kichinosuke. *Yonaoshi ikki no kenkyū*. 2d ed. rev. Tokyo: Azekura Shobō, 1970.

Shōji Kichinosuke, Hayashi Motoi, and Yasumaru Yoshio, eds. *Minshū undō no shisō*. Vol. 58 of *Nihon shisō taikei*. Tokyo: Iwanami Shoten, 1970.

Singer, Brian C. J. *Society, Theory, and the French Revolution: Studies in the Revolutionary Imaginary*. New York: St. Martin's, 1986.

Singer, Kurt. *Mirror, Sword, and Jewel: A Study of Japanese Characteristics*. Introduced by Richard Storry. New York: George Braziller, 1973.

Sivin, Nathan. "Chinese Conceptions of Time." *Earlham Review* 1 (1966–67): 82–92.

———. "On the Limits of Empirical Knowledge in the Traditional Chinese Sciences." In *Time, Science, and Society in China and the West*, ed. J. T. Fraser, N. Lawrence, and F. C. Haber, pp. 151–69. Amherst: University of Massachusetts Press, 1986.

Smart, J. J. C., ed. *Problems of Space and Time*. New York: Macmillan, 1964.

Smith, Thomas C. *The Agrarian Origins of Modern Japan*. Stanford, Calif.: Stanford University Press, 1959.

———. "Japan's Aristocratic Revolution." *Yale Review* 50 (1960–61): 370–83.

———. *Nakahara: Family Farming and Population in a Japanese Village, 1717–1830*. Stanford, Calif.: Stanford University Press, 1977.

———. *Native Sources of Japanese Industrialization, 1750–1920*. Berkeley and Los Angeles: University of California Press, 1988.

———. "Ōkura Nagatsune and the Technologists." In *Personality in Japanese History*, edited by Albert M. Craig and Donald H. Shively, pp. 127–54. Berkeley and Los Angeles: University of California Press, 1970.

Stambaugh, Joan. "Time, Finitude, and Finality." *Philosophy East and West* 24 (1974): 129–35.

Starr, Chester G. "Historical and Philosophical Time." *History and Theory*, Beiheft 6 (1966): 24–35.

Steele, M. William. "Edo in 1868: The View from Below." *Monumenta Nipponica* 45 (1990): 127–55.

Stevenson, Robert Louis. "Yoshida-Torajiro." In *Familiar Studies of Men and Books*, pp. 174–90. New York: Charles Scribner's Sons, 1902.

Strayer, Joseph R. *Feudalism*. Princeton: Van Nostrand, 1965.

———. "The Tokugawa Period and Japanese Feudalism." In *Studies in the Institutional History of Early Modern Japan*, edited by John Whitney Hall and Marius B. Jansen, pp. 3–14. Princeton: Princeton University Press, 1968.

Sturrock, John, ed. *Structuralism and Since*. Oxford: Oxford University Press, 1979.

Tahara Tsuguo, Seki Akira, Saeki Arikiyo, and Haga Noboru, eds. *Hirata Atsutane / Ban Nobutomo / Ōkuni Takamasa*. Vol. 50 of *Nihon shisō taikei*. Tokyo: Iwanami Shoten, 1973.

Takagi Shunsuke. *Ee ja nai ka*. Tokyo: Kyōikusha, 1979.

———. *Ishinshi no saihakkutsu: Sagara Sōzō to uzumoreta sōmō-tachi*. Tokyo: Nihon Hōsō Shuppan Kyōkai, 1970.

Takagi Zaichū. *Bakumatsu ishin Kyōto chōnin nikki: Takagi Zaichū nikki*. Edited by Uchida Kusuo and Shimano Michio. Osaka: Seibundō, 1989.

Talmon, Yonina. "Millenarism." *International Encyclopedia of the Social Sciences* 10:349–62. New York: Macmillan–Free Press, 1968.

———. "Pursuit of the Millennium: The Relation between Religious and Social Change." *Archives européennes de sociologie* 3 (1962): 125–48.

Tanaka Akira. "Bakufu no tōkai." In *Kinsei 5*, pp. 309–51. Vol. 13 of *Iwanami kōza Nihon rekishi*. Tokyo: Iwanami Shoten, 1977.

———. "Ishin seiken ron." In *Meiji ishin*, pp. 147–75. Vol. 5 of *Kōza Nihonshi*. Tokyo: Tōkyō Daigaku Shuppankai, 1970.

———. *Meiji ishin*. Vol. 24 of *Nihon no rekishi*. Tokyo: Shōgakkan, 1976.

———. *Meiji ishin to rekishi kyōiku*. Tokyo: Aoki Shoten, 1970.

———. *Meiji kokka*. Vol. 5 of *Taikei / Nihon rekishi*. Tokyo: Nihon Hyōronsha, 1967.

———. *Mikan no Meiji ishin*. Tokyo: Sanseidō, 1968.

Terror und Spiel: Probleme der Mythenrezeption. Edited by Manfred Fuhrmann. Munich: Wilhelm Fink Verlag, 1971.

Thompson, Edward Palmer. *The Making of the English Working Class*. New York: Pantheon Books, 1963.

———. "The Moral Economy of the English Crowd in the Eighteenth Century." *Past and Present*, no. 50 (1971): 76–136.

Thompson, William Irwin. *The Imagination of an Insurrection: Dublin, Easter 1916: A Study of an Ideological Movement*. New York: Oxford University Press, 1967.

Tilly, Charles. *The Contentious French*. Cambridge, Mass.: Harvard University Press, 1986.

Toby, Ronald P. *State and Diplomacy in Early Modern Japan*. Princeton: Princeton University Press, 1984.

Tōkyō hyakunen shi. Vol. 1, *Edo no tanjō to hatten* (*Tōkyō zenshi*). Tokyo: Gyōsei, 1979.

"Tora hachigatsu Koishikawa." In *Bakumatsu hishi shinbun waisō*, edited by Meiji Bunka Kenkyūkai, pp. 269–71. 1934. Reprint. Tokyo: Meicho Kankōkai, 1968.

Totman, Conrad D. *The Collapse of the Tokugawa Bakufu, 1862–1868.* Honolulu: University Press of Hawaii, 1980.

———. "Ethnicity in the Meiji Restoration: An Interpretive Essay." *Monumenta Nipponica* 37 (1982): 269–87.

———. "From 'Sakoku' to 'Kaikoku': The Transformation of Foreign-Policy Attitudes, 1853–1868." *Monumenta Nipponica* 35 (1980): 1–19.

———. *Japan before Perry.* Berkeley and Los Angeles: University of California Press, 1981.

———. "Tokugawa Yoshinobu and 'Kōbugattai': A Study of Political Inadequacy." *Monumenta Nipponica* 30 (1975): 393–403.

Tōyama Shigeki. *Meiji ishin.* Iwanami zensho, 128. Tokyo: Iwanami Shoten, 1951.

———. *Meiji ishin to gendai.* Tokyo: Iwanami Shoten, 1968.

Tsuchiya Takao. "Ishinshijō no nansensu." *Chūō kōron* 46, no. 12 (December 1931): 282–90.

Tsunoda, Ryusaku, William Theodore de Bary, and Donald Keene, comps. *Sources of the Japanese Tradition.* New York: Columbia University Press, 1958.

Tucker, Robert C., ed. *The Marx-Engels Reader.* New York: W. W. Norton, 1972.

Turner, Victor W. *Dramas, Fields, and Metaphors: Symbolic Action in Human Societies.* Ithaca, N.Y.: Cornell University Press, 1974.

———. "Myth and Symbol." *International Encyclopedia of the Social Sciences* 10:576–82. New York: Macmillan–Free Press, 1968.

Ueyama Shunpei. *Meiji ishin no bunseki shiten.* Tokyo: Kōdansha, 1968.

Varley, H. Paul. *Imperial Restoration in Medieval Japan.* New York: Columbia University Press, 1971.

———, trans. *A Chronicle of Gods and Sovereigns.* New York: Columbia University Press, 1980.

Veyne, Paul. *Writing History: Essay on Epistemology.* Translated by Mina Moore-Rinvolucri. Middletown, Conn.: Wesleyan University Press, 1984.

Vico, Giambattista. *The New Science of Giambattista Vico.* Translated by Thomas Goddard Bergin and Max Harold Fisch. Ithaca, N.Y.: Cornell University Press, 1968.

Wakabayashi, Bob Tadashi. *Anti-foreignism and Western Learning in Early-Modern Japan: The "New Theses" of 1825.* Harvard East Asian Monographs, 126. Cambridge, Mass.: Harvard University, Council on East Asian Studies, 1986.

Walthall, Anne. *Social Protest and Popular Culture in Eighteenth-Century Japan.* Association for Asian Studies Monographs, 43. Tucson: University of Arizona Press, 1986.

Waters, Neil L. *Japan's Local Pragmatists: The Transition from Bakumatsu to Meiji in the Kawasaki Region.* Harvard East Asian Monographs, 105. Cambridge, Mass.: Harvard University, Council on East Asian Studies, 1983.

Watsuji Tetsurō. *Sakoku: Nihon no higeki.* 1950. Reprint. Tokyo: Chikuma Shobō, 1964.

Weber, Eugen. *Peasants into Frenchmen: The Modernization of Rural France, 1870–1914.* Stanford, Calif.: Stanford University Press, 1976.

White, Hayden V. *The Content of the Form: Narrative Discourse and Historical Representation.* Baltimore: Johns Hopkins University Press, 1987.

———. *Metahistory: The Historical Imagination in Nineteenth-Century Europe.* Baltimore: Johns Hopkins University Press, 1973.

———. *Tropics of Discourse: Essays in Cultural Criticism.* Baltimore: Johns Hopkins University Press, 1978.

———, ed. *The Uses of History: Essays in Intellectual and Social History.* Detroit: Wayne State University Press, 1968.

White, James W. "Rational Rioters: Leaders, Followers, and Popular Protest in Early Modern Japan." *Politics and Society* 16 (1988): 35–69.

———. "State Growth and Popular Protest in Tokugawa Japan." *Journal of Japanese Studies* 14 (1988): 1–25.

Whitrow, G. J. "Reflections on the History of the Concept of Time." In *The Study of Time,* edited by J. T. Fraser, F. C. Haber, and G. H. Müller, pp. 1–11. New York: Springer-Verlag, 1972.

———. *What is Time?* London: Thames and Hudson, 1972.

Wilson, Elizabeth A. "Reading Ōgai's 'Sakai Jiken': An Exercise in Disclosing Meanings." Department of Asian Languages and Cultures, University of Michigan, Ann Arbor, 1989.

Wilson, George M. "The Bakumatsu Intellectual in Action: Hashimoto Sanai in the Political Crisis of 1858." In *Personality in Japanese History,* edited by Albert M. Craig and Donald H. Shively, pp. 234–63. Berkeley and Los Angeles: University of California Press, 1970.

———. "Changing Images of the Meiji Restoration in Japanese Historiography." In *Papers of the C.I.C. Far Eastern Language Institute,* edited by Richard B. Mather, 4:170–81. Ann Arbor, Mich.: Committee on Institutional Cooperation, 1973.

————. " 'Ee ja nai ka' on the Eve of the Meiji Restoration in Japan." *Semiotica* 70 (1988): 301–19.

————. "The Kyoto Intervention of 1858." In *Nihon kyōiku shi ronsō*, edited by Motoyama Yukihiko Kyōju Taikan Kinen Ronbunshū Henshū Iinkai, pp. 510–27. Kyoto: Shibunkaku Shuppan, 1988.

————. "Plots and Motives in Japan's Meiji Restoration." *Comparative Studies in Society and History* 25 (1983): 407–27.

Worsley, Peter. *The Trumpet Shall Sound: A Study of "Cargo" Cults in Melanesia.* 2d ed. rev. New York: Schocken Books, 1968.

Yamaguchi Masao. "Kingship as a System of Myth: An Essay in Synthesis." *Diogenes,* no. 77 (1972): 43–70.

Yano Yoshiko. " 'Okagemairi' to 'ee ja nai ka.' " In *Seikatsu / bunka / shisō,* pp. 317–57. Vol. 4 of *Ikki.* Tokyo: Tōkyō Daigaku Shuppankai, 1981.

Yasumaru Yoshio. "Minshū undō no shisō." In *Minshū undō no shisō,* edited by Shōji Kichinosuke, Hayashi Motoi, and Yasumaru Yoshio, pp. 391–436. Vol. 58 of *Nihon shisō taikei.* Tokyo: Iwanami Shoten, 1970.

————. *Nihon nashonarizumu no zen'ya.* Tokyo: Asahi Shinbunsha, 1977.

————. " 'Okagemairi' to 'ee ja nai ka.' " In *Minshū undō no shisō,* edited by Shōji Kichinosuke, Hayashi Motoi, and Yasumaru Yoshio, pp. 494–501. Vol. 58 of *Nihon shisō taikei.* Tokyo: Iwanami Shoten, 1970.

Yoshida Tsunekichi, Fujita Shōzō, and Nishida Ta'ichirō, eds. *Yoshida Shōin.* Vol. 54 of *Nihon shisō taikei.* Tokyo: Iwanami Shoten, 1978.

Yoshikawa Kōjirō, Satake Akihiro, and Hino Tatsuo, eds. *Motoori Norinaga.* Vol. 40 of *Nihon shisō taikei.* Tokyo: Iwanami Shoten, 1978.

Index